IN SEARCH OF STRUCTURAL POWER

For my parents, Paddy and Margaret

In Search of Structural Power

EU Aid Policy as a Global Political Instrument

PATRICK HOLDEN
University of Plymouth, UK

ASHGATE

Published by
Ashgate Publishing Limited
Wey Court East
Union Road
Farnham
Surrey, GU9 7PT
England

Ashgate Publishing Company
Suite 420
101 Cherry Street
Burlington
VT 05401-4405
USA

www.ashgate.com

British Library Cataloguing in Publication Data
Holden, Patrick
  In search of structural power : EU aid policy as a global
  political instrument
  1. Economic assistance, European - Political aspects
  2. European Union countries - Foreign relations
  I. Title
  327.4'0090511

Library of Congress Cataloging-in-Publication Data
Holden, Patrick, 1974-
  In search of structural power : EU aid policy as a global political instrument / by Patrick Holden.
    p. cm.
  Includes index.
  ISBN 978-0-7546-7333-0
  1. Economic assistance, European. 2. European Union countries--Foreign economic relations. 3. Economic assistance, European--Developing countries. 4. Economic assistance, European--Case studies. I. Title.

  HC60.H6642 2008
  338.91'4--dc22

                                                        2008031814

ISBN 978-0-7546-7333-0

Mixed Sources
Product group from well-managed
forests and other controlled sources
www.fsc.org Cert no. SA-COC-1565
© 1996 Forest Stewardship Council
FSC

Printed and bound in Great Britain by
MPG Books Ltd, Bodmin, Cornwall.

Contents

List of Figures and Maps

List of Tables

List of Boxes

Acknowledgements

I am immensely grateful to the various officials in EU institutions, national governments and civil society who granted me interviews or otherwise facilitated my research. Needless to add, the views expressed here are entirely my own.

Academically I have benefitted greatly from support and stimulation from my time at the Department of Politics and Public Administration in the University of Limerick (2000–2005) and the Centre for International Studies at Cambridge, where I had a visiting fellowship from 2004 to 2005. Special thanks are due to Nick Rees, Bernadette Andreosso-O'Callaghan, David Coombes, Eddie Moxon-Browne, Sean Molloy, Elaine Byrne, Geoffrey Edwards, Joyobroto Sanyal. My work has been aided enormously by the vibrant research culture and enabling atmosphere at the Plymouth International Studies Centre, and I would like to thank in particular Richard Gibb, Malcolm Williams, Mark Wise, Jamie Gaskarth, Taku Tamaki, Rebecca Davies, Brieg Powel, Shabnam Holliday, Alex Cunliffe, David Brockington, Karl Cordell and Tom Harris.

I would like to express my gratitude for financial support I have received from the Irish Research Council for the Humanities and Social Sciences and the European Union, via a Marie Curie Fellowship. Sincere thanks are also due to the Cartography Unit of the School of Geography at Plymouth for their excellent maps. Last but not least, I owe a special debt of gratitude to my many good friends and above all to my family (including in-laws), without whom none of this would be possible.

Preface/Permissions

This text was completed before the Georgia war of August 2008 and the financial crash of September 2008. These events will only intensify the dynamics analysed in this book.

Parts of chapter 3 were first published in 'Development through Integration? EU aid reform and the evolution of Mediterranean aid policy' *The Journal of International Development* 2008: 20, 230–244. They are reproduced with the kind permission of John Wiley & Sons Limited.

Chapter 2 includes some material from 'Tensions in the organisation of aid policy for foreign policy purposes: a case study of the European Union's Mediterranean Aid Programmes', in the *European Journal of Development Research* 2006, 18: 3, 387–412. This is reproduced with the kind permission of EADI, the European Association of Development Research and Training Institutes.

There is also material in chapters 2 and 3 that originally appeared in 'Partnership Lost? The European Union's Mediterranean Aid Programmes' in *Mediterranean Politics,* 10: 1, 19–37, and is reproduced with the kind permission of Routledge.

Some quotes in chapter 3 first appeared in 'Hybrids on the Rim? The EU's Mediterranean Aid Policy' in *Democratization,* 12: 5, 461–480 and are reproduced with the kind permission of the editor.

List of Abbreviations

AA	Association Agreement
ACP	Africa Caribbean and Pacific Countries
AECI	Agencia Española de Cooperación Internacional
AFD	Agence Française de Développement
ALA	Asia and Latin America Aid Instrument
AP	Action Plan
ASEAN	Association of South East Asian Nations
CAP	Common Agricultural Policy
CARDS	Community Assistance for Reconstruction, Development and Stabilization (Balkans)
CDF	Comprehensive Development Framework (World Bank)
CFSP	Common Foreign and Security Policy
CIS	Commonwealth of Independent States
CONCORD	European NGOs confederation for relief and development
CSP	Country Strategy Paper
DAC	Development Assistance Committee of the Organisation for Economic Cooperation and Development
DCI	Development Cooperation Instrument
DFID	Department for International Development (UK)
DG	Directorate General
EBRD	European Bank for Reconstruction and Development
ECA	European Court of Auditors
ECOWAS	Economic Community of West Africa
ECU	European Currency Unit
EDF	European Development Fund
EU	European Union
EIB	European Investment Bank
EIDHR	European Initiative (or 'Instrument' post-2006) for Democracy and Human Rights
EMP	Euro-Mediterranean Partnership
ENP	European Neighbourhood Policy
ENPI	European Neighbourhood and Partnership Instrument
ESDP	European Security and Defence Policy
FEMIP	Euro-Med Facility for Investment and Partnership

GATT	General Agreement on Tariffs and Trade
HDI	Human Development Index
IFIs	International Financial Institutions (the World Bank and the IMF)
IMF	International Monetary Fund
ISQG	Inter-service Quality Support Group
MDG	Millenium Development Goals
MEDA	Mesures d'Accompagnement
Mercosur	Common Market of the South (El Mercado Común del Sur)
NIP	National Indicative Programme
NIS	New Independent States (of the ex-Soviet Union).
PCA	Partnership and Cooperation Agreement
PHARE	Pologne Hongrie Aide pour la Reconstruction Economique
PRSP	Poverty Reduction Strategy Paper
RELEX	The External Relations DG (Relations Exterieurs)
SAP	Structural Adjustment Programme
SCAC	Service de Coopération et Action Culturel (France)
SCR	Common Service for External Relations (Service Commun pour les Relations Exterieurs)
SWAP	Sector Wide Adjustment Programme
TACIS	Technical Assistance for the Commonwealth of Technical Assistance for the Commonwealth of Independent States
UEPLAC	Ukraine-Europe Policy and Legal Advice Centre
UMA	Union Maghreb Arabe
UNDP	United Nations Development Programme
USSR	Union of Soviet Socialist Republics
WTO	World Trade Organization

Introduction

In a world where military threat is not a defining factor in most regions, economic instruments have become increasingly important in serving political, as well as commercial, objectives. The European Union has long specialised in this *modus operandi*, given its origins as an economic community with political ambitions. This gradual and economic-based approach has been explained in terms of civilian power, soft power and perhaps most appropriately as a form of 'structural foreign policy' (Duchêne 1972; Nye 2004; Keukeleire 2000). Aid policy is one of the EU's primary instruments here and it has played a role both in integrating Europe and in supporting Europe's interests worldwide. More generally, international aid has been one of the major forms of intervention by the developed world in developing countries. Although aid is often criticised as ineffective in achieving the rhetorical objectives of development and democracy, most would agree that it has always had other objectives (Schraeder et al. 1998). Indeed the prevalent and longstanding use of aid by states and international organizations, can hardly be explained by pure altruism, and implies that aid serves important interests. Accordingly, aid is evaluated as a 'political instrument' here in relation to political, geoeconomic and strategic objectives that are distinct from development and democracy. Given the recent failures of hard power, exemplified by Iraq, aid is likely to increase in importance as a means of forming the socio-economic and political institutions of other countries (and broader regional structures).

These two concerns, the external role of the EU and the power dimensions of aid policy, are investigated jointly in this book. Despite a healthy body of literature on both topics there is still a need for a critical, but non-ideological, analysis in both cases. Many studies of EU external relations/foreign policy focus on the normative and ethical dimensions of the EU's international role. While this is important, and intellectually interesting, as Sjursen points out it may lead to a rather naïve view of the EU (2006, 2), and minimise the power dimension of its activities. Also many observers increasingly view the EU as a type of superpower (McCormick 2006; Leonard 2005). These views are based on its subtle projection of influence worldwide, through economic and institutional cooperation which is boosted by its economic gravitational pull, and optimism about the long term prospects of European integration. Needless to say, there are numerous assumptions here that must be tested. On the other hand, because the EU seems subordinate to the major European governments and the US when it comes to crucial geopolitical issues, others tend to dismiss it as an actor, and this is also extreme.

This variance is mainly a function of different theoretical approaches and conceptions of power. As broad ranging studies necessarily offer little detailed empirical evidence on specific sectors and countries, there is a need for a detailed study of what the EU has actually done, as opposed to its values and potential. This book's focus on aid policy should make a valuable contribution to the debate on EU power. Regarding aid policy, the vast majority of studies and evaluations are in relation to the normative objectives of development and democracy. These are, obviously, worthy and entirely valid approaches. Yet, for example, studies of the democratic impact of aid may well miss out on broader political effects of aid (Burnell, 2004), and may neglect further institutional, economic and power effects. Those that adopt a more critical (left-wing) approach are highly conscious of such issues, and these, ironically, tend to view aid as highly effective, although in a negative sense (Robinson, 1996). Clearly there is still room for debate on the question of donors' capacity to use aid for political and institutional engineering, for better or worse.

Accordingly this book seeks to navigate between various perspectives and assumptions and contribute to our understanding of EU foreign policy/external relations and the politics of aid. It is designed to be of interest to a relatively broad sector of readers. For EU specialists it offers a meso-level analysis of a classic 'civilian power' instrument, to complement macro-level discussions of the EU's international role and detailed studies of the EU's policies towards particular countries and regions. The book also challenges the assumptions of those who regard the EU as an actor above power politics. While many of the points about aid, trade and power will be unsurprising (or perhaps even understated) for those with a more critical perspective, the detailed study of the operation and limitations of aid also challenges conventional opinions on the ability of international forces to shape the domestic structures of states. More generally the study of the EU, and its efforts to reform other states, addresses ongoing debates in International Political Economy in relation to globalization and national and regional power configurations. For aid policy experts, the holistic analysis of aid policy as a political and geoeconomic instrument offers a different perspective on evaluating aid policy, and helps explain the weaknesses of aid as a force for development. There are, of course, limitations to the detail of argument a study of this scale can make. These are fully addressed in the empirical and concluding chapters.

This book argues that EU aid policy can be usefully understood as an effort to develop its structural power. The concept was developed by Susan Strange, who defined it as the 'power to shape and determine the structures of the global political economy within which other states their political institutions, their economic enterprises and (not least) their scientists and other professional people have to operate' (Strange 1994, 24–25). As explained in chapter 2 it doesn't necessarily involve empire or hegemony (in the traditional senses of these words) but refers to deep-seated formative power in differing sectors. This notion of structural power is prevalent in the discourse of opponents and proponents of the European Union, although of course the language is different. Within the EU[1], much Eurosceptic

---

1   In this text the term 'EU' is used, as is conventional, to refer to the European Union which officially came into existence with ratification of the Maastricht Treaty in 1993, and

frustration and suspicion stems from how the European Court of Justice developed a preeminent European legal order on the basis of minor commercial disputes, and this legal supremacy is a classic example of structural power. In the external sphere, those who advocate the EU as a means to control globalization, and talk-up the 'gravitational pull' of the EU, are thinking in terms of structural power. The concept captures the depth and comprehensiveness of the EU's external relations objectives, which go beyond direct commercial and security benefits, to seek a deeper type of power. EU efforts to, for example, shape the rules of the world trade regime, promote the Euro as a global currency, reform other states in line with EU laws and rules, and politically and economically integrate them with the EU, can be understood as efforts to develop this form of power. Competition for structural power could be seen as a natural and not necessarily problematic feature of contemporary global politics. It is not intended to depict the EU as a sinister monolith, indeed it is self-evidently a highly complex entity with multiple interests and objectives. The argument is that these interests coalesce around Europe's structural power, and that this is in fact a major function of the EU. The pursuit of structural power is not *a-priori* incompatible with support for development and liberal democracy (although it does imply a dilution of democratic empowerment). For example, many would accept that the Marshall Plan was a successful effort to promote development, liberal democracy but also American structural power in Europe. The focus here is on EU efforts to use aid for objectives that are quite different, but are also essentially structural in nature.

'European aid' includes EU member state aid as well as EU-level aid, which is managed and delivered by the EU institutions. The latter is the main interest here, as the subject is the collective policies of the EU that are working for long-term European interests. Nevertheless the degree of coordination between the EU and member state aid is obviously important. There is also an extensive web of cooperation within the international aid community more generally, which cannot be ignored. EU-level aid has historically been managed according to varying rules and institutional procedures. As described in chapter 2, the basic format is that the member state bodies (in the Council of the European Union and lower-level groupings), the autonomous European Commission (which is supposed to serve the supranational European interest) and in some cases the European Parliament devise the basic policy and budget for aid instruments. Although the system is quite fragmented it is argued here that there is a substantial degree of political control and direction of aid funding. The programming and planning of the aid is handled by the European Commission and monitored and controlled by member state bodies at different stages.

The empirical focus of this book is on the EU's mainstream aid instruments for countries and regions. As chapter 2 outlines these receive the bulk of the EU's external aid funding. There are of course many other smaller specific instruments related to human rights, environmental protection, borders and migration, which

---

the previous European Communities which existed from the Treaty of Rome of 1957.

will be considered insofar as they are relevant. The mainstream aid instruments are more directly linked with the EU's objectives in the geographical areas in question. Even their official objectives go beyond 'development' to include reform and integration with Europe. Geography matters in this case, and it is the regions neighbouring Europe where this use of aid is most developed. Aid to the 'Mediterranean' to forge a Euro-Mediterranean region and to the ex-Soviet Union to liberalize and integrate the successor states, has played a vital, if not always successful role in EU policy. Aid to Sub-Saharan Africa is delivered as a part of the EU's historical trade and development relationship with the ACP (Africa, Caribbean and Pacific) countries. Meanwhile EU aid to Latin America and Asia, in particular the emerging economic powers of this region, has increased substantially since the end of the cold war. In all cases the EU has a mix of security, commercial and normative objectives, as well as the constant theme of structural power. Always, aid is linked to broader EU efforts to deepen economic and institutional relations and it is analysed within this context. The aid in question may involve technical assistance for government, business or civil society, networking of elites, or direct budgetary support, or – relatively rarely – the kind of direct development investment in areas such as infrastructure, that the public imagines 'aid' to consist of. All of this is accompanied by conditionalities of different sorts, although there is much more to the politics of aid than conditionality. EU aid policy is constantly in flux and the approach taken here is to offer a historical analysis of the aid in operation from 2001–2007. Apart from being the most recent period, this enables us to study the impact of radical reforms to EU aid policy in 1999–2001, designed to enable aid to be used more strategically. Case studies of key countries and regional organizations – Morocco, Ukraine, Ghana and Mercosur – are used to clarify what is a necessarily broad analysis. In 2006 and 2007 EU aid policy was again overhauled, and the impact of this is also discussed.

A Note on the Theoretical and Methodological Framework

It must be stressed that structural power is not a theory per se, but a concept used as a framework for an analysis. It does not lend itself to a specific worldview, apart from the principle that political entities tend to try and develop their own power. As such it accords with what has been called 'new realism' (although the terminology becomes problematic), in that it recognises the centrality of power to understanding international relations, but has a broader view of this concept and is not obsessed with the state (Strange 1997). [2] As outlined in chapter 1, the approach here is heterodox, in line with most forms of International Political Economy (Murphy 2001). The guiding concept used here is harmonious with that

---

2   In fact Molloy argues convincingly that the originators of realism also had such a broader approach and have been misrepresented as state-centric, but this is not the issue at hand (Molloy 2007).

developed by Susan Strange, but adapts it somewhat. A wide variety of theoretical approaches include arguments congruent with the basic concept of structural power. Critical political economy theories are most obviously relevant here and comprehensively inform this work. They involve a deeper sense of power than direct, easily observable (and measurable) definitions, are more inclined to understand economic relationships in terms of power and have a broader sense of what is 'political' in general. Although Strange was no Marxist, Neo-Marxist and Neo-Gramscian theorists have developed concepts of hegemony, which are in fact highly congruent with structural power (Kelly, 2002). Also insights from the dependency and structuralist schools are still relevant, in that acute economic asymmetry is one form of structural power, but only a very basic kind. The more potent form comes from broader legal, institutional and ideological structures. Many constructivist insights can also be clearly related to hegemony and structural power, although they are not focused on in the empirical studies for methodological reasons explained in chapter 1. The more mainstream, neo-positivist schools of IPE also have relevance in that structural power also includes the power to purposefully shape the rules of institutions and 'regimes'.

Aid policy itself is a direct form of intervention. The hypothesis that this is used to increase the EU's structural power is not taken for granted and a great deal of the empirical chapters is devoted to discussing the purposes of aid, in terms of the legislation and funding priorities. In most cases the search for structural power is deemed to be the dominant tendency, but it is freely accepted that there are multiple purposes to aid, as to other forms of public policy. Beyond this, the question is to what extent the EU has the capability to use aid strategically for its structural objectives (such as free trade areas, extension of European law, and the dilution of national configurations of power). This involves an analysis of the EU's operating procedures and strategy formulation and also draws on literature on the political economy of reform in the countries in question. Again critical and relatively liberal perspectives are considered, and I argue that their diagnosis of the landscape in developing countries is often quite similar, although their understanding of the underlying forces and the correct prognosis diverges widely. Generally, although quantitative data is used to support the argument, the reader is not bombarded with statistics and the ultimate argument is qualitative.

This book originated with a study of EU aid policy and democratization in 2001. It soon became apparent that the thrust of EU policy was geared to a different form of political and institutional engineering and a different conceptual framework was need. As the foregoing suggested, this is intended as a relatively objective study. I am not trying to justify or criticise the EU and globalization. Of course I have my own ideological and ethical predilections, which do not always neatly cohere. As a European citizen, I am broadly favourable to the concept of a European Union, although not necessarily to its specific format or policies. Like most people in the developing world I have natural sympathy with the poor of developing nations, which are disempowered and impoverished mainly due to systemic factors far beyond their control. While using aid for structural power is not automatically anti-development it is obviously a very different priority to development as normally understood. Intellectually the elephant in the room here is the question of whether the liberal economic policies that the EU supports will lead to economic development. I am not a trained economist but obviously have my own biases here. There is no question that the right combination of free enterprise and outward policies with strategic state support can kick-start development (albeit unequally), as demonstrated in the case of numerous Asian countries (Wade 2003); and Western Europe in a previous era. These are not blanket neo-liberal development policies however, and a totally open and laissez faire approach has rarely worked. Whether such policies could work if the developed world forsook its own extra-liberal powers (such as covert subsidies and protectionist trade instruments) is a moot question but is entirely hypothetical. Therefore I find this EU approach ethically problematic and am doubtful as to its developmental potential, although it is a more enlightened form of power projection than historically used by great powers. In any case I have no vested interest in arguing that the EU is succeeding in using aid to develop its structural power or not, and a nuanced picture emerges from the empirical studies.

The Organization of this Book

Two further introductory chapters are necessary before going on to the core studies. The first chapter is crucial to the argument of the entire book. It explains the concept of structural power, situating it within other theories and concepts, and relating it to the EU's international activities. It then articulates precisely how EU aid policy can be seen as an effort to develop this form of power. Lastly it explains the methodological approach to analysing and drawing conclusions as to the nature and impact of the EU's aid policies. Chapter 2 outlines the factual detail that non-EU aid specialists will need to understand the discussion in the later chapters. It also expresses the core assumptions about how EU aid policy works and how it relates to the rest of the international aid community. Following this there are four empirical chapters 3 and 4 look at how EU aid policy has worked in the core neighbouring regions, the Mediterranean/Middle East and the ex-USSR. It is here where the description of aid as an instrument of structural power fits most neatly, and it is from a study of these regions that the wider project was developed. Chapter 5 analyses EU aid to Sub-Saharan Africa, this takes place within a particular historical development partnership but nevertheless has a substantial power dimension. Chapter 6 deals with more distant partners, namely EU partners in Latin America and Asia where there is a less developed EU policy framework and where geoeconomic interests predominate. Chapter 7 discusses how EU aid policy has evolved in the period in question and whether the instrumental use of aid for EU power has been moderated or accentuated.

Chapter 1

The Theoretical and Methodological Framework: EU Aid and Structural Power

The relatively simple concept of structural power has great explanatory potential when applied to the EU's international role. It helps us avoid an overly liberal and idealistic understanding of the EU's role but also avoids an overly rigid and 'hard' definition of power, which would be inappropriate. Moreover, the structural power concept allows for greater differentiation, as is fitting for a complex and fragmented institution such as the EU. As outlined below it is by no means suggested that the tendency to seek structural power is peculiar to the EU. It is part of a general 'will to power' which percolates through the commercial and development policies of states and international institutions. The first part of this chapter is devoted to outlining this conceptual framework, starting with a brief exposition of how the EU is considered an 'actor' in international affairs and then discussing the concept of power in much more detail, drawing on a wide range of theories from international relations and international political economy. It then applies the structural power framework to the EU's development policy and other activities, before discussing the role of aid instruments in particular. Following on from this, I outline more specifically how I evaluate the EU's use of this instrument. This starts with a more general discussion of approaches to evaluating aid then discusses the methodology of the empirical studies in more detail.

1.1 The EU as an Actor

Although there is a growing acceptance that the EU is an actor worthy of study, it is necessary to clarify in precisely what sense this is the case. Defining what amounts to an actor in international relations is not unproblematic. Smith argues that the traditional theoretical prerequisites for a 'strategic actor' are unrealistically high. Rather than expecting an actor to be 'monolithic, possessing a unified set of preferences and capable of unified action' it is more reasonable to evaluate whether it is capable of 'collective action' and 'strategic impact' (Michael Smith 1998, 80). This is because the former criteria would, arguably, not be entirely fulfilled even by the major nation states. Bretherton and Vogler define the basic criteria for an actor in terms of degree of autonomy, coherence and capability (Bretherton et al. 1999, 18–23/36–42). Crucially, the EU takes different forms for different spheres of activity. In the case of the Common Foreign and Security Policy (including the European Security and Defence Policy), there is room for debate.

Given its highly intergovernmental structure, whether the EU can be considered relatively 'autonomous' from the member state governments is questionable. Arguably even these intergovernmental structures for policy making have become so institutionalized, that the EU cannot be considered a mere mechanism to be instrumentalized by member states (Michael E. Smith 2003). But there are serious question marks over whether there is political autonomy from the United States, given the very close links many member states have with the Superpower and that unanimity is required for nearly all CFSP actions. Coherence is another big question mark. A lack of coherence was one of the essential reasons, according to Hill for the 'capability expectations gap' (Hill 1998, 23). The concept of coherence is, admittedly, qualitative and depends on what principles and objectives one has in mind (Tietje 1997, 211–214). Nevertheless it is clear that the EU has lacked unity at fundamental strategic conjunctures (most notably the Iraq invasion). Thus the questions asked by Hill are still salient. Certainly the CFSP is a fascinating case study of the Europeanization of EU policy-making (Tonra 2003), and its potential importance is enormous. However its impact in crucial strategic situations has been limited and it is still debatable whether actorness can be ascribed to the EU here. Without prejudging the issue, the argument here does not presuppose that the EU is an actor in the realm of traditional foreign policy. This focuses on another form of EU foreign policy (centred on its 'external relations' policies) where a much clearer case can be made.

In regard to EU external relations, the first pillar of the EU (the European Community) is predominant and it has solid, autonomous, supranational institutions such as the Commission and the Court of Justice. Also the Member State channels often use qualified majority voting which gives them a supranational dimension. All of this improves coherence. General studies of the EU's foreign policy place a great weight on these civilian/external relations instruments (Hazel Smith 2002). Even Hill's original critique noted the 'highly structured political economy dimension of collective, autonomous, external, commercial and development policies' (Hill 1993, 322). In Smith's opinion the EU's strategic capacity increased significantly due to further integration and the European Community (specifically the Commission) may be understood as the 'strategic agent' of the EU (Michael Smith 1998). In this sphere, enlargement and general trends in European integration have not necessarily reduced supranationality. In some cases the delegation of significant tasks to the European Commission has expanded. For example, the Nice treaty of 2000 gave the Council and Commission control over most aspects of trade in services, whereas before, this was the prerogative of individual governments. Likewise in administering aid policy the member state committees have adopted a less hands-on role, as their increased size (now 27 members), makes management impractical and so more power has been delegated to the Commission (interviews, European Government and European Commission officials, 2004–2005). Apart from the institutional set-up the less politically charged atmosphere in these areas of activity (as opposed to, for example, the Middle East conflict) allows for greater coherence and unity. Certainly there is *prima facie* evidence that the EU has significant capability here and thus it can be considered an actor, but what kind of power may this lead to?

1.2 Concepts of Power

This section will first discuss popular ways of conceptualising the EU's power before outlining a more comprehensive typology of power and situating the concept of structural power within this framework. One of the original paradigms for the EU's role in the world was that of a civilian power, which encapsulated the EU's use of non-military instruments to project its influence on the international stage (Duchêne 1972). Of course, due to the ESDP, the EU is no longer a purely 'civilian power' and many contemporary scholars seek to go beyond this term (Whitman, 1998), although the concept is still found useful (Orbie 2006). Deeper criticisms include that the civilian power approach is predicated on a conservative 'interest-based' ontology of the international system (Manners, 2004). This may or may not be a problem as long as these limits are understood and indeed the concept can be adapted to incorporate constructivist insights. Nevertheless it is true that the term has strong 'normative' assumptions (and distinctly echoes the French idea of a 'mission civiliatrice'), which are problematic. Even when the civilian power paradigm was introduced others were discussing the EU's world role in much more critical terms (Galtung 1973). A concept of power is needed that addresses these critical arguments and that has more of an analytical edge. Some similar criticisms may be made of Nye's concept of 'soft power'. It was originally described in very broad terms as 'non-command power' and is now conceived as the influence and security benefits which stem from the attractiveness of a state or group of states (Nye 1990; Nye 2004). It is a useful descriptive term but again can be a little vague. This is not surprising as the concept is part of a public debate on the use of aggression in US foreign policy (Nye 2005). This 'rhetorical' utility of the term partly explains why it is not such a precise analytical tool.

Manners develops the ideational underpinnings of 'soft power' and the ethical implications of 'civilian power' with the notion of normative power (Manners, 2002). This conceives the EU as a changer of norms in the international system, partly through its very existence (see also Maull 2005, 778) and partly through conscious efforts. As Manners outlines, normative power can encapsulate various critical approaches to theorising international politics, one example being the neo-Gramscian concept of 'ideological power' further discussed below. Normative power is more commonly related to social constructivist approaches. These have been particularly prevalent in studies of the EU's international role, partly due to the clear importance of shared norms, socialization processes, discourse and identity in European Integration (Haas 1958; Christiansen et al., 1999). Constructivist approaches to Europe's international role focus on its use of discourse and dialogue to spread moral norms regarding values such as human rights, and multilateralism, a clear form of normative power. Yet many would argue that social constructivists in general have tended to underemphasize the power dimension in the study of IR (Barnett and Duvall 2005, 40) and this is certainly true regarding the study of the EU's international role. Again this is partly because constructivist studies of European integration have underplayed the issue of power, probably as a reaction to excessively interest-based and power-centric theories of integration such as Moravcsik's liberal intergovernmentalism (Moravcsik 1993).

This emphasis on the role of norms, values and identity in EU foreign policy is certainly valid and of intellectual interest but an exaggerated focus on values may blind us to the importance of more material configurations of power. Also a 'normative power' approach can fall into the trap of implicitly accepting the loftier rhetoric of EU policy-makers (Sjursen 2006, 2). In fact there is strong evidence that normative considerations in EU foreign policy are interacting with and essentially shaped by self-interest considerations: 'The way in which norms are conceived and incorporated into external policy reveals a certain security-predicated rationalism' (Youngs 2004, 435). It is argued here that they also reveal a certain power-centred rationalism. Thus a stronger conception of power is needed but conventional realism has little relevance and therefore 'new realist' IPE approaches have much to offer. Before discussing this however we must look more comprehensively at the concept of power.

Barnett and Duvall's taxonomy of power

It will already be apparent that this book uses a relatively broad definition of power, as opposed to the more explicit coercive notions of power. At the same time, if nearly all forms of persuasion and discourse are regarded as an exercise of power the concept uses its usefulness. Barnett and Duvall's definition is a useful starting point, 'power is the production, in and through social relations, of effects that shape the capacities of actors to determine their circumstances and fate' (Barnett and Duvall 2005, 42). As they argue, this definition is broad enough to accommodate many forms of power but not so broad as to render it applicable to all forms of social interaction and thus lose its analytical usefulness. They outline, based on this definition, a comprehensive taxonomy of the various concepts of power, which offers a useful basis for discussing structural power (although their vocabulary is different). They derive four primary types of power from two sets of variables, see figure 1.1. The first relates to the standard agent-based (power exercised by an agent) versus social relation (power as a feature of a relationship) distinction. The second is whether power must operate 'directly' or in a more diffuse manner. This is a more problematic distinction but the four types are worth treating discretely as a basis for further discussion.

The first type of power is the simplest – power exercised by a specific agent over another – and needs no more explanation. The second type also involves agency in that it involves an agent setting the rules (and agenda) of institutions, for example one great power setting the rules of an international organization or a less formal 'regime' (Krasner 1983). This institutional power is relatively diffuse

	Direct	*Diffuse*
Agent-based	1. Compulsory power	2. Institutional power
A property of social relations	3.Constitutive/structural power	4.Productive power

Source: Barnett and Duvall 2005, 88

Figure 1.1   Barnett and Duvall's categorization

in that it takes effect (shapes the choices of others) over the long-term in a variety of instances. Such approaches to power are used by mainstream neo-realists and neo-liberal institutionalists (Ibid; Keohane and Nye 1989).

What they call structural/constitutive (referred to here as 'purely structural') refers to the power relationships inherent in a social structure beyond any conscious exercise. One example they give is the Marxist understanding of the capitalist system as a social structure that automatically empowers the owner of capital and dis-empowers the worker. One example from an international relations perspective, is World Systems Analysis. This divides the world into centre, semiperiphery and periphery based on long-term historical processes and the spatial relations of the contemporary mode of production (Caporoso 1989, 103–109). Capacity and choice is primarily a function of a state's location in this system and thus the system itself 'constitutes' power. There are also more ideational concepts of power along these lines. The aforementioned Neo-Gramscian school posits that intellectual structures and normative principles (the prime example being neo-liberal economic philosophy) intrinsically empower and dis-empower certain groupings (Cox 1983). Thus ideological hegemony has material and institutional effects, benefiting certain classes and countries. While many constructivists do not focus on power, systemic constructivism can clearly be related to structural power. This focuses on how international normative and ideational structures determine identities, roles and interests. Just as the patriarchal social system intrinsically constituted gender identities and roles (empowering the male and dis-empowering the female) so the international social structure constitutes identities and roles. Obviously the Westphalian ideational structures privileged states as actors over other forms of organization; the ideational structures of sub-systems like the Warsaw Pact communist block privileged the role of the Soviet Union and its leadership (Wendt et al. 1995). Changing ideational structures could empower or disable other actors. Wendt stresses that the underlying social structure in which states are embedded help determine the interests and capabilities of states. In other words the underlying social structure is a deeper form of power and thus 'power is constituted primarily by ideas and cultural contexts' (Wendt 1999, 97).

Their final form of power is also conceived in terms of social relations but 'productive power' is more diffuse and multi-directional than the previous form which is basically uni-directional with clear winners and losers (capitalist-worker, core-periphery).[1] Such conceptions of power are related to post-modernist and post-structuralist thought. Hardt and Negri's understanding of an a-territorial 'Empire' empowering and disempowering at multiple levels, is one example of the application of this to international relations (Hardt and Negri 2001). This form of power is not further discussed here as this book is based on a more conventional ontology, see section 1.5. 'Productive power' can of course remain in the background as an alternative understanding to the arguments posited.

As the authors of this typology accept, in practice these different forms of power will interact. Of particular interest is the link between purely structural power and question of agency, see figure 1.2. The former type of power can be sought in the same way that actors pursue 'mileu goals' (Wolfers 1962). The post World War II global economic system was to a large extent created via US agency in developing international economic governance, European integration and Japan's economic revival (Panitch 2005, 106). Thus the US was forging a system whose structural qualities would privilege its role. Likewise, ideological hegemony, or roles and identities with power effects, are projected by actors (states, international organizations etc.) Indeed this is the essence of the structuration principle, that agents and structures are co-constitutive. Also what Barnett and Duvall call agent-based institutional power can also be described as structural in that it is structural in effect; the rules created shape the choices of others. Accordingly, what is needed is a concept of power that incorporates structure and agency.

Strange's conception of structural power

Strange defined structural power as the 'power to shape and determine the structures of the global political economy within which other states their political institutions, their economic enterprises and (not least) their scientists and other professional people have to operate' (Strange 1994, 24–25). This can be purely structural, for example, the mobility and size of private finance in the current system means that states and other agents must respond to its cues and must obey rules regarding property rights/monetary systems and thus 'capital' has structural power. Also one state (the US) may be deemed to have structural power in that its sheer economic

---

1   Barnett et al. describe the difference in terms of the *direct* effect of structural power as opposed to constitutive power. In my opinion this is more problematic but the distinction between the two forms is justified nevertheless.

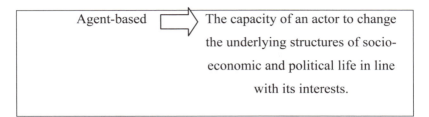

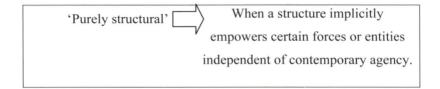

Note: Agent-based structural power includes what Barnett and Duvall call 'diffuse institutional' power

Figure 1.2   Different meaning of structural power

size relative to others (and their dependency on its markets) means that its internal rules and systems will spill over to others whether it wants to or not. A region or state may have structural power in trading terms if (beyond any discussion of purpose) its size leads to a gravitational attraction and inherently asymmetric trading relationships. However Strange's theory is not based on a structuralist/ determinist ontology and it also includes agents that possess the capacity to mould the formal institutions and deeper material and ideational structures of the international system (Ibid). Thus in her view a state like the US possessed and exercised structural power in terms of the ability to mould economic, financial and other systems. Indeed a major theme was that the US had the *responsibility* to act to change the international system. This is significant for two reasons. Concepts of structural power are often criticised for 'not sufficiently stressing the fundamental agent reference of power' (Guizzini 1993, 469), but while this may be true of some approaches is not so of Strange. Also, if structural power can be an attribute of an actor (and can be exercised by it) it can also be sought by an actor.

Strange sub-divided power into four structures (1994). These are not applied in the empirical analysis but are worth noting as the principle that structural power can be heuristically divided into distinct (but interconnected) sectors is important.

The primary structures (of which only two are economic) delineated are:

- Production: productive economic activity (not limited to 'industry').
- Finance: the allocation of credit.

- Security: viewed in a traditional sense. Structural power here would include technological capacity and the strategic position of an actor.
- Knowledge: this is used in two senses, relatively technical issues regarding information and scientific capacity but also deeper issues regarding perceptions and beliefs. This can be clearly related to Neo-Gramscian and Constructivist approaches. Although it is fair to say that Strange did not fully explore the epistemological implications of this form of power (Tooze 2000, 188).

Structural power is particularly useful as a framework for the following reasons. It captures the relationship of agency and structure well in that it, obviously, appreciates the importance of structural factors but is far from any kind of tautological structuralism. It allows for agency and purpose. Related to this, structural power analysis has a strong political economy dimension (appropriate given the crucial role of economics in the EU's external relations) but does not fall into economic determinism. The concept allows for a nuanced approach in several ways. Although it is obviously power-centric it is not as extreme as the neo-realist approach that offers a purely neo-mercantilist interpretation of the EU supporting its commercial interests in a zero-sum world (Gilpin 2001, 10). It is supporting its commercial interests but we may also perceive the EU's activities as a more subtle project that goes beyond short-term direct self interest to develop structures ultimately favourable to Europe. The following section will give examples of this. Structural power analysis also strikes the right balance between a rigorous neo-realist approach that precludes any role for normative forces and an unhealthy assumption of EU benevolence. Indeed structural power is capable of different ethical interpretations. It does not imply that the EU's actions are ethical but neither does it preclude this possibility. It could be argued, and Strange herself argued this, that it is responsible and good for Europe to increase its structural power in a world otherwise dominated by 'casino capitalism' and one superpower (Strange 1995). The point is that it allows for an ethically neutral analysis without dismissing ethics in principle. Structural power also lends itself well to empirical studies. It has been argued with some justification that the concept can be vague, but it can be specified, indicators can be derived (even if the concept itself is essentially qualitative) and a substantial argument can be made. Crucial is that it can be divided into different sectors which should allow for a richer picture of the EU's role than an 'is the EU a superpower?' kind of debate.

1.3 Contemporary EU External Relations from a Structural Power Perspective

The specific form of globalization over the previous four decades can be interpreted in terms of changing forms of structural power. Efforts to develop a political economy insulated from the global market failed. More modest efforts to develop mixed-economies or 'developmental states', which involved a major role for the state in the economy, have also come under enormous pressure. Thus national public power has been attenuated, especially in the first and second worlds. This springs from the structural pressures of a changing global economy but also from the agency of states and international organizations promoting 'neo-liberal' reforms. This, probably overused, term is central to the understanding of EU external policies. Neo-liberalism is broadly defined here as the belief in the economic efficacy of free markets, free trade and individual enterprise; and that this economic freedom is inextricably linked with individual political freedom and democratic constitutional government (Hayek 1962; Friedman 2002). In these decades, development theory and practice became explicitly politicized incorporating these tenets on economic policy, economic governance and general governance (Gibbon 1993). Whatever about the rights and wrongs of this as a development strategy it is clearly a political venture that involves altering the socio-economic and political power structure of a country. If national networks of power are being denuded who is being empowered?[2] Is it private financial and economic actors, global institutions, or is the process used to reinforce the traditional repositories of power?

The question is intimately related to debates on the meaning of globalization in the contemporary world and this can in turn be related to structural power. The standard formulation is a contrast between 'hyper-globalists' who believe that territorial power is being superseded and 'sceptics' who reckon that states and possibly regional entities still are the core actors (Held et al. 1999). This also relates to long-standing Marxist debates about whether we are moving towards transnational truly global governance with global institutions such as the IMF and the transnational capitalist class or whether territorial political institutions (great states like the US) still hold ultimate power and are essentially in competition (Callinicos 2002). According to the latter only the weaker states are being denuded of power and globalization is a trojan horse for the dominant powers. This can overlap with neo-realist perceptions of contemporary international political economy. I start from Held et al.'s compromise position, that globalization is a reconfiguration involving the increased salience of global space and the empowerment of transnational actors but not entirely superseding state and regional power structures (Held et al. 1999). Another important compromise position is that capitalist states/regions will support their specific commercial and power interests but will also seek to support global capitalism as a whole (Cammack 2005). The point of this book is to investigate what this means in practice and how the European Union is seeking to accumulate structural power in the context of this global reconfiguration. The EU does this through adopting a skewed approach to

---

2   It should be noted here that this is not a simple process and many argue that domestic power structures are not really being superseded, this is investigated in the empirical chapters, and also there appears to be a resurgence of territorial power, as discussed in the conclusion.

promoting neo-liberalism, diluting the political freedom element when necessary, (and moderating its hyper-capitalist principles somewhat within Europe).[3]

The 'internal' process of European Integration can in itself be understood in terms of structural power, although the term is rarely used by practitioners or academics. A core tenet of the original 'integration theory' was that lobbyists and interest groups would gravitate towards the 'new centre of power' in Brussels (Haas 1958). The best example of structural power is the legal power developed by the European Court of Justice, as it established that European Community law went beyond the state to apply directly to individuals and that it was supreme over national law. These principles, established in early rulings, ensured that the EU legal order placed structural constraints of the choices of member state governments and other actors. In less subtle terms the UK government clearly understood the political implications of having a unified customs union in mainland Europe. When MacMillan complained of the 'continental blockade', a reference to Britain's struggle against Napoleon (Young 1999), he echoed Britain's long-standing opposition to a single hegemonic power in Europe. The decision of British policy makers, however grudgingly, to be at 'the heart of Europe' is a recognition that to shape Europe's future they must be a part of the EU. The alternative is, like Norway, to accept Europe's economic law without a say in determining it (Leonard 2005, 90). On the international level the desire to have a stronger voice in the world has become a more salient motive for integration. Policy initiatives such as the Single European Act (1986) and the creation of the Euro have been promoted as efforts to increase Europe's power in a globalised world (McCormick 2006).

The rest of this section reviews the relevant external policies and instruments of the EU. Policies are understood as a set of principles and objectives in a specific area, and instruments as the means to attain them. The latter are often based on the EU's economic weight and take the form of conditional legal economic cooperation agreements, financial and technical assistance of different types (also made conditional on various criteria) and structured dialogue at many levels. It will first go through the policies and instruments, (briefly) outlining how they are political/interventionist, and then relate them structural power. Many of these instruments are based on a degree of structural power the EU already possesses but the focus here is on how the objectives, if fulfilled, would greatly expand this.

Development policy is a major EU external policy and 'development' is an intrinsically political concept, implying a *transformation* of society beyond economic growth. EU practice has followed global trends in becoming more proactively political, as a cursory glance at its policy towards the ACP (Africa, Carribean, Pacific) states makes clear. The comprehensive development policy

---

3   The common agricultural policy is not discussed at any length in this book, but (while its effects may not be as uniformly negative as some suppose) it best exemplifies this selective approach of the EU to neoliberalism.

objectives outlined in 2000 established six priority thematic areas for EU intervention (Commission 2000b). These included good governance and the rule of law and, notably, integration into the world economy. Thus the role of development policy in supporting 'globalization' is made explicit. The basic instruments have been multilateral developmental partnerships, namely the Lomé conventions begun in 1975 which offered trade preferences and extensive financial assistance. In accordance with general thinking funding priorities have been diverted from directly supporting socio-economic development towards policy and institutional reform. Also both punitive and allocative (rewards based) aid conditionality have been introduced. As implied above the tendency towards liberalizing markets has been notable. The Cotonou agreement with the ACP countries (replacing the Lomé convention in 2001) is an example of this.

EU support for human rights and democracy, an obvious form of intervention, has been salient in the post cold-war period (Youngs 2002). The Maastricht Treaty (1992) outlined one of the objectives of the EU as 'to develop and consolidate democracy and the rule of law and respect for human rights and fundamental freedoms' (Article JI). This policy gives the EU purchase over other states' political institutions, legal systems, public administration and society in general. The instruments used here are broadly similar although dialogue plays a greater part and traditional diplomatic instruments such as demarches are used. Since 1995 all EU agreements with third parties have a standard clause, outlining that respect for human rights and democratic principles are an essential part of the agreement and that it can be suspended in case of non respect of these. Development aid is supposed to be conditional on human rights criteria and small-scale aid instruments have been established to support human rights/democracy, and civil society organizations in general. More coercive methods are available also such as the use of smart sanctions against noted human rights abusers.

The EU's Enlargement policy is judged by many to be its most effective foreign policy activity, at least in terms of impact (Hazel Smith 2002). Joining the EU requires a transformation of a countries economy and society, the famous Copenhagen criteria of 1993 made clear that states needed to be liberal democracies with free market economies and to have the ability to take on the EU's 80,000 pages plus of legislation. New types of aid instrument such as PHARE (*Pologne Hongrie Aide pour la Reconstruction Economique*) to Eastern Europe were explicitly designed to further not development per se but transition. It offered technical assistance to establish the regulatory and institutional system of a market economy and had conditionality built in. A deeper form of conditionality involved progress towards membership being calibrated according to whether the candidate was reforming sufficiently. In this case there is quite rigorous monitoring and extensive interaction between the Commission and the candidate country.

On a more general level the EU attempts to develop forms of global governance conducive to its modes of operation and its values. This includes the legalization of the World Trade Organization and the development of international law in general. One noteworthy aspect of this is the EU's efforts to develop region-region level cooperation (Edwards et al. 1990). It has enthusiastically signed cooperation agreements and initiated other forms of cooperation with entities such as the Gulf Cooperation Council (1989), Mercosur (1995) and the Association of South East Asian Nations (1980). In the latter case EU recognition played no small role in legitimating ASEAN as an entity in its region (Robles, 2004). The EU also offers technical assistance of to these bodies, none of whom are integrated to anything like the level of Europe.

In all of these cases there are multiple objectives and they can be interpreted in terms of normative/idealist, security, commercial and strategic objectives, but in particular as structural power objectives. Development policy may well be rooted partly in a sense of responsibility and it helps promote the EU's identity as a force for progress and solidarity in the world. Specific initiatives like debt relief are not based on self interest calculations (apart from gaining favourable publicity). However there are also geoeconomic and political motives to aid and development policy, which can be related to structural power. These go far beyond the traditional use of aid to support friendly governments to include more structural objectives. While the original Lomé agreement was relatively generous and genuinely developmental, arguably EU policies discouraged economic diversification and locked the economies of its ex-colonies into a 'complementary' relationship with Europe (Kahler 1982, 201). This situation has developed beyond that of creating simple economic dependency to intervening internally to support institutional reforms. Specific reforms supported by the EU, for example in the area of competition policy have enabled it to spread its own model of regulation and promote it in international fora (Foster 2001). This is a prime example of how structural power goes beyond creating dependency in developing countries to include shaping legal and institutional frameworks.

With regard to the EU's promotion of democracy and human rights, there is also a self-interest dimension. Robinson argues that for the US and other great powers 'democracy support' is a means of furthering the interests of transnational capital. According to him liberal low-intensity democracies or 'polyarchies' are models for governance as these are more likely to adapt their forms of economic governance and regulatory systems in the desired manner than 'mass democracies' or authoritarian states (Robinson 1996). They are more pliable in general to the forms of pressure that can be exerted by the EU. This argument is obviously controversial and is not unproblematic. A simpler argument is that in the EU's neighbourhood EU support for democracy is compatible with a drive for EU hegemony; in supporting political liberalization in Serbia or Ukraine the EU is effectively also supporting their incorporation into its sphere of influence. This is clearly understood in Russia, the only other potential leadership power in the region. In the rest of the world, although prominent, EU democracy support is not a major part of EU policy and is tailored by other strategic objectives (Santiso 2003, 161). Note its treatment of Saudi Arabia for example.

Concerning Eastern enlargement, that there was a normative dimension to the policy is indisputable. Yet again there was a clear self-interest motivation for the

EU as a whole. There was a power vacuum in Eastern Europe after the end of the cold war that something had to fill. As Commissioner Patten put it, 'the planned enlargement to Central and Eastern Europe accomplishes a specific foreign policy objective' (Patten 2002). In regard to its support of regionalism, certainly this is seen as a progressive form of governance and one that Europe could share with the rest of the world. It is also clear that in a 'world of regions' the EU is almost bound to be *primus inter pares* due to its greater level of coherence and economic weight. EU efforts to develop free trade and economic integration agreements with other regions, although these are stalled at the moment, are also an effort to develop a form of insurance in case of problems within the multilateral World Trade Regime (Aggarwal 2004, 1–2).

To summarise the foregoing these policies are – in their totality – better described as efforts to gain structural power than either altruism or pure commercialism. They may also be described in terms of security but the EU's objectives (assuming they are effective) involve increasing Europe's power in several ways. For example, one could describe its relationship with African countries as an effort to promote its economic security, to ensure the flow of key commodities to Europe, but the policy framework described above has gone very far beyond this. Generally the policies and instruments described seek to

- Further increase its economic weight and gravitational pull. Develop economic relationships that are highly asymmetric, in which the partner's economy is complementary to that of the EU (in line with traditional dependency theory).
- Alter domestic legal and economic structures in line with its internal rules, or in some cases literally extend its regulatory system (directly making rules for outsiders). Also, while liberalizing partners' economies and polities denudes regimes of power, the EU retains its own autonomous power and authority.
- Develop international legal and institutional frameworks favourable to its values and interests, such as a 'world of regions' and international economic rules according to its models.
- Encourage patterns of behaviour, modes of thinking and modes of governance favourable to the EU's interests, seeking a world based on liberal capitalist and multilateral values where its economic weight and institutional expertise gives it a central role. They also promote the EU's role as a partner and a teacher.

It should be noted that these policies serve also serve to increase the power of the EU institutions within Europe, as more and more aspects of Europe's global relationships are managed in Brussels. Externally, if successful, they will create structures intrinsically empowering to the EU and give it the power to shape institutions and structures. These features of structural power can be seen in bilateral/regional relationships, and also in the broader global context. Although different vocabulary is used these comprehensive policies, (as well as optimism about the CFSP) are behind predictions of the EU as an emerging superpower. For example, Leonard (2005) argues that the EU is well placed to take a leadership role in the world due to its economic weight, general attractiveness, its use of the instruments cited above and its general skill at multilateralism and spreading its legal order. However, there are major question marks over this vision. Can the EU really use its instruments to this effect?

1.4 Economic Assistance as an Instrument of Power

International assistance of different types has long been a diplomatic tool of states and empires. In the contemporary world aid may relate to military assistance, policing, environmental protection and humanitarian relief as well as economic and political development. The concern here is mainstream economic and civilian aid (for public administration or civil society development). The most prominent use of economic aid as a political instrument is American 'Marshall Aid' to Western Europe after World War II, which served a variety of strategic goals from cementing alliances to supporting European Integration. Generally, the purposes of economic aid are manifold. In a comprehensive survey and analysis of major Western aid donors' funding priorities, Schraeder et al. (1998: 319-321) divine four major objectives on their part:

- Humanitarian/altruism.
- Strategic, in the sense of building security alliances and developing patronage networks. Both the US and the Europeans used aid to this purpose in the cold war period.
- Commercial, generally promoting economic penetration by the donor country and securing access to raw materials.
- Ideological/political,[4] particularly in the cold war capitalist governments would be supported by the US and communists by the USSR, while Scandinavian donors supported 'progressive' left leaning regimes. The Marshall plan itself was essentially concerned with bolstering liberal capitalist forces in European states.

Only one of the objectives, 'humanitarian', is not dominated by self-interest considerations and this is judged not to have been a paramount incentive. One may argue that this is not surprising and that rather than the straw man of pure altruism, enlightened self interest is a valid interpretation of aid policy. Yet the power effect of these other incentives is unmistakable. This study concentrated on the cold war period and these incentives pertain in slightly different forms today. Aid is usually less directly tied to purchases from donor companies but it performs a subtler role,

---

4   This could be extended to include cultural support in the case of France.

often through multilateral donors, in encouraging reforms that create a favourable regulatory climate for donors'/commercial interests. Ideological factors are apparent in Western donors support for 'liberal' forces; this is most obvious in areas of ideological conflict such as the Middle East. The use of development aid for geopolitical reasons still exists of course. Another security dimension emerges with the new concepts of security (Nye 1991; Buzan 1998) more focused on soft security threats, often caused by politically and economically weak states. Recent EU policy documents such as the 'European Security Strategy' (Council 2003) are explicit about the role of aid in promoting Europe's security. In securitizing the domestic political and economic structures of other countries the EU is also claiming a right to shape these structures itself. These geopolitical, geoeconomic, ideological and 'new security', objectives are patently congruent with the concept of 'structural power'.

As to defining the assistance analysed here the (Organization for Economic Cooperation and Development) OECD, definition of 'overseas development aid' (ODA) and 'official aid' (OA) is an adequate starting point. ODA is aid:

> provided by official agencies, including state and local governments, or by their executive agencies; and is administered with the promotion of the economic development and welfare of developing countries as its main objective; and is concessional in character and conveys a grant element of at least 25 per cent (OECD, 2007,1).

OA is equivalent aid for transitional countries, such as Ukraine. Of course from a critical point of view the assumption that 'economic development and welfare' is 'its *main* objective' rather begs the question. However it does describe the kind of assistance analysed here which is that primarily engaged in this realm, as opposed to military aid or policing assistance. The modalities of aid are many. Old fashioned 'development projects' which involve an input of capital to develop infrastructure and new industries are relatively rare. More popular methods are technical assistance ('advice' and training) for public and private actors and direct budgetary grants or loans either for structural or sectoral adjustment. Aid may also have an impact purely as a process (it can lead to new relationships between donor and recipient and can also alter the balance of power within recipient governments). Essentially, the aid in question has a direct impact through the expertise and advice offered and the general input of funding and capital into the recipient country. It can also have a less direct impact through conditionality, in which aid is used as a lever to shape governments behaviour.

Within the EU aid has been used a tool of integration in several senses. Firstly, as a side-payment to poorer nations and regions to accept further integration (Moravcsik, 1993). Secondly, the Commission's management of aid gave it a certain purchase over regional (and to an extent national) governance and policies. The degree to which EU aid funds did foster 'multi-level governance' is debated (Bache 1998) as but Commission policy certainly encouraged a process that was already in play. Aid has also played a major role in the EU external policies outlined in the previous section that work towards developing structural power. Aid itself is a relatively direct resource-based form of intervention, but the intended effects are essentially structural, and so this understanding of the role of aid policy links the different forms of power outlined by Barnett et al. The salient feature of aid as an instrument is that, unlike broad trade and cooperation policies, aid is a more focused instrument which can be controlled and targeted for specific purposes. This is all in the abstract however and the question at hand is to what extent the EU really can use its aid as a targeted instrument to support its structural power.

1.5 Methodology of the Empirical Studies

In analysing and evaluating this use of aid, the principle that there are different forms of structural power is important. The 'deeper' form of structural power (asymmetric cognitive and legal/economic structures) automatically constitutes power and does not require conscious agency to be 'exploited'. The other form is to gain the institutional leverage or economic and political weight that enables one to consciously shape the choices of other actors. We must also note that structural power can be divined within different sectors, and at the national/bilateral, regional and global levels. Thus EU interventions must be evaluated at these different levels, and one would expect considerable variety.

As discussed below there are many challenges to the use of aid for this purpose, and there is still a question mark over what degree of coherence the EU has as an actor. Therefore the key question isolated is whether the EU has the capability of using its substantial aid funding strategically? 'Strategic' is defined here as conscious planning on the part of an organization to change the external environment in pursuit of certain medium to long-term objectives (Mintzberg et al. 1998: 3–22). This definition is intrinsically related to notions of purposefulness, knowledge and coherence. The latter is a key element for the EU, if it can use its aid policies in tandem with its enormous economic weight this would make it a uniquely powerful actor on this level.[5] This question about aid policy chimes with broader questions about EU external relations as to the 'capability' of an institution such as the EU to project its influence on the world stage (Hill, 1993).

The concept of capability may seem banal and rather crude compared to sophisticated contemporary EU research agendas. However, it is still of crucial importance and also relates to profound questions regarding the nature of the EU as an actor and the role of 'public power' in the world. There are some tensions in the approach adopted here. The focus on capability gives the empirical element of

---

5   Note that the coherence studied here is quite different to the official use of the term where 'coherence' is studied in terms of the harmony of the EU's other policies with its 'development' objectives. I do not presume that the EU is 'anti-development' but hypothesize that it is not the political priority.

this study a rather neo-positivist flavour and the case studies essentially analyse the EU's activities from a rationalist perspective. Yet the underlying theoretically framework is not 'positivist' and the concept of power itself, is essentially qualitative, although indicators can be used to trace it. Also, while they are not empirically researched, discourse and identity form an important dimension of structural power. The author appreciates the contribution of constructivist approaches to the study international relations but there is a need for analytical, empiricist studies based on causality to understand the role of actors such as the EU and complement more reflectivist approaches. Of course this will always involve assumptions which can be intellectually challenged.

The approach here is congruent with the broad principles of 'critical realist' social ontology (Bhaskar 1998).[6] This accepts the existence of a 'real reality', avoiding postmodernist excesses, and allows for social facts (nations, organizations) beyond the individual. It also avoids positivist overconfidence, accepting that social reality can only be imperfectly apprehended (either through qualitative or quantitative techniques). Causality is divined in terms of the relationship between the key concepts and 'social facts' rather than 'positivistic atomism' (Burnham et al. 2004, 61). Here data is interpreted theoretically via the key concepts such as development, liberalization, integration, power and the 'social facts'. In Wittgensteinian terms, the discourse of the empirical research takes place within a conventional 'language game' in which it is assumed that the EU 'exists' and can have an 'impact'. In sum, the rationalist element does not imply an entirely neo-positivist approach, and the book offers a reasoned, empirically-supported, argument rather than a 'measurement' of structural power.

Evaluating aid policy

The 'effectiveness' of aid is a perennial subject of debate. Space constraints preclude an in-depth 'literature review' but the following passages outline the key findings which have informed this study. The crucial point to note here is that aid can be evaluated from a variety of perspectives and according to different objectives. Naturally, the greatest focus is on the normative/altruistic objectives, not necessarily because of naivety but because these are important. Most studies of aid are concerned with its impact on economic growth and development more generally (Burnside and Dollar 2004). These are obviously relevant as while it is not supposed here that development is the primary objective, the EU cannot fulfil its broader objectives in the face of developmental crises. Given the incredible range of donors and types of aid, the basic question of whether aid 'works' for development can hardly be answered in a parsimonious fashion (Riddell 2007). There is powerful evidence that the foreign policy and economic interests of donors tend to detract from the development quality of aid (Browne 2006). This

---

6   Critical realism is not to be confused with the International Relations theory of realism.

book inclines towards the mainstream 'reformist' view that the specific form of capitalism exported is problematic for development (Stiglitz 2002; Wade 2001). The political impact of aid in recent years is overwhelmingly studied through the lens of democratization, or 'good governance'. Again these are important variables but there other political affects that may not appear through this 'lens' (Burnell 2004). There is also a vast bulk of literature on the aid process and the element of partnership. This is also relevant as the greater domestic consensus, the greater support there will be for the aid intervention. However if one accepts the structural power framework, the numerous studies debunking the rhetoric of partnership are not surprising (Development Initiatives 2002).

Most germane to my research agenda are the studies of the impact of aid on reform, which rigorously analyse the extent to which the outside donor can use conditionality to alter the policies and institutions of recipient countries (Mosley et al. 1991; Killick 1998; Devarajan et al. 2001). The question is generally approached through a rational actor 'principal-agent' framework. Although they tend to neglect the deeper economic and political pressures these studies are most relevant as they focus directly on the power issue and the capability of donors to affect individual change. For some time there has been a degree of consensus that the donor is rarely able to impose its will absolutely. Even with the poorest countries there is always a bargaining game (Mosley et al. 1991). The main reason for this is that recipient governments/regimes still have substantial autonomy and the capability to distort or block reforms (Dillman 2001). Beyond the formal government 'powerful vested interests of political groups may slow, divert, or even stop a desirable reform. The larger the number of interest groups the more complicated the implementation is likely to be' (Dinar et al. 1998:1). In terms of enforcing conditionality the 'information gap' as Mosley (1991) and Killick (1998) demonstrate is formidable. Quite simply it is difficult for donors to gauge whether the agreed upon reforms are being genuinely implemented. The famous World Bank (World Bank 1999, chapter 2) review of aid policy 'Assessing Aid' accepted (as academics have argued) that efforts to crudely enforce 'good policies' have not been successful, but did not (as is often suggested) give up on the concept of conditionality. Harrison (2001) argues that aid in Africa has in some cases managed to reform and improve public administration, but has not touched the 'deeper tectonics' of political economy structures, which nurture corruption and patrimonial systems. Therefore most agree that aid has had an impact but not the optimum one for developing liberal capitalism. There is still hope that allocative conditionality can act as a catalyst for governance reform (Pronk 2001; Deverajan et al. 2001). Aid donors have developed in sophistication, with Sector Wide Adjustment Programmes coordinated and monitored by numerous agencies. Yet, here too it has been argued that the degree of policy analysis behind SWAPs is often not substantial and information gap problems remain (Brown et al. 2001).

Accordingly, it is not presumed here that conditionality itself will achieve what the EU wants and must be analysed in conjunction with the direct impact of aid itself (the target injection of funding and expertise) on political and economic structures.

The particular challenges of planning for policy change and institutional reform are significant. The use of rigorous methods may not be suitable and arguable a comprehensive but qualitative context analysis is the best means of discovering an opening (Shotton 1999). The numerous studies of the impact of democracy aid shed light on the general capacity of donors to shape institutions. Common advice/ criticisms of democracy support strategies which are relevant to other forms of aid include:

- The need to go beyond a 'one size fits all' policy (Carothers 1999, 85) and to think beyond the 'transition paradigm' (Carothers 2000), to realise the plurality of possible outcomes for a process of change and to develop approaches for dealing with different political environments, especially 'semi-authoritarian' states.
- The need to integrate the economic and political reform agendas, to face up to power structures and to map the political economy of the target country (Burnell 2000; Carothers 2000).

In this arena in particular there are debates over the role and use of indicators, to measure success. Indicators may seem easier to derive for economic reform, but the more institutional dimension of this sphere is also qualitative and poses similar challenges. These challenges are central to the EU's efforts to use aid for structural power.

Another element of evaluating aid is assessing the 'performance' of specific donors. This is a major business in itself, performed by donors themselves and/or independent consultants. The most respected donor evaluation series is that of the Development Assistance Committee of the OECD. Their five standard criteria for aid evaluations are widely used. These are the Relevance and Effectiveness of the aid in terms of development objectives, the cost Efficiency of aid and the direct and indirect Impact of the intervention, and the financial and environmental Sustainability of the intervention. These criteria (which are pretty much common sense) can be applied to specific projects or an entire aid programme/instrument. Of course the devil is in the detail of the methodology, particularly with regard to measuring the effectiveness and impact. Again these criteria are applicable here but with regard to different principles. For example the concept of relevance is germane for a study of the use of aid for structural power but the major focus is relevance to the structural objectives of the donor, rather than the developmental needs of the recipient.

Many studies of aid agencies focus on their organizational structure as this to large extent determines the coherence of a donor's activities. Of course coherence can only be evaluated in terms of specific objectives. For the objective of 'development' there is a broad consensus among academics and NGOs that aid agencies should be autonomous from national foreign policy structures. Aidan Cox et al. (1997) argue that this ensures the development objectives are not contaminated by foreign policy considerations. Conversely in terms of foreign policy it may appear that to have the aid agency integrated into the foreign policy structures would be ideal. The optimum set-up for a unique institutions such as the EU is less clear, and as to the objectives in question are distinct from conventional 'foreign policy', it is not clear how the organizational status of the aid agency impacts upon this. Another salient issue is organizational intelligence, which involves developing the capacity to learn and adapt from previous experience. Aid organizations in particular, as Forss (1999 96) argues, need to foster this as they operate internationally in a generally unsettled environment, yet he argues that organizational intelligence has often being lacking. There has been a major drive on the part of agencies, including the EU, to increase their knowledge management and organizational intelligence. This will obviously have a major bearing on the ability to use aid 'strategically'.

As to evaluations of the EU, one point must first be established: the European Commission has historically been the target of coruscating criticism for its management of aid policy. Even compared to other donors it was singled out for poor performance by official and unofficial evaluations (Europeaid evaluation unit 1998; ECA 2000). Of course these are from a normative perspective but even so the comprehensive and vigour of the criticisms call into the question whether it can use aid as an instrument in any sense. These include knowledge management, cohesion, strategy formulation and methodology as well as issues related to implementation and cash disbursement (DAC 1998). Many of these failings are related to how aid policy was structured within the Commission, as discussed in the next chapter. It is also relatively under-resourced as an aid organization (Dearden 2002). For such reasons it has been argued that the EU is 'a political dwarf in the global aid regime' and a 'source of funds' rather than an actor in its own right (Santiso 2002).

Clearly these criticisms call into question the premise of this book, that EU aid can be used as an instrument for structural power. Firstly it should be noted that the title of this book 'in *search* of structural power' does not assume that the EU is being successful. Also there have been extensive reforms to the European Commission and the EU aid system in general. Apart from improved efficiency and increased staffing these have the specific objectives of improving the strategic capability of the EU and so the impact of these need to be investigated. More recent evaluations imply considerable improvements on all counts (DAC 2002 & 2005). Also the Commission should not be written off as an agent as, although a troubled institution, it has proved surprisingly effective and resilient in promoting the European interest and European Integration. The general points as to the limitations of the impact of aid donors are well-founded. However, using aid for 'structural power' is actually in many senses easier than using aid to support development or democracy (objectives which are hostage to many other factors). Some aspects through which aid can be used to support structural power (to support trade policy reform) are quite feasible. When one considers the enormous economic weight of the EU, which also support the reform and integration agenda, and the power of global economic forces that are in congruence with many of its objectives, the possibility that aid can be used to support structural power becomes more realistic.

Evaluating the EU's use of aid for structural power in specific regions

Given the scope of this book a primary evaluation of the impact of EU aid would neither feasible nor credible. The agency and capability of the EU is evaluated through qualitative and quantitative studies of its aid and other policies for discrete world regions. The EU's policies and objectives for each region are distinct but there are strong commonalities, EU policy invariably involves supporting reform, institutionalized cooperation in general and economic integration in particular. The political security and political economy dimensions of the EU's relationship with this region are then analysed and the EU policy framework is studied. A country case study is used to give depth and meaning to the argument. The EU's policy objectives are then interpreted in relation to structural power. This involves first of all analysing the political economies of states in the region, the mutual determination of economic and other governance structures, and how this relates to EU interests.

One thing all of the states in question have in common is that they do not conform to modern liberal models of economic and political governance. Apart from this, the contexts vary and there are a variety of conceptual approaches, from political science and political economy, to defining the systems in question. These are further discussed in the empirical chapters. Key variables here include the strength of the actual state, the concentration of economic power and the link between economic and political power. In fact there is often surprising commonality between more critical and liberal analyses of the domestic context although the theoretical underpinnings and prescriptions differ. For example, most agree that African societies are dominated by patronage-based economies and patrimonial political systems but the understanding of the historical reasons for this and the appropriate policy response may vary widely (Erdmann and Engel 2006). As our focus is not primarily on devising a development strategy some of these debates are superfluous and we can concentrate on mapping the structures of power. In understanding the EU's objectives one must gauge the likely effect of its reforms of economic, societal, legal and administrative institutions being successful, and how they would affect internal power structures, and the external posture of the state. It is argued that the primary effect in most cases would be to denude endogenous power structures and empower the European Union. (This is especially the case for the EU's neighbourhood).

Following on from this, the specific role of aid is then discussed and indeed this role may vary for different regions. Although it is an assumption that aid is used as an instrument of structural power, this is not taken for granted uncritically. The legal basis of the aid instrument is analysed first of all, in terms of to what extent it enables aid to be used for structural power. Then the thematic priorities in allocating funding are analysed, to further clarify the purpose of aid. Classifying aid is a thorny issue. The DAC (Development Assistance Committee of the OECD) does it in terms of sphere of activity: education, health, water, transport, communications, energy etc. However this does not tell us much about the character of the assistance. For example, a grant to build a bridge and a technical assistance programme on privatizing the rail system would both come under the rubric of 'transport'. For our purposes distinguishing between these forms of aid is obviously crucial. Therefore I make a distinction between

1. Reform orientated projects and programmes. Reform itself is unbundled into different categories including the various efforts at economic reform (structural adjustment programmes, aid for privatization programmes, technical assistance for policy reform), broader reform of the state including political development/political liberalization.
2. Support to the private sector, which is closely linked to the broader reform process, and integration with the EU.
3. Direct aid for socio-economic support and development, this includes 'traditional' development aid for infrastructure or rural development, and aid for health, education, water and environmental protection.
4. Other (emergency relief aid, migration control).

The first two categories are directly in line with the EU's structural power objectives, the third may support it indirectly. In practice a specific project may have an element of all four; in this case it is categorized depending on what the primary purpose is. There are also cases where the allocations are less than specific as to the precise breakdown, and so this is not an exact science, but the overall proportions are an accurate reflection of the EU's priorities.

Capability, the capability to use aid to alter the configurations of power outlined, is then evaluated. This involves analysing the use made of aid funding, the strategy and methodology, and the operation of control mechanisms such as conditionality in practice. In regards to the EU's funding priorities, these are analysed in terms of a variety of political, economic and strategic criteria. Some quite clear conclusions can be drawn even from this aggregated data. (A systematic multiple regression analysis is not offered as this would not further our understanding). A key question is the extent to which EU aid is operating in synergy with the other policies. The main sources here are planning and programming documents themselves buttressed by interviewing where possible. Official evaluations are also availed of.[7] This may seem problematic as the consultants involved are, to an extent, dependent on donor contracts, it is not unduly cynical to suggest that this colours (consciously or otherwise) the evaluation – they may not wish to kill the goose

---

7   Official evaluations from the past two decades are attributed to the 'Europeaid evaluation unit', from whose website they were acquired. It should be noted that this unit didn't actually exist until 2001, and the formal 'authors' are normally a range of outside consultancy firms.

that lays the golden egg (Carothers 1999, 287). I agree that pragmatism may lead to a muffling of overtly critical language, and certainly the terms of reference for an evaluation set the agenda. Yet from my own research and experience there is no reason to dismiss official evaluations, as long as the above caveats are considered. Their specific findings on issues relevant to structural power (for example trade promotion, macro-economic reform or EU performance in general) are assumed to be valid. Another focus is the degree of coordination with the EU member state aid instruments and the broader international community. The latter sheds light on the extent to which EU aid is supporting globalization and/or European structural power.

Evaluating the impact of aid is always problematic, even in purely economic terms as it is difficult to separate the role of aid from other endogenous and exogenous factors. In this case the causality cannot be proven but the basic impact of the EU's efforts can be derived from quantitative and qualitative data. (Its psychological and sociological impact is not analysed in any detail for practical reasons). The relevance of certain indicators will vary but the general issues are as follows:[8]

1. The extent to which the EU's association or cooperation agreements have been implemented (including free trade, investment provisions and joint institutions).
2. The degree of economic interaction, in particular trade and investment, as measured by relevant international organizations. In a sense this relates to previous efforts at measuring interdependence (Tetreault 1980) but not a great deal of stock is put on the raw empirical data; it is understood in the context of trends and institutional structures.
3. The degree of economic and institutional reform in general as measured by the international community (including ratings agencies and think tanks). The opinions of agencies such as the World Bank Institute are taken as they reflect and shape the opinion of the mainstream international community (including the EU) and so can imply its own measurement of success. The degree of change here has a major impact on whether the EU is achieving structural power and the type of structural power in question; the deepest form of structural power would involve a wholesale liberalization and Europeanization of the region, other, more likely scenarios lead to more nuanced and complex outcomes.

Progress in these areas can be taken as indicators of Europe's structural power just as poverty reduction statistics can be taken as indicators of its developmental role.

---

8   For the study of Ghana in chapter 5, point 2 is given less focus as contemporary economic interaction is of less importance relative to reform. The fourth case study is of the Mercosur grouping, where the opposite is true.

Conclusion

Many of the EU's external objectives are best understood in terms of structural power. This concept is congruent with ideas from different schools within politics and international studies. Rather than being a theory itself, it enables an analytical framework that can shed much light on the role of the EU. With regard to this is important to note that structural power can be divined in different forms and at different levels. The EU has always has structural power to an extent, and it is using its policies to further develop this. Admittedly, the EU is not a monolith and there are many logics and objectives to its activities. However, the thrust of its policies is more accurately described as the pursuit of structural power than the pursuit of normative objectives. If defined in terms of the latter the EU's policies would have to be regarded as pretty ineffective, but seen in terms of the former the picture is more nuanced. The precise role of aid policy in the EU programme is that it is potentially a more flexible and targeted instrument than its other forms of cooperation. Theoretically it can help reform the economies and institutions of partner countries in such a manner as to empower the EU. Of course there are major challenges to this, not least of which is the problems of liberalizing statist or patronage-based political economies and governance systems. The following chapters will outline in more detail precisely how the EU is attempting to operate its aid policy to develop its power.

Chapter 2
A Global Overview of EU Aid Policy

To describe the EU aid policy-making and implementation process as 'byzantine' hardly does it justice. A variety of institutions, each of them highly complex in their own right, and an array of outside actors play a role (or seek a role) in the fragmented EU system. This is further complicated by frequent institutional reforms, although there is a degree of clarity for the time period in question as a major set of reforms were completed by 2001. This chapter introduces the institutional context for EU aid policy in this period and further clarifies the type of aid focused on here. Lastly it explains the relationship between EU-level aid policy and the aid of European states and situates EU aid policy within the wider international aid community. This necessarily touches upon general issues regarding EU policy-making, but only very lightly as this a major field of enquiry in its own right and the main aim is to lay the basis for the empirical chapters. It is argued that, notwithstanding the fragmentation and complexity, there is substantial control (and direction) over EU aid policy on the part of the member states and the Commission. This expands on the argument that the EU has sufficient cohesion to, potentially at least, use aid for political and strategic objectives.

2.1 The European Union and its External Aid Policies

The EU's institutional architecture still derives from the Treaty of Maastricht in 1992, which launched the European Union itself. Maastricht resulted in a rather messy three pillar structure. Pillar one was the European Community (the essential structures of the European Economic Community and other Communities), while pillars two and three involved separate procedures for the Common Foreign Security Policy and Justice and Home Affairs respectively. In reality the distinction between each pillar inclined to blur (in terms of institutional roles and policy) but the legal distinction is clear. Pillar one is governed by the European Community Treaty while the overarching Treaty on European Union outlines the rules for the other pillars. The member state Council is still the highest executive power and the state which holds the 6-monthly Council Presidency also has agenda setting powers with regard to EU external affairs. The bulk of Council decisions are made by its lower level bodies of national diplomats and experts (Hayes-Renshaw and Wallace 2006). Within Pillar 1, the Council must combine with the two primary supranational institutions, the European Commission and the European Parliament, to form EU law and policy.[1] The European Commission has a prominent role in aid and other external policies and thus is the focus of much of this chapter. It is a hybrid organization, with a variety of institutions and roles; including proposing legislation, implementing policies, representing the EU and enforcing compliance with EU law. In practice these institutions are interconnected and on the whole pillar one has a strong legalized and integrated dimension. Of course there has been immense debate as to how to interpret this degree of institutional integration in terms of its effect on sovereignty (Rosamond 2000). For our purpose the main interest is to what degree it allows for a strategically directed external relations policy.

The history of 'pillar 1' external relations policy goes back to the establishment on the EEC and its Common Commercial Policy in 1957. Although some of the ambitions of the first Commission were restrained by national leaders (Nugent 2001, 31–33) it did carve out a major role in external relations. In accordance with the Treaty, the Commission was to represent EEC trade interests in international negotiations. The Council could decide on a mandate, within which the Commission would negotiate, while the Council would monitor its progress via a committee of experts. Although cumbersome, and undoubtedly frustrating for negotiating partners, this has proven on the whole to be a surprisingly effective method for the EU to promote its interests. As early as the Kennedy Round world trade negotiations of the 1960s the American's discovered the EEC to be a more cohesive and formidable negotiator than expected (Coombes 1972). Also various Commission missions and offices in the rest of the world were gradually transformed into 'Delegations', of which there were 30 by 1970 (European Commission 2004j, 19).

The Treaty of Rome included an implementing convention that allowed for free trade with 'associated countries' (colonies in the process of becoming interdependent) and also established a European Development Fund (EDF) to supply them with aid. The EDF was a strange birth for EU aid policy as it was, and is, managed in a hybrid manner. The funding is provided by member states outside of the EU's budget and it has retained other legal specificities. However, the Commission was established as the natural operator of the aid. Within Europe, aid also grew in prominence. The European Regional Development Fund was launched in 1975 with the aim of remedying regional imbalances within Europe. This was also a political and ideological endeavour, in that it implied recognition of a common European space (beyond a common market). The European Development Fund was greatly expanded with the launch of the Lomé agreement in 1975 and aid was also introduced for other regions, notably the Mediterranean. This was concurrent with the politicization of EU external relations policy, as it sought to steer economic relationships for broader purposes. Aid to these new areas

---

1   The ultimate legal authority is held by the European Court of Justice. There are of course many other bodies not discussed here, notably the European Central Bank, which has a significant external role also.

was more fully Europeanized than the EDF. The Council (and later the Parliament also) determined the framework legislation, together with the Commission, while the Commission would take the lead in operating the aid.

External aid policies would multiply rapidly over the following decades as the EU sought to use its resources for more objectives in more areas. Indeed such was the proliferation of aid types that until 2002, country programmers did not even have a master-list of EU aid instruments operating in the country in question (interview, Commission, February 2003). The range of aid formats has been reduced somewhat (see chapter 7) but for the 2001–2007 period a wide variety of instruments were in operation. An aid instrument is generally defined in legal terms, the rules, procedures and funds outlined in the legislation.[2] Given the nature of the EU each aid instrument must be enabled by a specific regulation. Indeed specific democracy and human rights instruments had to be suspended in the 1990s as the Court of Justice ruled that there was no specific legal basis for their activities. Various Treaty articles serve as the legal basis for aid legislation. Title XX outlines the EU's development policy objectives. Yet it is significant that few of the instruments in this period (and none of the major ones studied here) were based solely on this Title. Aid could also be based on Title XXI/Article 181 (general cooperation with third countries) and the multipurpose Article 308, which basically enables legislation on subjects not specifically covered by the Treaty.

The panoply of EU aid policies

Table 2.1 offers a snapshot of the geographical and thematic priorities of EU aid spending, and the variety of instruments. By far the greatest single expenditure on external aid is on pre-accession aid (which actually includes several regulations) and aid to the Balkans, where there is an official EU membership perspective. In itself this is evidence of the self-interest dimension of EU aid policy. This form of aid is not focused on here as the question is whether the EU can exert power without enlarging ad infinitum. In regard to the truly 'external aid' the bulk is devoted to geographical aid as figure 2.2 illustrates ('other' also includes €125.12 million for South Africa which is similar in kind to these aid instruments). One particular form of aid included here is macro-financial assistance, in which concessional loans or grants are allocated to countries with acute public finance difficulties. This is on a conditional basis, in partnership with the International Monetary Fund. It is managed very much on an ad-hoc basis, and thus it cannot be considered as a part of a long-term EU strategy (Ecofin, 2008). The amounts involved have decreased substantially from €1,178 million in 1993 to €141 million in 2003 (Ibid).

---

2   Aid instruments may be further sub-divided for administrative/accounting purposes as there are distinct budget lines, but this is not necessary or useful here.

Table 2.1 EU external aid commitments in 2006 (€ millions)

GEOGRAPHICAL AID	
Preaccession aid (5 main instruments)	2663.57
Balkans (1 main instrument)	523.54
New Independent States/NIS (1 main instrument: TACIS)	527.58
Mediterranean & Middle East (1 main instrument: MEDA)	1177.67
Latin America (1 main instrument: ALA)	355.81
Asia (1 main instrument: ALA)	853.42
THEMATIC INSTRUMENTS	
Macroeconomic assistance	91.99
Humanitarian aid (managed by the ECHO agency)	645.53
Food aid	428.71
Co-financing NGOs	211.88
International fisheries agreements	192.02
The European Initiative for Democracy and Human Rights	145.14
Other	899.14
Total from the EU budget	**8716.00**
Add the European Development Fund	**3407.86**
Total EU external aid	**12123.86**
Total 'purely' external aid excluding (pre-accession aid and the Balkans)	**8936.75**

Source: Europeaid 2007

Most of the numerous global thematic instruments are very small and only the largest are included in table 2.1. It does show the variety of tasks for which aid is performed, which run a gambit of moral and practical purposes, from supporting human rights to fishing agreements. There are also instruments to support environmental protection, curtail anti-personal mines and provide access to information technology. In terms of funding, humanitarian and food aid are by far the most important thematic instruments. Duffield argues that even this form of aid can be viewed as a political intervention and a control mechanism (Duffield, 2001). This may be so but they are not considered here as instruments geared to expanding the EU's structural power. Similarly, apart from the EIDHR, the other

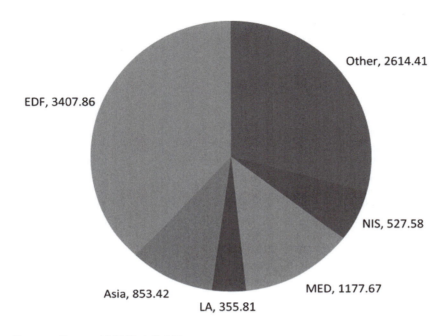

Other, 2614.41

EDF, 3407.86

NIS, 527.58

Asia, 853.42

LA, 355.81

MED, 1177.67

Source: Europeaid 2007, 143-144

Figure 2.1   Comparing EU geographical aid commitments in 2006 (€ millions)

thematic instruments are not studied in any detail as they are not structural power policies (some EIDHR interventions may be understood in this sense). Taken in their totality these policies do add to the EU's influence and they are considered as a part of the overall impact of the EU in a country. However, the main focus is on the major geographical aid instruments. These apply most of the funding for any given region and they have holistic long-term programming procedures that are supposed to ensure a strategic EU approach.

2.2 The Management of Geographical Aid Instruments

At the beginning of the period in question major reforms of EU aid management were implemented. At the highest political level the Development Council was incorporated into the General Affairs (External Relations) Council (2001). This meant that all major external aid instruments now came under the one Council grouping (although the actually significance is debatable as lower level working groups take care of most issues here). More importantly for our purposes, a common programming format (in terms of methodology and procedures) was agreed on for all the geographical EU aid schemes and there were detailed reforms of the Commission. The following passages outline the power of the different EU entities in aid policy. It is necessary to first subdivide EU aid policy into three levels:

- Forming the aid regulation itself.
- The programming of aid over six-year/three-year periods. This includes allocating funds on a non-contractual basis.
- Yearly planning and actual implementation. This includes specific commitments (contractual agreements to fund specific projects) and 'disbursements' (actual payments).

In analysing EU policy in the following chapters, figures for allocations or commitments are generally used as they better reflect EU priorities, while the rate of disbursement is hostage to various other practical issues.

As regards forming the regulation, the situation is relatively simple. The Commission proposes the legislation while the Council has the final say in allowing it. The Commission's right of initiative is obviously a substantial power, but the member states can also be informally involved at this stage. Generally the Parliament has an increasing role in EU aid legislation (see chapter 7) but for the instruments in question it has had less of a role. The legal basis for the regulation is of crucial importance. If the regulation is based on Article 179, the co-decision procedure is used, in which the Parliament has much greater powers. However, for Articles 181a and 308 the Parliament only has a consultation role. So for example, the MEDA, ALA and TACIS regulations were based on Article 308. In these cases the Parliament can make suggestions, some of which were taken up, but there is no legal obligation to do so. As chapter 7 outlines, civil society groups are becoming increasingly effective in combining with an empowered Parliament to shape the debate but, during the period in question, their influence was limited. Neither could partner governments be deemed to have any influence here. Thus it can be safely concluded that the dyad of Council and Commission have shaped these policies, and, as in all EU legislation, the former has the ultimate power.

Yet the legislative framework is necessarily always quite broad, to allow for a certain degree of flexibility. As one interviewee put it, 'the beef is in the programming' (interview, Commission, December 2002). At this stage the allocations for each country are decided, as well as the broader aid strategy (the sectors to focus on and type of activity) and the specific projects. Here the Commission has the primary role. It takes the lead in formulating the Country Strategy Papers and Indicative Papers where these elements are decided. In deciding the actual country allocations the major member states will also have an informal input. Regarding the actual content the Commission is very much in control, although extensive consultations are envisaged, see figure 2.2. As discussed in the following chapters

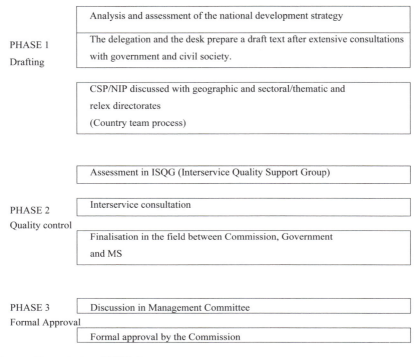

	Analysis and assessment of the national development strategy
PHASE 1	The delegation and the desk prepare a draft text after extensive consultations
Drafting	with government and civil society.

CSP/NIP discussed with geographic and sectoral/thematic and
relex directorates
(Country team process)

	Assessment in ISQG (Interservice Quality Support Group)
PHASE 2	Interservice consultation
Quality control	
	Finalisation in the field between Commission, Government
	and MS

PHASE 3	Discussion in Management Committee
Formal Approval	
	Formal approval by the Commission

Source: Commission, 2001F, 8

Figure 2.2   The official CSP programming process

in most cases the consultation with civil society has been very limited while even partner government's views, although obviously important, have not diverted the Commission from its own strategy.

The formal member state role comes via the 'Comitology' Committees involved at several levels of aid policy. This term is used to describe the variety of Committees of national officials by which the member states monitor the Commission's administration of agreed policies. They work according to varying procedures, which determine how constraining they are on the Commission (Docksey et al. 1997). For the regulatory procedure any proposed Commission action must be approved by a qualified majority to be passed. This process is the most constraining vis a vis the Commission. For the management procedure, actions are approved unless the Committee has a qualified majority that demands an alteration to the document. Comitology Committees on aid policy generally use this less constraining procedure, (of the instruments focused on here TACIS, MEDA and the EDF used the management procedure while the ALA use the regulatory procedure). Their official input into the programming process is at quite a late stage and in the period in question they have not had a major role in shaping the strategy. For example there have been no referrals to the Council by the Mediterranean Committee and interviewees could think only of minor changes to the documents (alterations to a project's focus or methods rather than a change in strategy) made by the Committee.[3]

Regarding the more specific level of implementation and planning. Here again, the different elements of the Commission are in the lead. The exact configuration has altered somewhat since 2001. A new agency, Europeaid, was established in 2000 to handle the planning and implementation of all aid programmes (except pre-accession and humanitarian aid). But also in 2001 a process of management of responsibility to Commission Country Delegations was begun, in which most implementation and planning tasks were devolved to them. Comitology committees are also involved at this level, as they have to approve annual plans(sometimes called finance plans) and in some cases had to approve each individual project (this was mostly phased out by 2001 as it was not time efficient).

2.3 Inside the Commission

While noting that ultimate authority lies with the member state institutions, the foregoing has established that the Commission is the major player at the business end of aid policy. It is a fascinating institution because of its hybrid nature, it in some ways takes the form of a civil service but also has more explicit political powers, and indeed the President of the European Commission is often seen by the public as the 'EU President'. Accordingly it has a dual structure with appointed Commissioners which provide political leadership and a permanent bureaucracy based on Directorates General. Each college of Commissioners is renewed every five years. Over the 2001-2007 period there was the Prodi Commission (from 1999-2004) and the current Barroso Commission (2004-2009). Its highly particular organizational make-up and role lend it to all kinds of interpretations. For Eurosceptics it is viewed as the embryonic government of the European superstate. For Marxists it is the apotheosis of the liberal capitalist tendency to insulate key areas of governance from the popular will. It seems an archetypal example of a 'relatively autonomous' institution (Cammack 2005), designed to manage competing national and business interests in favour of the broader interests of European capital. Objectively, the Commission is best understood as a 'statist' organisation in line with continental European traditions of strong autonomous (or extra-democratic) institutions (Nugent 2000; Featherstone 1994). Idealistically, it is 'at heart, an enlightenment artefact, based on the triumph of rationality over the molten magma of human chaos' (Middlemas 1995).

---

3   The minutes of Comitology committees are available via the Comitology register on the Commission website (Secretariat General 2008).

Needless to say the Commission hasn't always succeeded in its enlightenment project. The incredible range of tasks it has to perform is part of the reason for its shortcomings. Writing in 1970 Coombes divined contradictory forces in organizing the Commission. As an originator of law and ideas it required a quite flexible organizational format, whereas its administrative role implied a more rigid Weberian bureaucracy (Coombes 1970). The range of administrative and operational tasks has expanded over the years, partly due to its own political ambitions (Cram 2001). The period leading up to 2001 saw extensive reforms at the systemic, external relations and aid policy level. The dismissal of the Santer Commission over corruption was the spur for systemic reforms of its management procedures and culture. Also in 1999 the external relations DGs were revamped, as part ongoing effort to get the optimum balance between thematic and geographical structures, see figure 2.3. The delineation of specific Trade and Enlargement DGs had a compelling rationality, while the distinction between the External Relations and Development DGs had more to do with institutional history. External Relations (or 'Relex', from the French acronym) deals with political and economic relations with most of the world, including most aid instruments, while Development handles the relationship with the ACP countries. All four DGs and the two agencies come under what is called the Relex family, within which the External Relations Commissioner has pre-eminence.

1995	1999	2001
DG1: External Economic Relations and East Asia, North America, Australia.	External relations	External relations
DG1A: CFSP Central and Eastern Europe, New Independent States, external missions.	Development	Development
DG1B: Med, Latin America, South East Asia.		
DGVIII: Development co-operation with ACP countries,	Trade	Trade
	Enlargement	Enlargement
	SCR	Europeaid
	ECHO[1]	ECHO

Source: Nugent 2001

Figure 2.3   Organizational changes in the commission

Aid policy had been managed by the relevant DGs but, as discussed in the previous chapter, the Commission's performance was almost universally criticised. In 1998 the Common Service for External Relations (SCR) was created to ameliorate aid management but actually had a disastrous impact. It was disbanded in 1999 and was replaced by the Europeaid office. This body deals solely with aid implementation and evaluation (excluding pre-accession and humanitarian aid), leaving the DGs to concentrate on programming and other long-term factors. An Inter-Service Quality Support Group was also set up, consisting of a permanent secretariat (three people) and a group of experts 'borrowed' from the various DGs for the purpose of evaluating programming. It is itself physically located within DG Development and is run by this DG. Its input into the production of the CSP itself is at quite an early stage (see figure .3) in the process. Thus the reforms, and the new Country Strategy Paper format, were designed to improve the Commission's strategic capability as well as its basic efficiency. Since 2001, the only change has been the increased role for the Delegations in implementation, with aidco taking a more advisory and monitoring role. The current division of labour for programming and implementation is outlined in figure 2.4.

Although this division does not correspond with best practice models it suits the Commission's needs. The DGs have proven incapable of handling all aspects

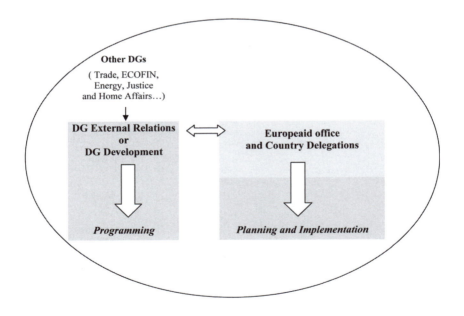

Figure 2.4 Inside the Commission

of aid administration, now left to Europeaid and the Delegations. The latter may be presumed to have the most country knowledge and expertise but having one centrally located entity dealing with programming facilitates the political guidance of aid. The DGs are well positioned to offer this political direction as they are involved in all dimensions of the relationship. This is particularly true for the External Relations DG whose officials are attuned to their role in promoting the European interest. The difference between it and the Development DG is striking. Officials interviewed within External Relations from 2002-2004 felt that the other DG was overstaffed and not focused sufficiently on the EU's external relations goals. So, for example, at the first round of CSP programming (2001) several Mediterranean aid officials were unhappy with the role of the Inter-Service Quality Support Group. Individuals felt that it was too developmentally orientated and were not convinced that the official guidelines and methods for the CSP were suited to a strategic aid instrument such as MEDA. The Development DG on the other hand still sees itself as the basic source of policy for economic and financial assistance and regularly produces communications outlining guidelines on various issues. As one External Relations official put it: 'I really do see a real problem there – of finding so many comms (communications) defining what you can and can't do that you end up in an enormous, complex and bureaucratic straitjacket' (interview, Commission, December 2002). Clearly there have been tensions between differing conceptions of the role of aid policy within the Commission, with External Relations more in line with the use of aid posited here. It is this DG that controls the aid instruments for crucial strategic regions like the Mediterranean and the ex-Soviet neighbourhood.

2.4 'EU Aid' in a European and International Context

'Europe' is the greatest donor of aid in the world, but this includes the member states' aid as well as EU managed aid. Aid policy is different in kind from EU trade policy and EU agricultural policy as EU member states retain their own autonomous aid policies, which is not the case for these other issue areas. Given the variety of political and economic objectives aid furthers it is not surprising that member states want their own aid policies (or that aspiring international actors such as the Scottish and Catalonian governments also have aid policies). The major European donors are France, the UK and the Germany. In terms of aid as a percentage of GDP per capita, Denmark, The Netherlands, Sweden and Luxemburg are far in advance (Orbie 2003, 399). These are the only ones to have reached the .7% of GDP level that all developed countries have committed to, and they and other smaller states seek to play an active role in shaping European aid policy.

The development chapter of the Treaty calls for coordination and complementarity between EU and member state aid policy. Coordination involves the exchange of information while complementarity is much more far reaching and implies a division of labour; with the EU and member states applying themselves to specific sectors. Given the scale of combined EU and member state aid this could massively increase the influence and impact of EU policy. General trends in aid policy have created a favourable environment for their realisation, specifically an increased consensus on policy issues and the use of modalities such as sectoral reform programmes, which require cooperation amongst donors. As outlined in the empirical chapters there was little progress towards detailed complementarity in the period in question. Coordination on the ground is constantly improving but strategic coordination (of the long-term strategies) which enables full complementarity is still an ideal. Regarding European collaboration within international fora, the European Commission has tried to develop a common European position on key aid and development issues (Orbie 2003). Yet it is significant that while European states have a very large percentage of votes in the boards that control the World Bank and the International Monetary Fund, they do not necessarily speak with one 'EU' voice. As Chapter 7 discusses there have been recent efforts to further harmonize European aid policy.

Beyond Europe there is a highly institutionalized international aid community to consider, including public multilateral and bilateral/state donors; and private transnational donors (NGOs and foundations). Here the European Union straddles the division between multilateral and bilateral institutions. The EU has a seat in bilateral fora, of which the most important is the Development Assistance Committee of the Organization for Economic Cooperation and Development. This attempts to lay out guidelines on all aspects of aid and development policy and also evaluates donors in regard to these. As table 2.2 shows the major bilateral donors outside of Europe are the US and Japan. Pressure to coordinate aid policy and procedures has increased markedly in the past decade, due primarily to the need to attenuate the workload of recipient countries in dealing with multiple donors. Key aspects of policy conditionality have been harmonized under the leadership of the International Financial Institutions (IFIs: the World Bank and the IMF), at least among Western donors. There are other substantial aid donors that are not in the 'international community' as represented by the DAC. Most notably oil rich Arab states and China have offered large amount of aid of different types, often for nakedly political/ideological and economic purposes.

Regarding multilateral bodies, the United Nations agencies and programmes are major players in humanitarian and food aid. The UNDP (the United Nations Development Programme) also tries to try to play an agenda setting role in international development policy and governance related aid but the World Bank is by far the most important in this respect.[4] Its unparalleled research capacity has allowed it to set the agenda in many ways for thinking on development and public

---

4   The World Bank and IMF are technically within the UN family but entirely independent in reality. These institutions also derive power from their general role as providers of public finance in general (not concessional and not any kind of 'aid'), thus their influence cannot be divined merely from the amount of aid they give (Riddel 2007, 80).

Table 2.2 DAC members net ODA/OA in 2007 ($US millions)

EU member states (including contributions to EU aid budget and EDF)		Other DAC	
Austria	1797.95	Australia	2470.89
Belgium	1953.17	Canada	3921.92
Finland	973.48	New Zealand	315.46
France	9940.19	Norway	3727.05
Denmark	2563.02	Japan	7690.69
Germany	12267.13	Switzerland	1680.27
Greece	500.82	United States	21752.83
Ireland	1189.79	**DAC total**	103654.54
Italy	3928.64		
Luxembourg	364.66		
Netherlands	6215.30		
Portugal	402.51		
Spain	5744.04		
Sweden	4334.08		
United Kingdom	9920.65		

Note: total EU-level ODA/OA in 2007 was 11770.91$ millions

Source: DAC database 2008

management (Gibbon 1993; Wade 2001). It is conscious of this power and has launched a major drive to transform itself into a 'knowledge bank' and develop its 'knowledge management', defined as 'capturing and organizing systematically the wealth of knowledge and experience gained from staff, clients and development partners' (World Bank 2004a). The EU's own collaboration with the World Bank is extensive, as detailed in the studies of Morocco and Ukraine. The World Bank led the way in operating harsh structural adjustment to break-up statist economic regimes in the 1980s and also, under the tutelage of Wofehnson (Wade 2001), pioneered softer, coordinated international efforts at promoting development within certain policy guidelines. In regards to the poorest developing countries World Bank and IMF-led debt relief has been one of the most significant sources of 'aid' in the past decade. The Heavily Indebted Poor Countries (HIPC) initiatives (1996, 1999) have released hundreds of millions for eligible countries (Callaghy 2004). Recipients must produce a Poverty Reduction Strategy Paper that complies with 'pro-poor' and standard neo-liberal conditionalities. After the Gleaneagles G8 summit of 2005, further multilateral debt relief was announced with the prospect of 100% relief from debts to the International Financial Institutions (Moss 2006). The Bank has also promoted Comprehensive Development Frameworks for less poor developing countries, which are supposed to serve as a template for international and domestic development policies.

Thus there is a degree of convergence within the public international aid community, which promotes development along lines complementary to first world needs and in accordance with liberal values. However, as long as donors have control over their allocation of funds and final say over the activities funded they can still be regarded as having an autonomous aid policy. For example, extensive pressure from the DAC and other bodies to focus more aid on the poorest of the poor has not prevented the EU from using aid according to its priorities. A high proportion of EU-level aid goes to relatively well-off middle income countries with strategic importance, as opposed to least developed countries, and for this it is much criticised (Open Europe 2007, 6). Indeed the EU has dramatically reduced the percentage of its aid going to the poorest in the previous two decades (Riddell 2007, 62).

Conclusion

EU aid policy is essentially controlled by the member states and the Commission. While the former have ultimate legal authority, the latter has been delegated control over programming and implementation. The policy procedures ensure that key member state interests must be taken into account but, once the legislation is established, the Commission is the single most important player in shaping and implementing aid strategy. The EU's use of aid policy increased dramatically in the post-1989 era, far beyond the capacity of the Commission to manage it. The extensive reforms over 1998–2001 were an effort to redress its numerous deficiencies and these were explicitly designed to improve strategy formulation, as well as general efficiency. A more powerful External Relations DG, which handles programming and general political and economic relations for most countries, should in theory enhance the EU's ability to use aid for long-term political purposes. In the global context, although there is a certain degree of harmonization of public aid donors worldwide, the EU still retains its specificities and its agenda. Certainly it is not to be confused with purely multilateral organizations, such as the UN agencies, as it has a particular geographically-based configuration of interests to support (in this sense it is more state-like). EU aid policy can also be distinguished from the various EU member state policies as it tends to work towards the long-term European interests in coordination with other EU-level policies. Ultimately, it is more appropriate to evaluate it in relation to these policies than as a part of a European or global development effort.

Chapter 3
EU Aid and Euro-Mediterranean Integration

Since the 1970s the EU has singled out the Mediterranean region for close attention. As with the Western element of the former Soviet Union, the Mediterranean is considered a part of Europe's 'near abroad'. Due to its geographical proximity there is a far greater degree of interdependence in its relationship with Europe than for other developing countries. Or as Hager put it, the two shores of this sea are linked not precisely by interdependence, but by two distinct kinds of dependence (Hager 1973, 196); Europe is dependent on North Africa and the Middle East for energy supplies and has clear security interests, while the other shore is highly dependent on Europe economically and commercially. The notion of a Mediterranean region has highly symbolic connotations, apart from its historical resonance it is a microcosm of the North-South economic divide and a crossroads of civilizations. These contrasts help throw the political dimension of the EU's economic diplomacy into sharp relief.

What is especially striking about EU Mediterranean policy is that, while security is the greatest single concern, the means of tackling this involves economic and institutional reform and integration with the EU. This is because the instability of the Arab states in the region, is attributed in large part to socioeconomic failure and poor governance.[1] As the region was very much in the Union's economic sphere of influence it presented an opportunity for it to use its various instruments to intervene in these countries and help to shape the future. This chapter will outline the policies the EU has adopted here (some of which are similar to those for the EU's Eastern Neighbourhood) and how they may be interpreted as efforts to extend its structural power. The essence of EU policy is an effort to support a transition process and forge a Euro-Mediterranean economic space. The chapter will look in detail at the MEDA aid programme, designed explicitly to support this process, and evaluate its operation as an instrument of structural power. The course of the chapter is as follows. First the basic historical context is outlined. Then the EU's policy framework is discussed and related to the theoretical framework. Following on from this the aid instrument is analysed in some detail. Finally there is a detailed analysis of the EU's strategy for Morocco, this is one of the EU's closest partners and is finely balanced between reform and reaction.

---

1   Turkey and Israel are not considered here; as one is an accession country and the other does not receive aid. Libya is not included as it has not taken part in the Euro-Mediterranean Partnership.

3.1 Historical Background

As in other parts of the world the North-South relationship in the Mediterranean became highly asymmetric once European superiority in military and economic terms emerged. By the 19th century the European states were beginning to colonize the region. In Morocco, Tunisia and Egypt the pretexts for intervention were economic/financial failure, the ensuing breakdown of order and consequent threats to the international community. Other areas were won through conquest and war. The colonial moment was relatively brief in these countries, with the exception of Algeria the British and French had left in under a century. Yet their influence was substantial, particularly in encouraging a form of economic development geared to the *métropole* market. This took the form of agro-exports, for example food and wine in the Maghreb, cotton in Egypt (Richards & Waterbury 1998, 35/41). Independence was achieved between 1945 and 1962 for the entire region, and the nature of the resulting states has been the subject of some debate. Richards and Waterbury argue that the colonial experience actually strengthened the domestic institutions of the Arab world and that far from being 'weak' the Arab state has been too strong (Ibid, 35, 41). Others, in particular Ayubi (1995), would disagree with this and argue that although 'fierce' in terms of security policies the states are weak in terms of their capacity to act. White (2001) has also emphasised, while recognising the obvious importance of structural economic factors, the autonomy of these governments and the strategic choices they make.

Unquestionably, these states were vulnerable since inception to external or internal security threats. They sacrificed notions of democracy in favour of a push for national security and development. As there was no strong 'private sector' it was the State-led development efforts. In tune with development thinking in the immediate post-colonial era, there was state capitalism with a protected economy in which the public sector was the major force, while the private sector fed off the state and its extensive bureaucracy. Indeed patrimonialism was and is a common feature of their political economies. For the 'populist revolutionary states' (Algeria, Syria, Tunisia and Egypt) it was 'bureaucratic' (Ayubi 1995, 196–223), in that patronage was based more on interest groups than organic ties. In the case of Morocco and Jordan it was more organic, based on personal/familial ties (Ibid, 224–255). While these modes of governance proved enduring, economic policies were altered due to internal financial difficulties, mounting debts and greater external pressure as neo-liberal globalization gained momentum. This started in the 1970s in some cases, but nearly all had adapted by the 1980s. As they turned to the international financial institutions for emergency finance and longer term investment, they had to accept core conditions in return for this. All of this led to a more outward-looking approach to development and export-led growth focused on light manufacturing industries, which pointed them towards Europe (White 2001). From the beginning many of the newly independent states looked towards the European countries as the major economies of the region. This was especially true for the Maghreb.

The EEC/EU had begun to engage more proactively in the region in the 1970s. This was in response to clear indications that the instability in the region was having an impact on Europe's security. It constructed what it called a Global Mediterranean Policy (GMP), an effort to formalise and harmonise the EU's Mediterranean relationships through signing trade and cooperation agreement with the riparian states (Jawad 1992, 20–35). These included several European states at the time (Spain and Greece).[2] The GMP agreements waived tariffs for most industrial products and also offered financial assistance to the poorer countries. Naturally this further encouraged the Euro-orientation of the trade policies of the Mediterranean Partner Countries (MPCs). Yet these agreements were not entirely generous and the Europeans, although eager to promote development, were firm in defending their own interests. Key agricultural products were not included in the tariff waiver and the EU reserved the right to impose quotas on these and on sensitive industrial products such as textiles (Fontagne 1997, 20–34). This left the EU's partners rather vulnerable and this vulnerability was greatly increased by the Mediterranean enlargements of the EU and the Single European Act. The Greek (1981) and Spanish (1986) enlargements of the EU introduced countries whose agricultural products were competitive rather than complementary with Mediterranean partners (Jawad 1992, 38–44). Agro-exports would be further restricted. To add to this the renewed efforts at European Integration, the Single European Act (1986) and the 1992 programme led to renewed fears of revived European protectionism (a 'fortress Europe) even in countries as powerful as the US and Japan. The fear of being 'locked out' was very real (White, 2001). This gravitational pull of European Integration (based on the fear of exclusion) is the real 'soft power' of Europe. Morocco and Tunisia led the way in this Euro-courting as their export-led growth policies had linked them most closely with Europe (Ibid).

Generally, the (albeit limited) liberal economic reforms in the region had removed a plank of legitimacy from the state (the traditional provider), which combined with the failure to develop participatory political systems helped provide the basis for powerful Islamist opposition movements (of many types) throughout the region (Burgat, 2002). Yet these partial reforms had failed to engineer substantial economic growth and at the turn of the century Arab states ranked poorly on most levels of political, economic and human development (UNDP 2002; Zaafrane and Mahjoub 2000). Such stagnation was exacerbated by rising demographic pressures and the various conflicts in the region, leaving a series of states with latent or actual crises to the South of Europe. One forewarning for Europe was the strong anti-western sentiment shown by the Arab peoples (and in particular North Africa which might have been felt to be distant from such forces) during the Gulf Crisis of 1990–1991. When financial crisis led to a botched democratization and civil war in Algeria (Dillman 2000) Europeans were given a clearer warning. Direct threat from terrorism was also a factor then although not as

---

2 Communist South East European States were not included.

prominent as now. Generally there was a fear of the rise of radical 'anti-Western' Islamic movements, perhaps spreading to European Arab populations. Rightly or wrongly, migration (mostly of young unemployed) was felt to be a security threat. Such factors were cited by the Commission in arguing for a more proactive Mediterranean policy (Commission 1994).

3.2 The EU's Policy Framework

Led by Spain the EU stumbled towards a comprehensive Mediterranean project from 1989 to 1995 (Gillespie, 1997). Dilemmas as to the scope of this project are apparent as policies such as the Renovated Mediterranean policy (RMP) in 1990 were concerned primarily with the Maghreb (Gillespie 2000, 147). Optimism regarding the Middle East peace process extended this strategy to the entire Mediterranean region (and to include a region-building component), including Egypt and the Levant. The EU's new vision was articulated in the Barcelona Declaration of 1995, which set out the Euro-Mediterranean Partnership (EMP). It was signed by the EU and the 12 partners: Morocco, Algeria, Tunisia, Egypt, Israel, the Palestinian Authority, Jordan, Lebanon, Syria and three accession states, Malta and Cyprus (both of whom would join the EU in 2004) and Turkey. The EMP envisaged intensified cooperation between the EU and its neighbours on a variety of levels. It was divided into three 'baskets': basket 1 dealt with political/security cooperation, basket 2 with the economic/commercial sphere and basket 3 with social/cultural affairs.

Although no hierarchy of objectives or sequence is outlined, clearly basket two is the primary one and it is relatively detailed as to how the economic objectives will be met. The bilateral Association Agreements are the key instruments here, these involve free trade in goods (excluding agricultural products) and have gradually been realised (see table 3.1). It is important to note that the EU had already given free access for most goods to these countries and was now opening them up in return. This is done in a graduated manner: tariffs for non-sensitive products are removed first whereas tariffs for products likely to be affected by European competition are removed from years four to twelve. Beyond trade in goods, liberalization of trade in services and harmonization of regulations in areas such as competition policy is envisaged, as the process develops. This process should be accompanied by integration between non-European states, leading to a common Euro-Mediterranean free trade area by 2010.

The Agreements also have a political dimension in that human rights and democratic principles are essential elements, and cooperation can be suspended in case of non-respect of these principles. This more idealistic element has been relatively toothless. On another political dimension there are numerous common institutions established, including a high level Association Council and more functional Association Committees and working groups. A rich web of 'functionalist' cooperation has also been developed at the Euro-Mediterranean

Table 3.1   Status of the Euro-Mediterranean Association Agreements with Arab partners

	Status
Algeria	Signed on 22.04.02 In force 1 September 2005.
Morocco	Signed 26.02.96 *In force 1.03.00*
Tunisia	Signed on 17.07.95 *In force 1.03.9*
Egypt	Signed on 25.06.01 *In force 1.06.04*
Lebanon	Signed on 17.06.02 *In force since 01.03.03*
Syria	Negotiations concluded. Initialled 19.10.04 Council to decide on signature
Jordan	Signed 24.11.97 *In force since 01.05.02*

Source: http://ec.europa.eu/comm/external_relations/euromed/med_ass_agreemnts.htm

level. Again this includes high-level ministerial meetings (mostly on issues such as trade, transport, environment and energy) and also a lot of 'technocratic' activity. As stated above the EMP includes a need for integration on the south side also. The various Euro-Med fora contribute to this. Also the EU has supported the Agadir process, an agreement signed in 2004 to build a free trade area between Morocco, Tunisia, Egypt and Jordan.

A new financial aid programme MEDA, (*mesures d'accompagnement* – 'accompanying measures') was set up to support the Association Agreements and the reform project. Modelled more on pre-accession aid than traditional 'development' aid, the aim of MEDA was essentially to further transition and integration of national economic systems. The legal objectives of MEDA are threefold (Official Journal, 1996a, Annex 2):

- To support the process of transition
- To support regional integration
- To help maintain social cohesion.

The first was clearly the overarching goal (Holden 2003). MEDA I was allocated € 3.345 billion for 1995–99 (substantially more than previous Mediterranean aid) MEDA II had €5.350 billion euro allocated for the period 2000–2006. The MPCs could also avail of other aid including an instrument to develop civil society movements (the MEDA Democracy programme) and other relatively small scale programmes. Loans from the European Investment Bank have also been made available to Mediterranean countries for infrastructure, development projects and a specific facility FEMIP (Facility for Euro-Mediterranean Investment and Partnership), was established (2002) to channel funds to the private sector.

The European Neighbourhood Policy (ENP)

The overarching policy framework of the EMP has been overshadowed, although not superseded, by the European Neighbourhood Policy (ENP) launched in 2003 (Commission, 2003a). This policy, for Eastern and Southern neighbours is an intensification of previous EU efforts in both regions. It continues the attempt to encourage reform through integration (and is based on the same economic strategy) borrowing from the Accession Partnership technique used for accession countries. . Agreed short to medium term Action Plans outline reform targets and countries are offered greater access to the EU internal market and certain internal programmes, as well as aid. The ENP aims at much greater integration, the end goal being the effective extension of the EU's internal market rules and harmonization of many other areas of public policy. While the EMP had an element of multilateralism the ENP is almost totally bilateral. Only some countries, Morocco, Tunisia and Jordan in the Mediterranean, were included in the first wave of Action Plans in 2004. Egypt and Lebanon followed in 2005, while Algeria is not considered ready for this process. As it didn't significantly alter the EU's objectives (merely intensifying them) the short term impact of the ENP on aid policy was limited.

Interpreting the EU's objectives

To summarise the EU's policy objectives: the proximate goal is to alter the regulatory system directly related to trade and commercial interaction. Yet there is also a deeper form of transformation sought. This involves reforming/ modernizing the economic, legal and administrative institutions and policies of the Mediterranean partners, in line with liberal 'rational economic models'. The process should include liberalizing the economy in terms of the legal framework and actual situation, reforming the administration in terms of formal structures and quality and more generally altering the patrimonial system of governance and policy-making. Hopefully, this will in turn reinvigorate economic and social development. The political reform element is best described as political liberalization. This involves an 'expansion of the public space' (Brynen et al. 1998, 3) but falls short of democratization *per se*, which would involve radical (regime) change.

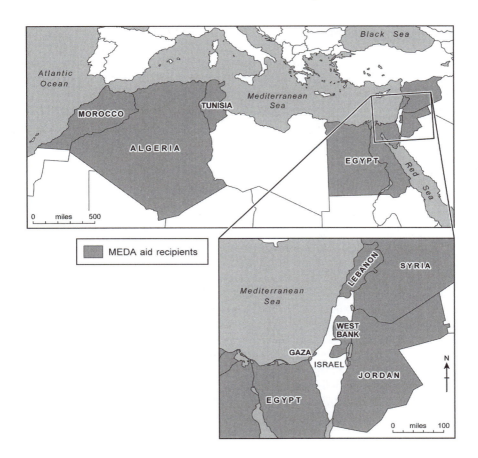

Map 3.1   MEDA recipients

Given the multidimensional nature of the policy framework there is ample material for various theoretical interpretations. Youngs points out that in fact different logics (and motivations) coexist within EU policy-making (Youngs 2002, 199). Obviously one overarching goal is security and stability. This is to be achieved through reform of the state (including limited political reforms) and economic development. It is undeniable that the securing of Europe from potential threats was the overwhelming motivational factor. Given that this is a broader conception of security, EU policy-makers sought 'a redefinition of internal and regional stability through the restructuring of internal socio-political processes' (Munoz 2000, 97). The instruments chosen to do this (reform and integration) inevitably involve increasing the EU's influence and role in the region, developing its latent structural power. Europe is also using its position to promote its own regulatory and economic models in the global economy, and this was an explicit part of the Commission's rationale for the EMP (Commission 1994, 6).

In the economic and commercial sphere, reforms to boost the private sector and develop free market capitalism mean that partner governments and businesses will be brought into the European Union's economic block in relation to the global geoeconomic environment. In this sphere the situation will be closest to domination due to the massive asymmetries between the partners. Economists have predicted that diversion of other international trade to Europe is a long-term likely consequence (Tovias 1997). Partner countries will remain free to pursue economic links with outside actors in Asia and America (a customs union would inhibit this but this has not yet been proposed). Yet even without a customs union and even if trade diversion does not actually occur, the EU's weight is preponderant and the regulatory models proposed are designed according to European templates which makes them a form of indirect European control. The fact that the EU is also supporting intra-Arab integration does not detract from this essential truth as this is secondary to the thrust for Euro-Mediterranean integration. Given the overwhelming weight of the European Union the freeing up of trade and other commercial barriers almost inevitably leads towards a hubs and spoke system. The level of intra-Arab trade is so low that this is inevitably a feeble sideshow.

Beyond economic integration, other levels of civil and political society would be brought further into the EU's orbit. Western style NGOs are being supported which will be linked to Europe in terms of funding from the EU itself, partnerships with European NGOs and in regard to general outlook/ideology. Political development too would also be steered although again not crudely dominated. While the more radical (and totalitarian) Islamist models would be rejected, Islamist politics may still be pursued but within certain limits. It should be clear that this trajectory does not imply the incorporation of the partners into a geopolitical block in terms of traditional foreign policy; in fact the EU itself is not a 'geopolitical' block in this sense of the term. What would occur is a diffuse soft hegemony in which in various sectors (and to a greater or lesser degree) European power would be increased via deeper asymmetric interdependence. The Commission, member states, business or civil society institutions may articulate this power in the relevant spheres. This may be related to the concept of Europeanization, which describes the process by which the norms and institutions of EU members (national governments and political/civil and economic society) are harmonised with certain key 'European' characteristics (Emerson et al. 2004). The key objectives of MEDA have already been outlined and are clearly in line with this dual vision of imposing reform and European influence.

3.3 MEDA in Operation

MEDA was explicitly conceived as a proactive instrument, which would catalyse (as opposed to merely support) a reform process in partner countries. It would accomplish this through positive or allocative conditionality and through adopting a 'strategic approach' to its financial and technical support activities (Holden, 2003). That is to say it would target its financial and technical assistance at key sectors in line with a long-term plan for reform of the MPCs economic systems. The MEDA 2 regulation for the period from 2000-2006 contained new procedures to ensure more efficient disbursement and also further emphasised that aid should be conditional and strategic (Official Journal 2000a).

While member state priorities are taken into account in the level of country funding the Commission has been in control of the programming and planning. It formulates the CSPs, which provide the fundamental analysis upon which the EU's aid and indeed other activities should be based and the NIPs which outline the specific content of the aid strategy for a three-year period including the funding levels. The Mediterranean Committee is the primary channel for member state input; although this comes at quite a late stage in the process and member state experts can also get involved in the country team discussions, see below. The EU's Mediterranean policy is, rhetorically at least, very much a partnership and the partner governments have to be consulted obviously as aid cannot be imposed on them. However, as a rule, the essential features of the strategy are determined in Brussels and then the details negotiated with the governments (Holden, 2005b). It was widely felt that an effort at a joint strategy would be a disaster, and would be reduced to a haggling exercise. The very nature of MEDA was not based on partner government wishes as they would have been happy enough with increased old-style development aid rather than the highly conditional, reform-focused instrument that was created (interviews, European Commission, 2002–2003).

Other groups within the Commission can be consulted for the country team process. Official literature (Commission, 2002a) cites 'sector policy specialists' of different types from the Trade DG, Development DG, the Economic and Finance DG and the human rights and democracy unit. An internal survey of programmers involved in the preparation of the CSPs revealed that for MEDA only the Trade DG had a significant input (Commission, 2002a, Annex 4). In brief it can be concluded that the Commission, specifically Directorate F in the Relex directorate, dominates the programming process. Here there is a specific 'culture' and ideology in terms of their commitment to the EU's Mediterranean reform objectives. The general efficiency of the system has also been greatly improved from the pre 2000 period when it was sorely criticized (Europeaid evaluation unit 1999, 27–34). This conclusion is backed up by official evaluations (Europeaid evaluation unit 2005: 16–17), which naturally emphasizes that things could still be further improved.

The following section analyses how this affected the EU's strategic use of aid. It concentrates on two axes:

- The analytical approach: Is EU aid based upon a deep and holistic analysis and understanding of the local context to provide the basis for a comprehensive intervention and to enable conditionality to be applied in a credible fashion?
- EU funding priorities/actual strategy: Are EU resources being used to further the declared strategic objectives? Is conditionality applied in practice?

The Country Strategy Papers

The common format for CSPs agreed by the Council (Commission, 2000a) specifies that there should be a systematic and holistic (political and economic) analysis of the country, making use of benchmarks and indicators. This should include the following information and categories:

- the policy agenda of the partner government
- the political and the socio-economic context
- the medium term challenges for the country
- an account of previous EU cooperation
- other EU aid instruments and policies
- and other donors' activities.

Apart from the format however, the guidelines available were not specific regarding the methodology to be used and indeed many programmers interviewed complained of this (interviews, European Commission, 2002–2003). The basic framework of a six-year long-term vision and a three-year NIP was not foreign to Mediterranean programmers. However, as discussed in terms of aid management there was always potentially a certain tension as CSP guidelines posit a general analysis of socio-economic development whereas MEDA is geared more specifically towards the regulatory/institutional framework. Several officials interviewed felt the CSP model was not quite appropriate for MEDA.

Over 2001 the CSPs for 2002–2006 were elaborated by the External Relations staff. The Mediterranean CSPs in general were highly regarded within the Commission for their degree of focus and rigour of analysis, relative to those for other geographical areas (interview, Commission official, January 2003). Officials themselves take pride in their achievement; one senior official noted that the CSP for his country was 'better than what the government itself could have done' (Commission official, interview, April 2004). They do form the basis for a strategic intervention but in view of the ambition of the EU's aims they have some deficiencies. Dearden had noted the CSPs (for developing countries) lacked analytical rigour in terms of their poverty reduction objectives (Dearden, 2002). This is also true for the MEDA countries and the MEDA objectives. Unsurprisingly the political analysis sections of the CSPs are not at all rigorous (these sections are very weak and haphazard in all CSPs). But also the sphere of economic policy and governance contains practically nothing in indicators and benchmarks. Some may argue whether this kind of methodology is appropriate for these objectives anyway. What is undoubtedly necessary is an awareness of the politics of economic reform in countries with highly politicized economies (with entrenched and inter-related forms of economic and political power). Although there is no hint of a detailed analysis of the likely opponents and supporters of change, programmers are clearly aware of such issues. The lessons learned sections are mostly concerned with implementation issues: there is some recognition of the 'political' problems experienced in the past but no real indication of how these might be overcome apart from ensuring the agreement of key stakeholders beforehand.

There are limits to any organization's ability to plan interventions in complex social systems. It is worth noting some particular challenges of the EU system. Rather ironically this is a feature of the quite cohesive policy-making and programming system which is run by a select group in strict accordance with the neo-liberal reform strategy. Despite the new CSP procedures, the processing of complex and qualitative knowledge' from the wider world is constrained. The fact that programmers (although obviously of very high calibre) do not usually have an academic background in their country and that there is a high turnover of staff also affects knowledge management. One positive aspect is the revamped evaluation unit already mentioned. Evaluations are fed back but they often have limited frames of reference and do not question the fundamentals of the EU's approach. Member state officials and experts should also be a crucial form of knowledge for Commission planners. Hitherto however member state involvement has been more concerned with financial control than the formation of a comprehensive strategy. There is coordination on the ground but more at the tactical level, within the constraints of the programmes. There are various other international networks that the Commission is plugged into. Notably, the EU can combine with the World Bank and avail of its intellectual resources. Above all the Euro-Mediterranean Partnership provides a rich web of communication with the partner governments and elements of civil society. The problem is that this communication takes place mostly at the tactical level – the precise focus of a sectoral reform programme etc. – rather than the deeper question of development/reform strategies. The neo-liberal framework implicit in EU policy excludes many approaches.

The EU's funding priorities: the National Indicative Programmes (2002–2006)

The basic point about MEDA as an instrument for reform and 'institutional engineering' was that financial resources should be used to support reform projects and serve to reward and encourage those MPCs that are on the path to reform. In practice this is not so easy as there are the various organizational/procedural constraints and, to an extent, the wishes of partner governments to consider. MEDA II funding was supposed to be (under MEDA II) more focused on EMP objectives. As Patrick Laurent (then head of unit B in Directorate F) put it the EU 'noted that five years after the Barcelona conference much had been done but that efforts had been spread too thin and that it was now necessary to strengthen the link between the MEDA program and the implementation of reforms initiated by the Mediterranean partners under the Association Agreement' (Laurent 2001). As the foregoing outlined EU aid has been streamlined to make it more suitable for the kind of targeted approach MEDA called for. The actual funding priorities of MEDA in this period can be divined from the projects selected and the amounts allocated in the National Indicative Programmes which are then implemented in yearly National Finance Plans. Space constraints preclude an analysis of the content of each NIP. The following passages will outline the EU's funding priorities according to the key classifications outlined in chapter 1:

1. Reform orientated projects and programmes including:
   * political development,
   * structural adjustment programmes,
   * sector-wide adjustment programmes, aid paid directly to the government (in tranches) conditional on certain reforms.,
   * privatization programmes,
   * various efforts to reform public administration.
2. Support to the private sector to upgrade to compete in a Euro-Med market, thus closely linked to the reform process.
3. Aid for socio-economic welfare such as rural development, health, education, water, environmental protection.
4. Other (migration management, humanitarian aid).

Where specific projects involve different elements they are categorized according to what the primary purpose is deemed to be. Table 3.2 makes clear that while there is a substantial amount devoted to directly maintaining social cohesion and combating poverty, aid for reform and private sector development takes up the lions share of funding. Aid for democracy is not a large part of this (even when supplemented by the specific funding instrument for democracy and civil society, which is a small scale instrument). The vast bulk of reform assistance is for economic and public administration reform. Accordingly the NIPs are very much geared to the EU's strategic objectives. This might seem a banal conclusion but it hasn't always been the case for the EU and there are substantial pressures to the contrary in this region.

Were it left to the partner governments, most agree, there would be much more funding devoted to job creating and infrastructure support activities (interview, Commission, April 2004). In terms of the instruments used one notes a greater reliance on budgetary support mechanisms for sectoral reform (aid paid directly to the government conditional on specific reforms) than previously. This facilitates the Commission's stated desire to focus on key sectors and also lightens the administrative burden on the Commission and helps it to increase the disbursement rate. They do however place a heavy demand on the aid donor in terms of monitoring and research/preparation. The next section will look in detail at an NIP for one country, Morocco. In general one may conclude that for each

Table 3.2   Programming priorities for the seven state recipients of MEDA 2002–2006 (€ millions)*

	€millions	% of total
1. Reform	1215.15	50.5
2. Support for the private sector	177	7
3. Socio-economic welfare	952	40
4. Other	62	2.5
Total	2406.15	100

Source: National Indicative Programmes
*This table also appeared in the Journal of International Development (Holden 2008, 239). Category totals differ slightly due to a reclassification of the Tempus programme and one aid project in Jordan.

country the Commission is evidently specialising in certain sectors rather than launching a broad range of projects and, as in the global picture, the main focus is on 'reform'. This conclusion is also borne out by the official evaluation of MEDA (Europeaid evaluation unit 2005, 15).

How did things develop within this period? The ideas and principles of the ENP are meant to influence ongoing MEDA programming, although its noteworthy that the Action Plans for the ENP were released after the NIPs for 2004–2006 had been drawn up. The Commission separately declared a new drive to improve democracy support in the region. New NIPs produced for the period 2005–2006, were based on a mid-term review of the CSPs informed by the new policy initiatives and lessons learnt. In the case of the Mediterranean, it was felt that there was no need for any dramatic change to the basic strategy (Commission 2005a). There is a reflection of the greater priority given to democracy in that there are more small programmes devoted to civil society development (generally for human right and development NGOs) in many countries. Essentially the focus of aid remains the same and there is no obvious impact from the new ENP. Other changes to the policy framework include a new range of desiderata related for example to the Doha development agenda, and the conclusions of the Johannesburg Summit on sustainable development. Again, the substantive influence of these is negligible.

The national strategies are complemented by region wide activities outlined in the regional indicative programme (RIP), see table 3.3. The Commission

Table 3.3   Regional Aid (€millions)

Regional Indicative Programme 2002–2004	
Pool of technical assistance	4
Training of pub administration	6
Transport/energy/telecommunications (re-regulation)	17
Environment programme	15
Education training and unemployment	5
Enhancing participation of women	5
Judicial cooperation – police co-op re drugs	6
Euromed heritage,audiovisual, information	35
Total	**93**
2005–2006	
EuroMesco (academic network of political scientists)	5
FEMISE (network of economic researchers)	5
Free trade – regulatory approximation	20
Intercultural foundation	5
Cooperation between towns and local administration	5
Justice and Home Affairs 2	15
Youth	5
Total	**60**

Source: Commission 2001a 2004c

recognises the difficulties of regional programmes and clearly states that the goal of region wide activities is, through limited training and networking activities, to complement the national strategies and the broader EU goal of facilitating cooperation. Thus we have technical assistance programmes for developing free trade between non-member Mediterranean countries. The provision of technical assistance to trade policy units will, officials feel, give the Commission an *entrée* into the sphere of intra-Arab trade policy for the future (interview Commission, December 2003). Also for the future, aid programmes to liberalize and interconnect the energy systems and transport systems of the partners are laying the basis for further economic integration. (Officials recognise that at the moment the political climate is not propitious for this). There are also programmes to support reform of the public administration and cooperation in the field of justice and home affairs to complement national activities.

Conditionality in practice?

The MEDA II regulation and programme was designed specifically to ensure the system of allocative conditionality would be operational and that the flow of funds would be calibrated according to countries' progress in making reform. Patrick Laurent (2001); 'This issue (conditionality) lies at the heart of the indicative allocation of funds within MEDA II. In this respect MEDA I had already broken with the underlying logic of previous protocols. The main message in MEDA I, which *had not always been well understood* was that no country had a right to a certain financial amount. Our approach is based upon competition between countries.' (Author's emphasis). Indeed the EU's ability to adjust funding according to whether partner countries are making progress (or at least efforts) towards structural reform is potentially a powerful tool. However attempting to calibrate payments for each year according to progress in the partner country is difficult.

Article 5 of the MEDA regulation, the legal basis for conditionality, states that allocation of funds should depend on 'progress towards structural reform' (Official Journal, 1996a). As outlined in chapter 2, there is a consensus that effective conditionality must be transparent and be based on clear criteria. The legal criteria are, perhaps understandably, vague but the Commission has not produced anything, which outlines more specifically what is expected, and how conditionality might operate. As stated in the previous section the CSPs do not fulfil this function. The Commission's intellectual resources are rather limited but there are a number of methods and studies (see appendices) that it could draw on. Of course there would always be a need for flexibility.

As a basis for this analysis, table 4 outlines the flow of EU funds to each country over time and other key statistics. Percentage of total aid and aid per capita figures give a clear indication of which countries have been most favoured. Based on the formal legal framework and this book's theoretical framework, I divine four broad criteria, which are expected to influence EU funding:

- Political reform.
- Reform of economic policy and governance.
- Progress in the EMP/openness to Partnership: this is related to the previous but not quite the same, it includes willingness to sign an Association Agreement, develop common institutions and accept the EU's principles.
- Geopolitical importance. This is likely to be significant although as the entire region is so sensitive to the EU there are not such stark contrasts to be made. It could be stated that a large power such as Egypt is more important that countries such as Tunisia. Countries like Morocco, which have a border with the EU, and Israel's neighbours could also be said to have exceptional geopolitical importance.

Table 3.4   Commitments per country over time (all figures are in € millions except aid per capita in €)*

	Morocco	Tunisia	Egypt	Algeria	Lebanon	Jordan	Syria	MEDA Total
country total 95–99	656.00	428.00	686.00	164.00	182.00	254.00	99.00	3060.00
% of regional total	21.4%	13.9%	22.4%	5.4%	6.0%	8.3%	3.2%	
2000	140.60	75.70	12.70	30.20	0.00	15.00	38.00	568.70
2001	120.00	90.00	0.00	60.00	0.00	20.00	8.00	603.30
2002	122.00	92.20	78.00	50.00	12.00	92.00	36.00	611.60
2003	142.70	48.70	103.80	41.60	43.70	42.40	0.70	614.70
2004	151.80	22.00	159.00	51.00	18.00	35.00	53.00	679.60
2005	135.00	118.00	110.00	40.00	27.00	58.00	22.00	734.60
2006	168.00	71.00	129.00	66.00	32.00	69.00	22.00	816.70
country total 00–06	980.10	517.60	592.50	338.8	132.70	331.40	179.70	4,647.00
% of regional total	21.09	11.13	12.75	7.29	2.85	7.13	3.86	
Aid per cap 00 –06	30.35	46.97	5.72	11.28	35.86	55.23	11.59	

*The differences between the total for the 7 states and the absolute total are aid to the Palestinian Territories and regional aid. This table is based on one that appeared in the Journal of International Development (Holden, 2008). The figures for Morocco and Algeria in 2005 are different to said table, which was based on EU announcements in that year.

Source: Internal Commission factsheet 2008

The first quality may be dealt with relatively quickly. In terms of political criteria a typical pattern asserts itself. The EU's official criteria are phrased not in terms of pragmatic political liberalization – which admittedly is hard to define – but in lofty normative principles. Thus the regulation does allow for punitive conditionality in outlining that 'human rights and democratic principles' are fundamental to the EMP and that aid may be suspended if these are not respected. However punitive conditionality is a clumsy tool and has rarely been shown to work, especially given that most Med partners, although in financial difficulties, are not dependent on EU funds. In any case it is unlikely that agreement could be found to suspend aid. Again even beyond the political difficulties there are methodological ones. Evaluating and monitoring countries human rights record or degree of democracy is problematic. Neither the CSPs nor the Council's Annual Report on Human Rights offer a basis for this. Thus while the political criteria are normative and principled they are effectively impotent. The same problems apply to allocative conditionality, although the EU has given signs that countries like Morocco and Jordan, which have liberalized, will be rewarded.

Divining the logic to the Commission's allocations is speculative as there are too many variables and no clear benchmarks. Morocco's generous funding would appear to be over determined in that it hits all four buttons. However, as described in the following section, its progress in economic reform is highly questioned. As for Tunisia it would appear to be rewarded for fulfilling qualities 2 and 3. This begs the question of what weighting is given to political reform. Tunisia's allocation was explicitly reduced by 13.5 % in 2004 to penalise the government's authoritarian crackdown. This still leaves Tunisia as third highest recipient (and the second highest per capita recipient) so clearly political reform is not the main criteria. Although it is tempting to dismiss any idea that there is logic to the Commission's actions one can, taking a long view, delineate certain principles. Geopolitical importance explains relatively high allocations for Lebanon, Jordan and Egypt (buttressed by substantial economic and political reforms in the case of the first two). However, clearly geopolitical importance is not enough in its own right. Countries like Syria and Algeria, which are highly relevant to Europe's security agenda but laggards in terms of economic, political reform and general cooperation are given substantially less funding. In conclusion one can state that a crude form of conditionality has been applied. It is clearly not the most subtle and transparent of mechanisms.

3.4 Country Case Study: Morocco

The Moroccan state is based on a historical polity in North West Africa, centred on the cities of Marrakesh and Fez, and consisting of Arab and Berber peoples. The current dynasty has been in power since 1650, emerging from the colonial period as a Monarchy. (From 1912–1956 it was a French protectorate, with the Spanish as junior partners controlling some segments). Contemporary Morocco is relatively liberal, pursues outward economic policies and is generally pro-western in orientation. Yet it also faces massive problems with acute poverty and inequality. It is also far from a democracy or liberal economy. The concept of the *Makhzen* dominates perceptions of Moroccan governance. The term has different meanings, it literally means 'storehouse' and was thus applied to the financial/administrative machinery of the sovereign (Pennell, 2001). In the contemporary sense it has come to be applied to a more diffuse network of powerful individuals linked to the throne, (but not synonymous with the official government), who hold political, security and economic power. This section will outline the key characteristics of Morocco's political and economic make-up, before analysing the EU's role.

The historical context

Not atypically, European colonialism in Morocco bolstered the power of some indigenous elites, as it used local institutions to govern the country. The protectorate's development policy also helped rejuvenate the traditional elite through fostering the development of a powerful economic-financial oligopoly in Morocco (Pennell 2001; Henry 1996). Enormously powerful economic institutions were established, initially controlled by the French but later passed to indigenous elites. In particular the *Office Cherifian de Phosphate* (OCP) was established to exploit the country's massive phosphate reserves and a broader industrial-financial conglomerate, the *Omnium Nord African* (ONA) was set up in 1919, this would become 'the jewel in the Makhzen's crown, radiating new beams to transport royal patronage into the 90s.' (Henry 1996, 142). Upon independence the Monarchy faced many challenges in leading a factious country suffering from mass poverty. Large-scale emigration to Europe began in the 1950s and remittances would become a crucial source of finance. The country remained dependent on agriculture but political considerations precluded extensive land reform (Hammoudi 1997, 29–31). In terms of industry the major entities, remained in state hands, or, such as the ONA, controlled by regime elites. Also the state invested in certain profitable sectors (such as construction) and there began an intimate relationship between the state and the 'private sector'. Regarding politics, the Monarchy managed to consolidate its grip on power and marginalize other popular and nationalist forces. Waterbury (1970) outlines how the Moroccan political elite quickly fractured and the Monarchy exploited this situation to divide and rule. Henceforth politics involved groups competing for patronage, rather than building up an independent power base. The Monarchy also resorted to repression particularly after attempted army coups in 1971 and 1972. Partly as a result of this King Hassan II, seeking to harness nationalist forces launched an effort to 'reclaim' the Western Sahara for Morocco in 1974. This resulted in a guerrilla war from 1976–1989 which has not yet found political resolution and dominates the foreign and security agenda of the government. Increased revenue in this decade helped the support the war and allowed the government to increase the public sector and adopt a policy of Moroccanization: the gradual takeover of French owned land and industries. This was used to reward allies of the monarchy.

The financial crises of the early 1980s forced the government to turn to the World Bank and the IMF. Initial efforts at stabilization, in particular reducing food subsidies, led to massive social disturbances 1981. Eventually (1983) a more gradual approach to adjustment was arranged with some success. The reforms that were implemented in the 1980s were mostly concerned with the macro-economic structure. Although there was some obeisance towards institutional reform this 'adjustment' was in fact very limited (Maghraoui 2002, 26). Yet the general trend towards economic liberalization continued and Morocco was in the vanguard here (White, 2001). Such financial pressure did help lead to a certain political opening. With a new constitution (1996) increasing the power of parliament, the Monarchy succeeded in persuading the traditional opposition parties to take part in the regime and form the government, with the Monarch still holding ultimate power. With the enthronement of Mohammed VI in 1999 reforms were accelerated. Old hardliners were dismissed and significant reforms made in the field of human rights, and women's rights in particular.

Morocco in 2001

Politically, Morocco was best described as semi-authoritarian. The king and his advisors, the security forces and regional executives (responsible to the monarch), as well as less formal networks, amount to a parallel government (Maghraoui 2002). The degree of freedom tolerated had oscillated: the year 2000 saw increased repression of the media (Amnesty 2000). Uncertainty regarding the direction of the regime, is related to confusion about the personality of the King. A well-connected French 'biographer' argues that his personality is highly autocratic (and traditional) in many respects, but this cannot be proven (Tuquoi 2001, 211–215; 243–268). The King also appoints the prime minister and key cabinet members. Most of the political parties were very weak with the exception of the 'moderate Islamist' party, the PJD (*Parti de la Justice et Développement*) which had built a strong support base through grass-roots social work (and remaining outside the government). It too is linked to the establishment, as it was founded, partly at the instigation of the Palace (Willis 2002), as an effort to incorporate political Islam. Other movements refused to enter the formal political arena under the current rules of the game. In the ensuing period, more violent forms of political Islam erupted.

Morocco had a steady growth rate until drought in 1999–2000 led to a contraction. The macroeconomic situation is recognised as generally stable. Yet the socio-economic conditions of its citizens remain low, Morocco ranked lower than the other Arab EMP members in the human development index. Despite efforts to develop the private sector, the Moroccan economy continues to be dominated by certain large groups, including the ONA and others originating in the Moroccanization of the 1970s. Legally it can be hard to define a business grouping, as the ties between its different entities are rather organic (Moore 1996, 150–154). Moore cites the Lamrani and Kettani groupings as the largest and typically both of these individuals are close to the palace (Ibid). The financial system reflects the complexity of Morocco's political economy. A small group of major banks dominate what amounts to an oligopolistic financial system. These are, 'privately owned' but may be understood as a part of the Makzhen and thus the broader regime. Moore (1996, 157–158) notes how, in 1991 World Bank efforts to support programme for *independent* banks were undercut by the monarchy. It ended up financing large banks which the King and allies (including the two individuals named above) controlled.

The Moroccan privatization programme started in 1984, but moved very slowly. In 1989 a law was passed for the first wave of privatizations, which was supposed to wholly or partially privatize 114 companies by 1995 (Najem 2001). In fact by that year only 56 companies had been privatized (Ibid) and the deadline was extended to 1999. Najem argues that far from being a genuine effort to liberalize the economy privatization was used as a new method of patronage. The argument is based on the following facts. Firstly, that due to the concentration of wealth in Moroccan society very few people outside of the *Makhzen* network could possible avail of the privatization offers. Secondly, the process of privatization was not so transparent – certainly up to 1999. Large telecoms privatizations in this year and 2001, attracted significant foreign interest (Goldstein 2003, 23). Generally, efforts to attract FDI have been a cornerstone of development policy. A new investment framework code in 1995 had simplified the situation greatly for investors, but there were still complaints about inefficiency and corruption.

The quality of Moroccan governance was frequently isolated as the major barrier to development (although it also faces severe structural and environmental constraints). The prevalence of patronage can be a large extent be linked to the nature of the political regime. The theoretical independence of the judiciary had not been a reality (Mouqit 2004, 47–48). It was also weakened by low pay and often poor education (World Bank 2000a, 5–6). As in other areas, corruption had been rife, although Minister for Justice appointed in 1997 was regarded as a credible reformer (Denoux 2002, 180 –181). The state of regional and local government is confusing as different functions of representation, efficiency, security and patronage interplay. The provinces (prefectures for large cities) have been directly controlled by the central government (Zyani 2002, 3). Local government has substantial financial autonomy but this has encouraged corruption (El Badaoui 2004, 159–162). 16 new regions were established in 1996 with substantial responsibility for economic development. There are elected assemblies but a governor (*Wali*) appointed by the king, has ultimate power. Thus their function is more to manage development than democratization. General criticisms of Moroccan public administration are focused on chronic corruption, administrative inefficiency and a tendency towards factionalism and 'empire building' (Osmane 2004). This is unsurprising as traditionally the civil service has been used as 'an instrument of power and manipulation' (Cherkaoui 2002, 11). A World Bank report in 1995 outlined in stark form the deficiencies and negative impact of the civil service, which inspired the King to take more interest in reform (interview, Former Minister, April 2004).

Concerning broader societal forces, the trade union movement in general in Morocco is, like the political parties, highly factious. There is little internal democracy, and many unions are private fiefdoms. As the numbers of unions increased in recent years actual representation decreased (El Badaoui 2004, 168); also the large informal sector in the country rather diminishes union influence. The major Moroccan unions are linked to international bodies and there is a confederation for the Maghreb as a whole (USTMA – *Union des Syndicats des Travailleurs du Maghreb Arabe*). However this is, 'an empty shell' (interview, European Commission, December 2003). The CGEM (*Conféderation Générale des Entreprises du Maroc*) is the primary business association. Traditionally linked with the regime, since 1994 it had opened up to new businesses and developed its autonomy (Sater 2002, 16–17). As the Moroccan reform process develops it has been increasingly active in attempting to set the agenda. Houdaigui (2002, 98) notes that it has fostered relations with American and European associations and governments, arguably another sign of greater independence. Sater (2002, 23–24) argues that the rise of the CGEM may herald the emergence of a genuinely autonomous private sector, which supports the rule of law and a voice for 'economic rationality' linked to global economic forces, exactly the type of changes to governance that the EU wanted. Yet the expansion of the CGEM could also be understood as the *cooption* of new entrepreneurs into the Mahkzen system rather than the growth of a truly autonomous private sector.[3] A vibrant civil society has emerged in the past thirty years clustered around certain key sectors, mainly human rights and development. Other NGOs have arisen that (like the CGEM) may represent the rise of economic interest groups seeking a liberal internationalized economy with the rule of law. *Transparency Maroc*, the Moroccan branch of the international anti-corruption movement, was founded in February 1996. Initially it was not warmly received by the authorities, but it persisted and launched a well publicised drive against corruption (Denoux 2000, 170–171). The NGO has since been accepted by the government and works closely with some ministries. Other similar organizations, also with transnational connections, were active (Denoux 2000, 168).

Conceptualizing the Moroccan system

The Moroccan system poses many questions as to the complex interplay of economic power, political power, sociological and cultural factors. The country presents bemusing challenges for comparative political scientists and political economists. What is relatively clear is that the system has been patronage based and quite distinct from the liberal 'rule of law' ideal. Even the official government sponsored report evaluating 50 years of independence admits this (Government of Morocco 2006). Key questions for our purposes pertain to the power and objectives of the government and the broader regime (defined in terms of the Makhzen), the links between economic and political power and the question of how diffuse or concentrated the former is. The dualistic structure to Moroccan governance, with formal legal institutions permeated and deformed by patrimonial/ informal power networks, accords with the definition of a neo-patrimonial state (Erdmann 2002, 3). The latter concept implies a direct link between political power and political and economic patronage, and this is in line with the standard interpretation of the Makhzen system. The direct economic power of the Monarchy and allies, including

---

3   Desrues (2005, 59) suggests something similar may be occurring in relation to agricultural policy making in that there are new forms of interest intermediation but they are still essentially guided by the Makhzen and thus may amount to a reformulation of the Makhzen system rather than a sea-change.

governmental powers of patronage, bears this out. On the other hand the notion of some kind of unitary nexus of economic and political power seems excessive, given the extent of liberalization that has already taken place. Many Moroccans tend to see perceive the anti-liberal forces as more heterogeneous 'rent-seeking interest groups' at various levels of the state and the society (Mansouri 2003; El Badaoui, 2004). The difference is significant as the latter scenario means that the regime can tolerate and even support further liberalization (in view of the anticipated economic gains and aid) and the dissolution of certain power blocks. This gives the EU a certain space within which to operate and catalyse structural change that will fully liberalize and Europeanize the country. However, true liberalization of the commanding heights of the economy, directly linked to political power, is likely to be opposed. Although the Moroccan system has deep historical social and economic roots, it is not immutable, as indeed policies had already changed significantly in the previous period. There have been noteworthy, if incomplete legislative reforms in the political and particularly in the economic sphere. Also there are forces emerging from society, linked with trans-national networks, pushing for political and economic reform. Henry and Springborg cite Morocco as one of the few countries in the Middle East where a potentially sustainable political and economic liberalization process has taken place and where the private sector has developed some structural power (Henry and Springborg 2001, 171–178). The regime had hitched its star to an outward-facing development strategy and was heavily reliant on international aid, trade and investment. Thus the EU had the opportunity to use economic forces for deeper societal and possibly even political change and to inscribe Morocco within its own system.

Upon independence Morocco maintained close relations with France, and naturally it would also seek close relations with the new European Economic Community. All the more so as its economy had been routed towards European (French) markets in the protectorate years (White 2001). Thus Morocco pressed for a Trade and Cooperation agreement with the EEC as early as 1963, and one was agreed in 1969. As with its neighbours, this was regularised in a new agreement (which allowed for financial cooperation) in 1976. The early aid programmes to Morocco were geared towards traditional socio-economic development objectives (see table 3.5). There was no conditionality at this stage. Gradually Europe intervened more, introducing structural adjustment. Also the European Parliament obstructed the 4th aid package in 1992 on human rights grounds. Despite this less convenient aspect of the relationship the government continued to lobby for closer ties.[4] When it signed the Barcelona Declaration in 1995 it had already begun negotiations for an Association Agreement, which came into force on the 1st of March 2001.

---

4   Morocco actually applied to join the EEC in 1987. This was rejected.

Table 3.5   EU Protocol aid to Morocco from 1976–1996

Financial Protocol	Commitments (Ecu, millions)	Breakdown
1.1976 –1981	130 (including 56 from the EIB)	51% for rural development and general infrastructure support. The remainder went to support the private sector, social support and training.
2.1981 –1986	199 (90 from the EIB)	71% for rural development and general infrastructure support. The remainder went to training and social support.
3.1986 –1991	324 (151 from the EIB)	67 % for rural development and general infrastructure support. The remainder went to support the private sector, social support and training.
4.1991 –1996	438 (220 from the EIB)	45% for rural development (including agricultural credit schemes), 26% for social support 15% for the private sector and the rest for training.

Source: European Commission, 2001c: 6-12

EU-Moroccan relations since the Barcelona Declaration

The EU-Morocco relationship has not always been smooth. Migration remains an ongoing sore point as Morocco is seen as a source of illegal immigration. Fishing is another contentious issue as the government for some time refused to renew the EU- Morocco fisheries agreement – wishing to develop its own fishing industry. Also the stalemate has continued in regard to Morocco's claim to the Western Sahara; which the EU does not recognise. However, generally the Moroccan government has not been in conflict with the EU concerning international issues. There are some special bilateral relationships between Morocco and the former colonial powers. France has had a major role in terms of its historical shaping of Morocco and ongoing political and economic links. It is the largest bilateral aid donor to Morocco and the major trader and investor. It has also courted the Moroccan leadership assiduously in recent years. The relationship of the other colonial power, Spain, with Morocco is also quite profound but more troubled. Spain, the initiator of the EMP process, has attempted to cultivate a positive form of interdependence at the bilateral level (Gillespie 2000). Yet there have also been several explosions of hostility between the two neighbours in this period. These relate to fishing, migration, territorial disputes and terrorist fears. Nevertheless Spain is Morocco's second largest economic partner.

Morocco has been in the vanguard of the EMP process. It's enthusiasm was reinforced by the accession of Mohammed VI (1999) who, like his father, was French educated and had even spent a period doing a *stage* in the office of Commission President Jacques Delors. Upon the entry into force of the AA in 2000 Morocco took a proactive approach to institutional cooperation. The Association Agreement established two bodies for two thematic areas of major interest; a working group on migration and social affairs and a customs cooperation committee. Then there are six sub-committees established by the 3rd Association Council, based on the work programme of the Association Committee: the internal market; industry, trade and services; transport, environment and energy; research and innovation; agriculture and fisheries; and justice and security. Another sub-committee on human rights was later established after lobbying by civil society groups. The esoteric details need not concern us overmuch. The purposes of these bodies are to monitor (on the EU's side) and to generally keep each other informed and exchange information. They also serve to anchor various units and levels of the Moroccan administration into the EMP/ reform process. The Moroccan government has substantial political capital at hand due to its enthusiasm and reform credentials. 'In integrating Morocco into the *circle of friends* we are acknowledging all its efforts at reform', as the head of the Commission Delegation put it (Moha 2004). Thus there was no question of Morocco not being made one of the pilot countries ('circle of friends') of the ENP, and it was among the first wave to sign Action Plans in May 2004 (Commission 2004d).

This plan further specified the reform path for Morocco, but the essential thrust of the EU's policy has been similar since 1995. From the previous section we can deduce what the effect of this would be. At its most ambitious the deep reform and integration agenda would involve the effective dissolution of Makhzen economic, and eventually political power. Comprehensive modernization and liberalization to create a competitive free market would reduce the norms and modes of patronage and in a sense rectify the dualism developed by French colonialism, although given that the ultimate legal frameworks and economic trajectory would be European this could be viewed as neo-colonialism. On the other hand, if the impact of EU intervention was more limited this could help reinforce a new kind of dualism, with reforms in some sectors, but the essential Makzhen system unchanged. Lastly, the other prospect is that EU trade and aid policy has no real impact at all, and is merely an empty shell or a diplomatic gesture.

MEDA up to 2001

As table 3.6 illustrates a relatively large amount was devoted to socio-economic cohesion during the period 1995-1999. The programmers did include trade enhancing and reform related objectives though. These included a Structural Adjustment Programme, coordinated with the World Bank and the IMF, which was disbursed in three tranches dependent on the conditions stipulated. These were relatively vague, apart from the macro-economic consideration (reducing

Table 3.6   MEDA 1 Commitments 1995–1999 (€ Millions)

I. Reform (including private sector support)	283.245
II. Development/social cohesion	333.59
Total	616.835

Source: Delegation 2004

Table 3.7   MEDA Activities 2000–2001 (€ Millions)

2000 –2001	
Water Management sectoral adjustment programme	120.00
Modernization of the law courts	27.60
Participatory rural development in the Central Atlas	9.00
Financial sector adjustment programme	52.00
Health sector adjustment programme	50 .00
Urban solid waste management in Essaouira	1. 94

Source: Commission 2000c

expenditure). Each tranche was disbursed, so obviously it was decided that the conditions were fulfilled, although an official evaluation (ECA 2002, 12) was more sceptical. The support to privatization programme was an example of a technical assistance programme, where European expertise is used to facilitate and encourage reform, the main focus was on the telecommunications sector, major international privatizations would take place here, which, primarily, French companies would avail of (Goldberg 2003; Tozy and Hibou 2002). Complementary to direct aid for reform is support for the private sector. This includes support to business associations managed by the *Confédération Générale des Employeurs Marocains*. There followed an interlude between the launch of MEDA II in 2000 and the launch of the new programming system in 2001. In Morocco, the impact of the MEDA II regulation is striking in that several large sectoral adjustment programmes were introduced in 2000 and 2001.

The aid strategy 2002–2004

The new programming procedures were intended as a qualitative leap in programming. How does the Moroccan CSP measure up? The 'policy agenda' section of the CSP outlines the government's policy objectives (Commission 2001d). It notes the principal challenges cited; to support economic development, institutional reform (to 'modernise' the public sector, the administration and public finance). Nothing is said about the quality of the governments planning or about the degree of political will to implement the reform programme. The socio-economic section notes that the privatization process is continuing, and that in many ways the legal and regulatory framework for doing business and investing has improved. The next section on 'medium-term challenges' cites the acute need to improve the efficiency of the public sector and hopes that the ongoing process of deconcentration (within the Moroccan government) will help this situation. In terms of the environment for the private sector, it emphasises that the reformed legal framework must be fully implemented.

Concerning the political analysis section proper the Moroccan paper notes the process of liberalization. The primary symbol of this is the incorporation of opposition parties into the government in 1997, and the appointment of socialist (opposition) leader Youssoufi as prime minister. These and several other 'symbolic' events are recounted. Concerning the method of government it argues (controversially) that the dependence of the executive and legislature on the Monarchy is being reduced. It also notes that the coalition consensus government works quite slowly. It is stated, correctly, that the media and civil society are much freer than elsewhere in the region but that there are still impediments. Corruption is cited as a major barrier to democratic and economic development and the need is emphasised to expand on the current efforts to reform public administration and the legal system.

The section on risks notes that there are very strong expectations on the Moroccan side. It also admits that the cooperation projected is ambitious in terms of the amount allocated and the number of sectors involved. As for the budgetary support programmes it emphasises that public finance must be 'in order' for these to go ahead. Interestingly it also points out that the election of 2002 could, depending on the results reduce the drive for reform (in fact it did not do so, not that the 'drive for reform' had been overwhelming). This is a tacit admission that the economic agenda may not dovetail with 'democracy'. In the section on 'lessons learned' the CSP outlines previous EU cooperation (from the financial protocol era to MEDA). The initial difficulties with the new MEDA procedures are noted. Also the previous evaluations of Mediterranean aid are cited although the precise lessons learned are not specified. Generally it accepts that there have been major administrative problems in implementing aid and it is proposed that the deconcentration process may improve this. Sectoral and other budget support mechanisms are noted as useful in that they give the Commission leverage over the government and help to develop synergy and consensus among Moroccan ministries.

The EU's funding strategy for this period follow the patterns begun in 2000, see table 3.8. There are large sectoral reform facilities, some technical assistance to support trade and investment (see boxes 3.1 and 3.2) and direct support to the private sector. The use of these sectoral reform facilities, which involve direct

Table 3.8   The National indicative programmes for 2002–2004 and 2005–2006

NIP 2002-2004	€ Millions
Public administration	81
Transport sector reform	66
Aid to implement Association Agreement	5
Adaptation of the industrial sector	61
Training programme	50
Tempus (educational exchanges/reform)	8
Emigration l	5
Border management	40
Development strategy for the northern provinces l	70
Environment	10
EIB loan subsidy(Environmental protection)	30
TOTAL	426.5

NIP 2005-2006	€ Millions
Fiscal Reform (direct budgetary support)	80
Aid to professional associations (2)	5
Aid to implement Association Agreement (2)	15
Aid to official human rights centre	2.5
Aid to civil society	2.5
Tempus	4
Kenifra	6
Canalisation of Water	30
Development strategy for the northern provinces 2	30
Subsidies of EIB loans	10
Aid for urban housing	90
TOTAL	275

Source: Commission 2001b, 2004a

financial transfers to the government, implies a high degree of trust on the part of the Commission in the Moroccan government's will to reform bona fides. This method also allows EU policy-makers to efficiently derive maximum leverage from the limited funds available by concentrating on reform in certain key sectors. Often development and reform are seamlessly intermixed. The budgetary support programme for reform of the transport sector is intended to help liberalize the Moroccan economy and strengthen the private sector. The objectives of this programme apply to three subsections of this sector (D'Averso 2003). Road haulage should be deregulated, allowing new economic actors to enter the market and compete with the (former) monopoly state company. Concerning maritime transport the office that had been in control of regulation, management and services in ports is to be split into two entities. The port services market in general will be opened to competition. Also in the sphere of air transport the grip of the major state institutions is to be loosened to allow for new actors. Direct aid for development and socio-economic cohesion is continued but there is a lesser proportion than for MEDA 1. This form of aid again has a large focus on the Northern Provinces, a region which relates to European (especially Spanish) security concerns as it is the launching pad for illegal migrants, drug smuggling and the hinterland of two European cities, Ceuta and Melilla. This focus, and the programme on border management, is an example of a more direct use of aid for security (the basic MEDA approach is indirect; the aim being that aid will support security via reform and development).

The following NIP does not change much, the Commission understood the official evaluation of the country strategy for Morocco to have confirmed, that its approach to Morocco was essentially correct (Commission 2004). MEDA now offered two (albeit small) human rights support programmes. Apart from this the broad contours of the strategy are familiar. The sectoral adjustment facility is, in this case, for reform of the fiscal system, this is linked with the previous reform of public administration programmes and is also a joint venture with the World Bank. A new support to the Association Agreement programme is launched with more funding to support technical assistance for reforms. Also there is a new programme to support professional associations, again in partnership with the employers' confederation. Aid to socio-economic cohesion is maintained, as is the interest in the Northern Provinces.[5] In particular the EU agreed to support the government's urban housing programme to the tune of 90 million. Long running concern over living standards in Moroccan cities has been given more salience with the rise of Islamic-based extremism, often based in large 'shanty-towns'. In brief the EU's funding strategy has been to try and leverage reforms in key areas (in line with the agenda of the International Financial Institutions) while maintaining some social support. During this period, Morocco was also a major actor in regional MEDA funded programmes. In particular it was a central player in the Agadir process,

---

5   In fact the provinces had not receive all the funding due to them in 2002-2004 as money was diverted to the Mediterranean Rocade, infrastructure project.

Box 3.1   The support to association agreement programme

This programme involves direct reform of the trade/customs procedures but also the deeper element of the AAs related to freedom of establishment, trade in services partners and harmonization of legislation in areas such as intellectual property rights, competition policy and state aid. The activities envisaged are mostly technical assistance related, including training for Moroccan officials by private consultants and EU civil servants (via 'twinning' exercises). Precise actions are not determined in advance but are decided by a joint steering committee made up of Commission and Moroccan government officials. Given the broad themes cited above a wide range of ministries are involved including Foreign Affairs and Cooperation, Finance, Transport, Industry, Trade, Energy and Mines, Agriculture.

The results expected range from the practical, the transfer of information regarding EU policy and the general direction of the partnership, to the ambitious – the wholesale reform of legislation and administrative practices in key areas. Four types of indicators are suggested, studies and research on how to reform, actual legislation and regulations, implementation of the latter and training of Moroccan officials. Of course the issue is what results to expect from the small-scale technical assistance programme (5 million for 2002-2004 and the 15 million in the next period) as opposed to the broader process. Also neither the general nor the specific planning documents outline the potential risks from vested interests opposed to reform. This is an obvious pitfall given the nature of Moroccan political economy, described in the previous section, and the elements in Morocco that may stand to lose from the liberalization of trade in services or the adoption of rigorous competition legislation and practice. In contrast to the documents, Commission officials directly involved with managing this project are well aware of the pitfalls, and indeed are sceptical about degree of change possible, especially given the lack of intra-governmental cohesion (Interview, 2004, March). Basically this aid programme is oiling the wheels of the Association process but will not in itself induce major change.

which is regarded as a relatively realistic effort at Arab economic integration (as it is purely commercial and less 'bombastic' than other efforts).

There are numerous other EU aid instruments active in Morocco. These include environmental and migration related assistance budgets. None are as important (financially) as MEDA. One programme that is worth mentioning is the small-scale democracy support instruments which provide direct finance for civil society organizations. The MEDA democracy programme[6] was active in Morocco from 95–99 and there were 18 projects funded. Unlike most other Mediterranean countries there were some projects managed directly with the government. These mostly involve training/sensitising government employees to human rights

---

6   There were other EU budget lines active in this period including the co-financing of development projects with European NGO's and Environmental aid projects.

Box 3.2   The reform to public administration programme

This programme is of particular interest as it goes to the heart of the issue of institutional reform. The EU programme is targeted primarily at cost cutting and managing the budget. This involves lessening the number of personnel, and granting more freedom to line ministries as opposed to the Ministry of Finance, but giving the latter more of a role in monitoring performance and planning. It also includes reforming the human resources system, to help rectify the chronic failures of the Moroccan civil service. These reforms are to be managed by the Moroccan government while the EU (and the World Bank) monitors the situation before disbursing cash. An array of risks is acknowledged. These include the (refreshingly honest) point that the reforms the EU prescribes may not succeed in increasing efficiency. More political risks included the fact that with 2002 being an election year the outgoing government may not be keen on introducing painful reforms and the new government may not agree the programme. Also it is noted that programme goal of reducing expenditure may be hampered by Morocco's ongoing process of decentralization.*

This programme was eventually put into place in October 2004, the fears about the elections derailing the reform process were not realised. However, barriers to the programme's success remain, including the perennial issue of vested interests. While the Ministry of Finance is losing a certain amount of power, a major effort has been in place to ensure it supports the reform, but there are more serious obstacles. A major function of the civil service has been to provide work for graduates, which the private sector has not been able to supply, and thus massive long-term cuts are politically extremely painful, and the public sector is not shy of strikes. Also at all levels of the administration there are those who stand to lose from increased transparency, including top-level mandarins but also people at lower levels. Thus the forces for inertia within the basic administrative framework are formidable. As this programme involves direct budgetary support the conditions for disbursement are crucial. Indicators to determine this are of several different types, including progress reports by outside consultants. From interviewing, this researcher has concluded that the government was not expected to fully achieve its objectives, especially in terms of cost cutting, it comes down to a bargaining game between Brussels and Morocco, with the Commission pushing for the maximum reform that is politically possible. It was not ineffective here and reforms made included over 35,000 civil servants taking early retirement in 2005 (Commission, 2006a). This programme was followed by a related one on fiscal policy.

*   Another example of a dissonance between supporting economic liberalization and democracy.

concerns. After 1999 MEDA Democracy was incorporated into the EIDHR, which had been engaged in similar activities on a global basis. From 2001 on a 'focus-country' system was devised to guide the allocation of EIDHR funds (Commission 2001d). This was a rather rigid system which concentrated funding on a limited group of countries, selected in terms of need and importance. It actually backfired as many of these countries were inhospitable to this kind of aid (Commission 2004b), whereas some cooperative countries were sidelined. Morocco was one of these marginalized countries and this led to much disillusionment on the part of Moroccan civil society groups, which understood the implication to be that Morocco did not need democracy related assistance. Moroccan groups did have the opportunity to participate in some region-wide EIDHR programmes. Activity later increased when micro-projects were launched in 2004 and the 'focus country' method was loosened up (Ibid).

Morocco is a major aid recipient and to further contextualise EU aid it is apt to briefly review the work of other key donors. In terms of other European donors France is the most important, and the various elements of the French aid system are deeply engaged in Morocco. The *Agence Française de Développement* offers concessional loans and grants and concentrates on traditional development topics. *The Service de Coopération et Action Culturel* (SCAC) devotes much funding to cultural cooperation, its 'scientific and technical cooperation' includes some activities of relevance to the EU reform agenda. Its priorities for the period, include support to the rule of law and institutional support to economic actors, also sustainable development and higher education (SCAC, 2005). To summarise the French approach, most funding goes to traditional development (and cultural) objectives, while there are diffuse but substantial efforts to promote institutional development (and Franco-Moroccan links) in many spheres (the state, business and civil society) but not a large emphasis on *reform* as such. As the second economic partner, and with a highly developed institutional relationship Spain is naturally also an aid donor. Like France, Spain has a rich network of decentralized cooperation with Morocco. However the amount of actual ODA is relatively meagre. Spanish government aid goes mostly to socio-economic development issues with some private sector business support also. The geographical concentration is on the Northern Provinces (AECI, 2006). Thus the reform element of Spanish aid is slight. The same can be said for other major European donors such as Germany[7], Italy and Belgium whose funding is also very much focused on socio-economic development issues in this period. What can be concluded from the foregoing is that a broad division of labour has emerged between the Commission and the member states, whereby the former concentrated on institutional and policy reform and the member states on other issues.

There are other international donors more engaged in reform. The two of most interest are the World Bank and USAID. Although not a major donor as

---

7   Although it should be noted that the various German foundations are active in supporting civil society involvement in public policy.

such, the Bank's loans are extensive and it is heavily implicated through its influential analytical work in supporting reform. It did the research for the public administration reform programme and in terms of design this may be described as a World Bank project, although it is the EU that supplied the grant financing. As well as ongoing technical assistance the World Bank is offering a loan of $100 million to support this programme. US government assistance to Morocco is highly politicized. Firstly, the US, like the EU, is using aid to further its own geoeconomic/ geopolitical vision. In particular to facilitate the signing/implementation of a free trade agreement and as a part of the general drive for political change in the region (interview, USAID office Rabat, April 2004). There is a relatively large focus on reforming governance and developing civil society. USAID is particularly rigorous in its use of indicators for planning, even for nebulous areas related to governance and democracy and this is evident from its documents (USAID 2005), although the usefulness of its mostly quantitative indicators is doubtful. There are also other instruments such as the Middle East Partnership Initiative (with small scale political and economic reform projects). For the period in question US assistance was quite low, under $20 million from USAID in 2006 for example (USAID 2007). However from 2007 Morocco has been granted $691 million from a special budget line to use for agreed development purposes over five years.

The impact of the EU in Morocco

For Morocco, the period in question was one of steady economic growth, with some signs of the increased foreign investment, although many argue that this growth is not engendering broad based development (Bogaert and Zemni 2009). It has also been a period of acute security challenges for the state. Fears of poverty leading to extremism appeared to be well-founded as evidenced by terrorist attacks in Casablanca (2003), Spain (2004) and many more recent incidents. The government has redoubled efforts to fight poverty with its National Human Development Initiative of 2005 (Martin 2006). However, Al Quaida affiliated groupings appear to be increasing activity in the Maghreb as a whole and tensions have not been helped by the ongoing Israeli-Arab conflict and the US-led war in Iraq. Despite these circumstances the Moroccan reform process has not been derailed. Politically it remains relatively liberal and open, and all in all it is one of the lead reformers in the region. Being the first country to host the US/G8 backed Forum for the Future in the Middle East (2004), further showcased its reform credentials.

The deepest reforms have been in trade and trade related areas. The AA is being implemented on schedule, and this is by no means a foregone conclusion, as there are clear losers from this, and there have been many failed free trade agreements in the Arab world. Morocco has also signed new free trade agreements with other Mediterranean states and the United States, further locking it into the neo-liberal path. The latter might appear an economic rival to the EU but in fact its economic presence is vastly greater and thus liberalization of Morocco is still

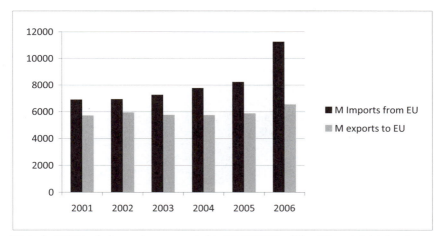

Note: in 2006 trade in services amounted to €5,172.713 million (Eurostat database). Trade in services figures are not included for other EU partners in this book as reliable consistent statistics were not attainable.

Source: DG Trade 2007a, 4/based on data from the IMF

Figure 3.1   Morocco's Trade in goods with the EU (25) 2000-2006* (€ millions)

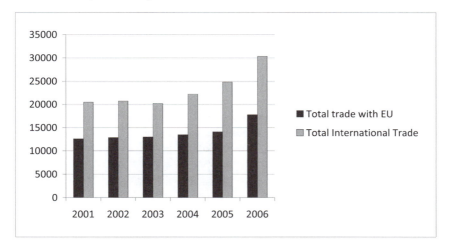

Source: DG Trade 2007a, 4/based on data from the IMF

Figure 3.2   Morocco's Trade in Goods with the EU and the rest of the world compared (€ millions)

Table 3.9   FDI inflows for Morocco,* \$ millions

	2000	2001	2002	2003	2004	2005	2006
Total	593.15	3,855.63	697.37	2,760.26	1,125.70	2,933.00	2,898.00
Europe	514.51	3,717.89	539.38	2,624.05	918.10	NA	NA
North America	36.60	84.21	46.24	68.43	54.69	NA	NA
North Africa	3.20	19.23	9.03	21.28	7.88	NA	NA
Other	38.84	34.3	102.82	46.5	145.03	NA	NA

* FDI stats are erratic in terms of the years they are available for. These UNCTAD figures are taken from national agencies which vary in terms of what they make available. Years 2000–2004 for Morocco are converted from the figures in Dirham in the UNCTAD country profile based on an exchange rate of 1\$:8.4 dirham.

Source: UNCTAD 2007

more likely to increase its influence than any other actor. While it is a little early to test the full impact of the EU's efforts on economic structures, there are certain indications that this hypothesis is correct. Trade had already increased by over 50% from 1995 (Eurostat 2006, 33-34) and figures 3.1 and 3.2 show trade with the EU is still increasing, although at a slower rate than trade with the wider world. As table 2.9 shows, in terms of foreign investment into the Kingdom the EU is clearly dwarfing other outside actors. The economic presence of the EU is likely to further intensify as the full impact of the EU's commercial agreements and aid-inspired reforms regulatory harmonization takes off. Thus this does amount to a degree of structural power for the EU. Morocco is adopting trade and other standards according to its rules. The weight of the Moroccan state in the economy has been substantially reduced, in the context of a greater European presence. Moroccan businesses, NGOs and other actors are working within contexts shaped not just by the government but by the EU. Morocco is definitely in the 'Eurosphere' (Leonard 2005, 145) in many respects, as exemplified by its joining the EU's Galileo satellite project and support for the Kyoto protocol.

However, it should be noted that there are limits to the change that the EU's aid and other instruments can catalyse. The deeper structures of economic governance, not to mention political norms and structures, are beyond the reach of the EU's aid programmers. It is significant that company law and competition policy have been areas with little progress (Commission, 2006a, 7-9), although the EU is still pushing for change here. There is by and large a consensus (amongst EU officials and the international community as represented by institutions such as the World Bank, Transparency International and investment ratings agencies) that Moroccan governance has not fundamentally changed, see table 3.10. In reality there is little aid programmers can do to prevent reforms being 'captured' by regime elites and their allies. There are several reasons for this. Governance reforms are essentially 'qualitative' and these are notoriously difficult to plan for as there is a need for

Table 3.10   World Bank institute measurements of Moroccan governance

Governance Indicator	Year	Governance Score (-2.5 to +2.5)
Government Effectiveness	2006	0.02
	2000	0.00
Regulatory quality	2006	-0.15
	2000	0.00
Rule of Law	2006	-0.03
	2000	0.1
Control of Corruption	2006	-0.06
	2000	0.04

Source: World Bank Institute

flexibility (to avoid rigid targets) but this means that the possibility of distortion due to organizational constraints or lack of knowledge is great. When it comes to deeper political and economic reforms, the Commission is not accompanied by the same weight of European pressure as commercial related reforms. More generally, while ownership of the reform process in Morocco is relatively strong it is still limited. While the upper echelons of the Moroccan business class declare enthusiasm many aspects of society are fearful of the impact of free trade on previously protected industries. Although the sacred cows of neo-liberal orthodoxy are never officially questioned there is widespread scepticism over the suitability of the development model posed, for Morocco. One ex-Minister interviewed summed up the feeling of many quite vigorously 'The Barcelona Process, Wider Europe! These are all just political games the EU is playing, with itself mostly. What we need is a Marshall Plan for the southern shore of the Mediterranean, with serious development of the infrastructure.' (interview, ex-Minister, April 2004).

Within these constraints, EU aid has been programmed and operated effectively in tandem with its other instruments. It has helped to change Morocco and adapt much of its economic system. But the emerging result appears to be a type of hybridization. Morocco is on a track in which much of the economic environment and in certain respects political governance will be liberalalized under EU tutelage but this coexists with older patronage systems and authoritarian political structures (Holden 2005a). This means that the EU's structural power in Morocco is likely to remain relatively thin (limited to certain sectors) and brittle as opposed to the deeper power that would come from a more comprehensive economic and institutional transformation of the country.

Conclusion

In this chapter the preliminary hypothesis that the EU uses aid to increase its own structural power has been borne out by the empirical evidence. How effectively the EU can actually do this is less clear, although certainly its policies are being used to more effect to promote structural power than democracy and development. The aid management system enables the strategic development of aid policy, despite the fragmented EU institutional set up. There is an institutional core, centred on the Commission, geared to working towards the long-term 'European' reform objectives. As for the EUs strategy formulation the CSP format is an improvement although there are still problems with knowledge management within the EU system. Concerning its broader strategic outlook, there is clarity of vision for areas directly concerned with the free trade objective, this clarity wanes when it comes to economic institutions and governance in general. Also the grasp of issues pertaining to the political economy of reform is limited. In terms of the use of resources MEDA became much more focused on reform and, apart from social cohesion, funding has been concentrated on a limited number of sectors. As predicted by some observers the Association Agreements enabled more coherent and focused programming (Europeaid evaluation unit 1999a; Phillipart 2001). Also the Commission has been attempting to engage with deeper economic & institutional reforms in a variety of sectors and through a variety of instruments (direct budgetary support and technical assistance). It is worth noting as well a general consensus that the basic efficiency of MEDA was vastly improved, which is obviously a prerequisite for other changes. Disbursement of funds increased from an average of 29% of commitments in the pre-2000 period to 77% from 2000-2005 (Commission 2005b).

What do the conclusions regarding the EU's capacity reveal about its ability to use aid to reinforce its structural power? It can use aid effectively to catalyse and support changes necessary to ensure the operation of the free trade area. Here of course the EU is partly acting as an agent of globalization. All of its partners are increasing trade with the rest of the world as well as Europe. Other actors, such as the US are moving in to make trade and cooperation agreements. Yet the global statistical picture describes the development of even greater European influence. In any case crude indicators cannot adequately convey the emerging relationship.[8] The framework that the EU has established in terms of the free trade arrangements and its vigorous efforts to ensure commercial cooperation and harmonization should ensure that its presence remains predominant and that the Euro-Med economic space becomes *a* reality, if not the all-encompassing community hoped for. This will certainly increase the EU's structural power in the economic/commercial sphere.

---

8   It is worth reiterating here that 'structural power' is not equivalent to the standard idea of dependency although there are some similar phenomena implied.

However this relatively thin penetration and integration will not ensure the deeper form of structural power postulated in chapter 1. A reshaping of broader economic and administrative and political institutions would be needed to ensure a deeper European political influence. Thin reforms of economic policy and governance will not provide the economic take off (even if one subscribes to the economic thinking) and political development essential to ensure stability and hence the European Union's security. A look at the situation of the 'best pupil', Morocco, is instructive here. Due to EU assisted (and imposed) reforms the state is being partially integrated with the EU and with the international economy. However, this coexists with older patronage systems and authoritarian political structures. If one visualises 'Morocco' as a constellation in Europe's vicinity, EU structural power may be conceived as a process bringing its constituent parts further into Europe's orbit. In fact due to the EU's limited capacity only certain groupings within this constellation are being pulled into the orbit, others are remaining aloof with their own centre of gravity. Needless to say this resistance is stronger in many other countries, where the environment for EU influence is less propitious. Thus the proactive use of aid to promote the EU's structural power is limited and the incorporation of the Mediterranean into the European sphere is not as comprehensive as the Europeans have planned. Given the uncertain geopolitical environment this means that the EU's entire Mediterranean policy is relatively fragile.

Chapter 4

EU Aid to the New Independent States: Shaping the Post-Soviet Space?

Following the implosion of the USSR a series of New Independent States (NIS) faced enormous challenges relating to security, politics and economics. Developments in the new Post-Soviet space would affect Europe's welfare and security in a variety of ways. The condition of Russia and the new European states was a particular concern, although the trans-Caucasian region and Central Asia also rose in importance. While this was an area too vast to be fully integrated into the EU, these considerations ensured European involvement in the effort to promote a political and economic transition. This was unchartered territory as a simultaneous transition from a totalitarian polity and a centrally planned economy to liberal capitalist democracy had never been attempted before (Balcerowitz 1995, 150; Kaminski 1996, 3-4). In a sense it seemed like the international community was presented with a *tabula rasa* to develop liberal institutions from scratch. In reality this was not the case and the transitions took different trajectories from those originally envisaged.

The European Union would have been expected to exert considerable influence here, as it was the major economic pole for the region and availed of unique political and cultural prestige. Indeed those attempting to preserve some form of unity in the imploding USSR looked to the Treaty of Rome for guidance (Herreberg 1998, 92). On the EU's part the Post-Soviet space was a land of opportunity as well as a threat, offering large mineral and energy resources, cheap educated labour and potentially large consumer markets (Fraser 1994). The EU has expended considerable time and effort on this region, with admittedly mixed results. Yet the integration of the NIS into the global economy has taken place as has a significant degree of integration and cooperation with Europe, not to mention a much larger European economic presence. Therefore it is worth analysing how the EU has used its aid in this region, what successes it has achieved and the limits of its political and institutional engineering. This chapter will trace the evolution of the EU's intervention in the region, highlighting the major objectives of this policy and the role of aid in this. The key aid instrument here was called TACIS: Technical Assistance for the Commonwealth of Independent States. The chapter analyses the use of TACIS as an instrument of structural power from 2000–2007. The case study of the Ukraine will illustrate in more detail the structural power dimension of the EU's activity and the effectiveness and limitations of its aid policies. Given its size and geopolitical power, the role of EU aid in shaping Russia's future was always going to be minimal, and it would not make for a representative case study. In fact

EU policies have become more focused on competing for influence with Russia than on reforming it. Its rather blunt coercive methods offer a neat contrast to the gradualist and subtle efforts of the EU to develop its structural power. Ukraine is the primary theatre for Euro-Russian competition and is of major geopolitical, security and geoeconomic importance.

4.1 The Political and Economic Context in the NIS

The countries of the former USSR faced a triple transition to independent statehood, to a new political system and to a more liberal market-based economy (Karaganov 1994, 233). Although the integrated command economy of the USSR meant that the NIS were highly interdependent, and most were dependent on Russia for energy, the Commonwealth of Independent States was not a 'Soviet Union lite' and most of the new states did gain a substantial degree of independence from Russia.[1] All of them had the legacy of centrally planned, militarised and specialised economies, severe environmental problems and undemocratic political structures (Schroeder 1996, 13). Yet there were massive differences in capacity and geography and they inevitably took divergent paths. The three core Soviet States (Russia, Ukraine and Belarus) and Moldova were the EU's closest neighbours. They availed of significant resources, industrial capacity (although industry was highly inefficient) and human capital. In the Caucuses region Georgia, Armenia and Azerbaijan were engaged in internal and/or external conflicts in the 1990s. The countries of Central Asia were at a very low base level of development and could be classed as developing countries rather than being in 'transition'.

The primary imperative was to change the defunct Soviet economic system. In ideal type terms the task was to transform from a centrally planned economy to a liberal free-market system (as allegedly practiced in the triumphant West). The hallmarks of the centrally planned system are that prices are fixed centrally (market forces blunted) by the political authorities. Thus the Soviet bloc amounted to an entirely different system insulated from the global economy: the value of its currency in world terms could not really be determined, and trade was managed by the Soviet state to gain 'hard' currency. From the 1970s the independent Eastern European countries had been reliant on Western capital (Mazower 1998, 371-374), and the Soviets were also more engaged in the global economy. The Gorbachev reforms involved substantial efforts to introduce market mechanisms and attract investment (Dyker 1994, 188-189), but the economy soon broke down to the degree that food aid and debt relief were necessary for the erstwhile superpower. The transition to a free-market economy involved several levels of reform. In terms of macro-economics, expenditure and foreign debt had to be got under

---

1   The Baltic States are not discussed here as they were soon fully integrated in Western political and economic structures.

control. A major part of this was the removal of subsidies and allowing prices to reflect market forces. The speed at which this was to be done was a matter of some debate, very rapid 'shock therapy' was actually quite rare. On another level the basic legal and institutional structure of a market economy had to be put in place. Privatization of state owned enterprises was obviously a key part of this but it also included the development of business law, a financial system, competition policy and the rules and norms of free-market capitalism more generally. Reforming and opening up to the global economy were seen as synonymous, for example currency convertibility was to go along with price liberalization. Forming a part of international trade was one key method of 'getting the prices right' and clarifying the correct 'value' of goods and services according to market principles (Robinson 1999: 534). Foreign direct investment would promote productivity and capitalist practices as well as (hopefully) supplying much needed investment capital. Linked to the institutional reforms was the broader project of developing a liberal democracy. Liberal optimists saw the political and economic transition in the ex-Communist bloc as a major step towards a globally integrated society of liberal democracies (Sachs 1995). Creating the formal institutions of a competitive parliamentary democracy in the new post-totalitarian states was certainly possible, but the development of the deeper institutions and norms of a capitalist democracy was a different kind of challenge.

Transition itself is a loaded term and has teleological overtones (Caruthers 1999; Braguinsk and Yavlinksy 2000: 10) which may cause policy-makers to assume that Western models will emerge. What happened in practice bore little resemblance to ideal types. It soon became clear that reformers (local and international) did not pay enough attention to 'institutions' in general and in particular to the legacies of the Communist system and the role of endogenous power blocks (Balcerovtiz 1995,1; Brabant 1996; Wedel 1998; Braguinsk and Yavlinksy 2000). The head of economic affairs at the UN secretariat denounced ' the blind faith in propositions, often of an ivory tower or heuristic textbook variety' (Brabant 1996: 6). Progress towards democracy was even more haphazard (in fact the ethnic tensions and conflicts made this goal unrealistic in some regions). Russia was the closest resemblance to shock therapy of the NIS. Dramatic price liberalisations occurred in 1992 (which spilled over into other countries in its orbit) and extensive privatizations took place under Gaidar and Chubais between 1992 and 1996 (Aslund 2008; Schroeder 1996). There was a more gradualist approach to reform in the other NIS. Inevitably the basic macro-economic changes were made. Efforts were made to develop the institutions of a market economy but these were incomplete, before the privatization of the economy. This was fatal as it meant that power elites (usually various elements of the former regime and well-connected businessmen) were able to capture and exploit the reforms (Hellman 1998). The power and resources they accumulated would further distort ongoing reform efforts.

All of this resulted in political economies quite far from liberal principles such as open competition, transparency and the rule of law. There are various ways to conceptualise the resulting hybrid systems. The term 'authoritarian corporatism' refers to how political elites with authoritarian tendencies structure interest intermediation and distort the economy to their benefit (Kubicek 1999, 58–59). The concept of the 'rentier state' which relies on income from resources rather than taxation on productive economic activity also has obvious relevance in some cases (Robinson 2004). Yet both of these may imply more coherence and a stronger state than is the case. Oligarchy denotes the unprecedented accumulation of power and wealth in the hands of a few private individuals. Resulting clientilist networks lead to a system that has been likened to neo-patrimonial systems noted in developing countries. Along similar lines Shlapentokh described the situation in Russia in 1996 as akin to medieval feudalism (1996). Gangster capitalism is also a phrase commonly used to denote the mix of marketization with lawlessness. Putin's Russia retains elements of this (Kagarlitsky 2002) but with a stronger central state. Integration into the global economy did proceed. All of the NIS joined the international institutions (they had little choice as they did not have access to private finance). Russia tried to use its weight and energy resources to promote integrative structures dominated by itself (Brzezinski and Page 1997) but any notion that it would form a coherent block in the world economy was soon disabused. As with the rest of the world, globalization (the forces of transnational capital and global markets) would serve to further fragment the post-Soviet space (Robinson 2004).

The effect of this form of transition on growth and welfare was nothing short of catastrophic. The limited reforms undertaken were not enough to encourage the Foreign Direct Investment needed, and there were far more attractive locations elsewhere (Bojcun 2004, 55). The chaos, corruption and numerous wars had predictably disastrous effects and so the (inevitable) recession after 1989 reached truly epic proportions. Despite considerable growth since the late 1990s only four of the NIS had reached their GDP levels of 1989 by 2005 (Popov 2007, 30). Given this situation it is unsurprising that democratic consolidation failed to take root. Thus it is fair to say that the liberal economic and political vision failed to materialise. Marxist-realists such as Peter Gowan scoffed at liberals like Sachs for naive views of the transition process. 'Objectives such as liberal capitalism, shared by Sachs and Western Governments have not been the exclusive goals of Western powers in the 1990s' (Gowan 1995, 57). Even by these standards the transition process was problematic in that the disorder gave rise to anti-Western sentiment. Yet the basic work of integrating them into the global capitalist system was achieved. The next section looks at Europe's role in this process.

4.2 The Evolution of the EU's Policies and Objectives

In the Cold War era contacts between the EEC and the USSR were limited. Soviet theorists viewed the latter as the 'economic arm of NATO' (Herreberg 1998,

88) or as a doomed effort to preserve European capitalism. Leninist thought viewed integration between capitalist powers to be unlikely (Baranovsky 1994, 59 – 62).[2] In any case the endurance of the EEC forced them to take it more seriously. Actual trade increased from the 1970s with the USSR exporting oil and gas (and other primary products) and importing manufactured goods. Under Gorbachev economic contacts further increased as did political overtures and a Trade and Cooperation agreement was signed in 1989. Needless to say it was soon overtaken by events.

Once the Soviet bloc started to unravel, the EEC and its institutions naturally took a keen interest. In fact the new geopolitical dispensation in Europe was a catalyst for efforts to intensify European Integration and the launch of the European Union. It had clear security interests and also extensive numerous economic interests, cited in the introduction to this chapter. Perhaps this element of self-interest is why the European Commission's economic report on the Soviet economy in 1990 was not accepted by the non-European members of the G 7 (Canada, US and Japan) who demanded a more 'neutral' report (Hardt and Rodkey 1996, 376). In any case initial action the EU took was as a part of the international community, in particular the G 7 and the international financial institutions, which now included the European Bank for Reconstruction and Development (a new institution set up to provide finance and advice to private and public bodies in the former Communist Block). Packages of emergency aid (food aid and technical assistance for reform) as well as debt rescheduling and new loans) were announced at various G7 summits in the early 1990s. Then as now the actual amount of 'new' assistance was limited once loans and already existing commitments were deducted from the public figures (Sachs 1995; Fraser 1994; Gowan 1995). The European Commission and IMF were charged with coordinating the various forms of aid to the East. A specific European level budget line was set up in 1990 to provide technical assistance and food aid to the independent Eastern European countries and the USSR (which would later become TACIS). The EU would gain a strong position due to its economic superiority and its role as one of the core elements of the international community engaged in assisting the transition, 'Because the European Commission was chosen as an essential coordinator and deliverer of aid to the countries in transition, countries building and maintaining relations with the EU provides a seal of approval for policies that are domestically unpopular (Brabant 1996, 418). Despite this leverage it is fair to classify the EU's policies at the early stage as 'essentially reactive', as events took their unpredictable course (Gower 2000, 196-197).

Nevertheless certain contours of EU policy soon became apparent. Crucially the distinction indicated in the different aid instruments for Eastern Europe 'proper' and the Soviet Union would percolate through other EU policies. The

---

2   As discussed in chapter 1, other forms of Marxism place more emphasis on the tendencies of capitalist entities to cooperate, leading to phenomena such as European integration and globalization.

former were gradually given the perspective of accession. For the ex-USSR the situation was less clear but a degree of formal integration was proposed. The EU became the greatest trading partner of the ex Soviet countries ' within a record short time span' (Brabant 1996, 384) while trade within the Soviet block decreased rapidly. It dealt bilaterally with the NIS, via Partnership and Cooperation Agreements (PCAs). These were political as well as economic agreements, involving a commitment to shared democratic values and human rights in accordance with international and European norms. They also provided for joint-institutions and dialogue similar to Mediterranean Association Agreements. Financial and technical cooperation was an explicit part of the cooperation package. The general aim was 'to promote trade and investment and harmonious relations between the parties based on the principles of market economy' (PCA Russia, article 1). The legal commitments were not so ambitious (Gower 2000), allowing for trade in goods under GATT rules, and reciprocal 'most favoured nation' status. There were other potentially highly significant clauses in which the EU's partners agreed to move towards harmonization of their regulatory system with the *Acquis Communautaire*, freedom of establishment and capital movements. In the Russian's case this was actually their request (Fraser 1994), a sign of their need to attract foreign investment. The Russia PCA also explicitly called for a free trade area while others were more circumspect. The PCAs themselves were to last ten years, with automatic annual renewal unless one partner decided to end it. Agreements were signed and ratified with all the NIS apart from Belarus and Turkmenistan, for political reasons.[3]

Thus we have the essence of the EU's approach established by the mid-nineties; legal agreements, economic and administrative cooperation, institutionalised dialogue and aid. Conditionality was latent in these instruments and this would be further developed. As the decade developed more reasons emerged as to the reasons for the EU's interest in the NIS, as a range of new soft security issues – including crime, weapons smuggling, illegal migration and people trafficking – emerged from the economic and societal chaos. Also the future Eastern Enlargement meant that the EU would now border some of these countries: there would be no buffer zone. These considerations would intensify the EU's efforts to reform and modernise the NIS, with a distinct approach towards Russia, the other proximate states and Central Asia.[4]

3　Note there were often problems in implementing their provisions as the case of the Ukraine illustrates.

4　On the CFSP level the EU adopted Common Strategies on the Ukraine and Russia. In fact these do little except reiterate core objectives and their main function is to remind and put moral pressure on member states to coordinate their own foreign policies to these interests. The Common Strategies are not further discussed here as they have not proved significant.

After Russia's financial crisis of 1998, the economy started to rapidly improve, fuelled mainly by higher hydrocarbon prices. Although clearly intending to build a stronger state than his predecessor Putin's new regime initially continue along the path of reform and engagement with the global economy. WTO membership was cultivated and Putin was also explicitly in favour of Russia's European and Western identity (Sakwa 2008). In fact some saw him as a 'Russian Pinochet' blending authoritarianism with economic liberalism (Kagarlitsky 2002, 265, 273). As a part of this policy he supported increased cooperation with the EU, both parties agreed to form four 'Common Spaces' in the fields of economics, security, research and culture in 2003. The economic element is in line with the ENP goal of extending the European Acquis although the discourse is less blunt about the partner taking on Europe's rules (to allow for the pride of a reviving Russia). The partners agreed a roadmap for developing these spaces in 2005 (which mostly involves regulatory dialogue) but progress has been slow due to political rows (Emerson 2006). In the meantime the economic implications of Putin's desire for a stronger state have become clearer. His ambitions did not stop at reconquering Chechnya and reigning in the regions but included re-nationalisation and the reinforcement of state energy companies, in particular Gazprom. Although he has not encroached on the private sector in all economic areas and has attracted significant FDI. Greater revenue from such concerns allowed the government to free itself from IMF conditionality. These efforts to build a powerful national economy are anathema to the EU whose own energy dependence on Russia has grown. Russia's willingness to manipulate its supply of energy for political objectives in the Ukraine, Georgia and Belarus has alarmed Europe and it has tried to push Russia to sign the energy charter, which attempts to regulate international trade in energy. Russia has resisted this as it would mostly require action on its part; including diversifying its supplier base and implicitly diluting its political control (Vahl 2001, 27). Nevertheless the EU still has potentially a great deal of leverage over Russia. The latter forms a far lesser proportion of EU trade than vice versa. It is the lack of coherence of EU member states that has reduced its impact. (One striking example is the then German chancellor Schroeder's signing of the Nordstream pipeline deal without consulting key stakeholders such as Poland). It is clear that Russia still needs foreign investment and know-how (Vahl 2001; Emerson et al. 2006). The EU has not given up on efforts to reform Russia and it argues that it offers Russia a more productive partnership that will avoid it being' trapped in the false strength of a hydrocarbon state' (Mandelson 2007a) but both it and America are now more blatantly concerned with modifying its power over its neighbours. The EU has no intention of 'accepting spheres of influence or private reserves of power over parts of the European continent' (Ibid).

For the other near neighbours of the ex-USSR the EU developed the ENP from 2003-2004, already discussed in the previous chapter. This was directly related to the Eastern Enlargement and the new geopolitical context it created. While it included the EU's southern neighbours in the Mediterranean it was clear that much of the ENP (with its focus on cross border cooperation) was geared towards the

Table 4.1   ENP action plans

Armenia: agreed 25.10.2006
Azerbaidjan: agreed 26.10.2006
Georgia: agreed 24.10.2006
Moldova: agreed 9 12 2004
Ukraine: agreed 9 12 2004

EU's new land borders to the East. It aims to intensify reform and cooperation on nearly all aspects of public policy. This is in line with previous policies but is more intense and more comprehensive. The basic process is that partner states sign Action Plans with the EU with short and long-term plans for reform. These will be differentiated according to each partners' needs and EU relationship. The main focus is on alignment of regulation with EU models, extending the EU's acquis. On offer for the partners are increased aid and deeper trade agreements. Action Plans have been agreed with all partners accept Belarus, whose authoritarian regime the EU is highly critical of, see table 4.1. There are substantial security and political components related to EU interests, including combating illegal migration and cooperation on policing issues. Again energy is a major concern, the ENP 'takes full account of the vital role that the EU's neighbours play in the EU's energy security either as supplier or transit countries' and the Action Plans aim for 'convergence of energy policies and legal/regulatory frameworks' (Waldner 2006, 3). On its part the EU offers greater access to the EU market and other EU programmes (such as research and development programmes) as well as increased aid. Yet it is not clear that what is offered is enough and the ENP may be a poor substitute for enlargement or a 'placebo' (Emerson 2004).

The countries of Central Asia have been relatively ignored (as the aid allocations show) and are treated in a more distant fashion. They have neither the same direct security implications of closer regions nor the same geopolitical importance of Russia. Yet the region is far from insignificant, and is a significant player in energy terms. The Commission is also working on converging their energy production and transit systems and legal frameworks with EU needs (Waldner 2006, 4). There are signs that the EU is becoming involved in the 'great game' in Central Asia (competing with the US, Russia and China) and it developed a Central Asia strategy in 2007.

Understanding the EU's objectives

Although the EU's activities can be understood through in liberal terms, its objectives also involve increased structural power, especially if one looks at its tangible specific objectives rather than the declaratory ones of peace and prosperity. It is attempting to form the internal governance of its partner countries and structure their role in the global political economy. It is seeking to liberalize the economies and, with the ENP and the regulatory dialogue with Russia, it is trying to extend the European *Acquis* to non-member countries. 'Europeanization' has different meanings (Olsen 2002) but generally refers to the impact of European Integration on the norms and institutions of member states. Energy Commissioner Piebalgs has called for the 'Europeanization of Russia', to promote EU interests stating that 'the best way to promote European energy security is to promote market values in countries like Russia' (Piebalgs 2006). The EU is seeking to blunt one potential lever against it by diffusing the control of energy supply, involving European companies also, and legalising the energy trade. The result of these policies, if they were successful, would be the dilution of the oligarchical blocks that control countries such as Ukraine (and are often closely linked to Russia), moving to a more open polyarchy (Robinson 1996) linked to the global economy and in particular to Europe. Civil society would also be linked in to European civil society (and even here there is inevitably a certain asymmetry due to disparities in wealth and other capacities). These policies would also unbundle (through dispersing and internationalizing economic power) the kind of strategic state Putin's Russia has become, that fuses economic and political power Also the dependence and vulnerability of many of the NIS towards Russia would be reduced. Essentially the defeat of the USSR would be complete in that the successor states would be integrated (via Europe) into the global political economy and accept Brussels made rules and regulations. These states would also be tied to the EU through joint institutions and political and security dialogue.

The dominant theme here is the EU's effort to shape the frameworks within which other actors (business, civil society and governments) develop. The structural power could be described as something that the EU possesses and could use. European policy makers could affect aspects of the regulatory systems and institutions of its partners by 'remote control', simply through changing laws in Brussels that they (like countries in the European Economic Area) would be required to adopt. The Commission could try and promote or disrupt efforts at regional integration within the NIS or engage in other more extensive efforts at institutional engineering. Business or political elites could use it to try and change structures and practices, for example Tony Blair's warning in 1997 that European investors may flee Russia due to irregular governance (Morgan 2007), would have much more resonance if the two entities were more integrated. It could also be understood as power that does not have to be operated but is inherent in the relationship. The likely economic pattern would be the locking in of the NIS into roles as low level manufacturing, energy and primary product suppliers to the European market. Dependency on the EU for trade and investment would mean that (even without intentionality) changes in Europe affect the NIS governments, businesses and citizens and changes their lives. Likewise the increased size of the European economic space would give European standards and regulations even more weight in terms of global economic regulation. On the cognitive level acceptance of the EU's policies would imply an implicit acceptance of the EU's role as a source of law and authority (albeit in limited areas). It must be stressed again that this is not complete domination. European power in the security sphere is not postulated and it is quite likely that the US and Russia would remain the greatest actors in the region here. Also, although the deep interdependence postulated would be highly asymmetric, there is always the potential for mutual influence. Generally, liberals were undoubtedly correct that liberal market economy (in this case under an EU leadership) is the least constraining form of governance available to the NIS, as opposed to rule from Russia or a local authoritarian regime (Hardt and Rodkey 1996, 371). The deep, diffuse, formative nature of European Union power is quite different from the coercive techniques of Russia, but the power dimension of EU activities cannot be ignored. The chapter now turns to how aid instruments were used to further its goals.

4.3 The Role of TACIS

TACIS was immediately distinguished from other EU development aid as it was devoted solely to technical assistance for transition; and other political/security objectives such as nuclear safety. Technical assistance is an 'intellectual' form of aid which involves the provision of advice, knowledge and training. The term 'technical' is Orwellian as it includes advice on political issues such as regulation and institutional design rather than purely technological/scientific issues. In this case the EU hoped for a political multiplier effect from its aid, to alter the legal, institutional and cognitive frameworks in the NIS. TACIS worked by offering policy advice (on reform and economic strategies), knowledge of how to run and administer a regulatory state, knowledge on the legal framework for free market democracies, and training and advice for private businesses. Initially quite short-term projects were the norm but longer term partnership arrangements were developed as the timescale for reform became more realistic. Also TACIS did start to provide some investment (development) finance as the decade progressed, but it remained primarily technical assistance. The main focus was on specific country programmes (involving the latter activities) but there were also numerous multi-country programmes. These included regional cooperation programmes such as INOGATE (to develop and interconnect energy systems) and TRACECA (to develop transport infrastructure).[5] There were also numerous distinct 'line instruments' such as TACIS democracy, which dealt specifically with civil society organisations (a cheap and highly visible form of aid).

The formal European Commission infrastructure was initially weak and it did not have formal Delegations in most countries. Aid was managed by contracting out projects to European consultancy firms. From 1991–2000 the EU committed

---

5   INOGATE: Interstate Oil and Gas Transport to Europe. TRACECA: the Transport Corridor Europe-Caucasus-Asia.

4.2209 billion ecu for TACIS (Commission 2007a). The greatest expenditure was on privatization/restructuring of state enterprises and reform of public administration (1.227 billion ecu), a large chunk was spent on nuclear safety and the remainder was spent mostly on important sectors such as energy, transport and agriculture. Russia was the greatest recipient, receiving almost 1.274 billion ecu, followed by Ukraine, which was granted a little under half a billion (Ibid). Clearly the sums in question are not very large given the time period and context, although there was also individual member state aid and the EU as a whole contributed 59% of aid in the initial period (Brabant 1996, 437). The EU was the greatest donor of technical assistance at this time (Fraser 1994, 212) and was also noteworthy for having a quite large grant component.

As with other aid programmes in the 1990s the operation of TACIS was severely criticised by academics and stakeholders. The primary official evaluation was relatively positive (Europeaid evaluation unit 1997). Commission management systems were severely criticised and the fact that the evaluation team could not actually determine how many projects there were speaks volumes. It decided that TACIS interventions were relevant to the objective of transition (but this in itself is hardly surprising). As to the all important question of impact the evaluators note that evaluating the impact of TA is extremely difficult. They come to the conclusion that TACIS did facilitate and speed-up some reforms underway, that it was effective in designing new organisations (as opposed to reforming older ones), that its training programmes were useful and that the people to people contacts promoted by longer TACIS projects were a valuable way of promoting sustainable reform. Other evaluations of specific instruments like INOGATE were also positive as to its general impact and potential, it had 'successfully promoted the ideas of international business law and project assessment among senior officials and politicians, creating a common language of debate and negotiation' while again noting administrative problems and the lack of real investment funding (Europeaid evaluation unit 2000, VI).

Outside observers were much less nuanced in their criticisms of EU aid policy. Many hoped that the EU, as the major economic power, would offer real financial support to the struggling NIS governments rather than TA (Hardt and Rodkey 1996, 369). EU leaders had rather disingenuously decided that as the investment needs were so great TACIS could never provide more than a small proportion of it, and therefore should not engage at all. There is a consensus that the coordination of EU aid and other European and International aid was inadequate (Brabant 1996; Herreberg 1998, 101). The failings of the Commission as an aid donor were widely recognised and Brabant argued that a new organisation should be set up to deliver aid, one with more expertise and flexibility (Brabant 1996, 447). TACIS was criticised for being unrealistic (Herreberg 1998, 101), including the lack of a coherent development strategy to justify the harshness of liberal reforms (Brabant, 1996, 447). More generally Wedel vividly describes how the misunderstandings of the entire approach to 'transition' (ignorance of local institutions and power networks) were replicated in the misuse and waste of aid (Wedel 1998).

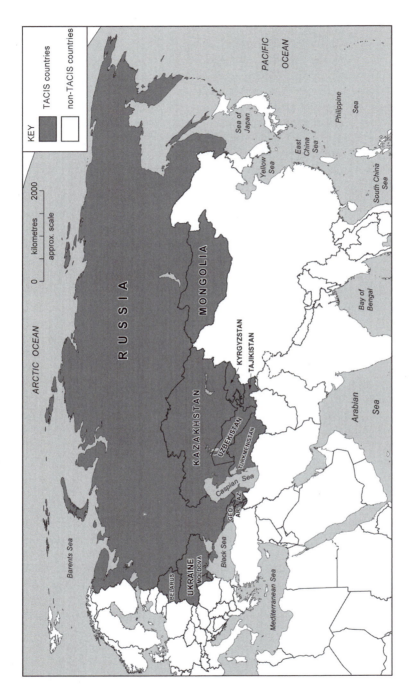

Map 4.1   TACIS recipients

All of these criticisms are undoubtedly valid but several factors should be noted. Firstly any innovative effort at institutional engineering is bound to be problematic. Secondly much of the criticism is based on the assumption that EU aid was designed to help the NIS. A more critical view would be that aid to the ex-Communist block was about helping economic expansion (especially European companies seeking to take advantages of privatizations), 'the task was not so much transferring Western information east as transferring Eastern information west' (Gowan 1995, 37). However this is perhaps excessively cynical and I take the view that aid was to serve Western interests in a deeper sense through inculcating structural changes amenable to its interests. The evaluations do indicate that TACIS was having some impact in supporting such changes and therefore may have been less of a disaster than supposed. But certainly the extent of its problems would preclude it from being an effective instrument of structural power and so the next section will concentrate on whether the Commission was able to further improve the instrument and realise its potential.

TACIS 2000-2007

There were some reasons to believe that TACIS could be improved, as the worst of the transition economic problems were over and the PCAs and other initiatives offered a more coherent policy framework for TACIS to operate in. The legal basis for TACIS in this period is clearly geared to making it more focused and gaining maximum leverage from the (limited) funds allocated (3.138 billion). It stipulates that aid for any one country should be geared to no more than three of six objectives:

- Support for institutional legal and administrative reform
- Support to the private sector
- Support in addressing the social consequences of transition
- Development of infrastructure networks
- Promotion of environmental protection and sustainability
- Development of the rural economy (including legal and institutional reform).

(Official Journal 2000b, Annex 2)

Article 2.6 of the regulation stipulates that funding should take into account the 'progress towards democratic and market orientated reform in the member states'. Regional cooperation and cross-border cooperation are still priorities. The primary form of aid is still technical assistance but it does allow for investment aid of up to 20%, hoping that this could be used to draw in other funding. This recognises that TA in itself can only have a limited impact. One facility that was not enabled by this legislation was direct budgetary support, used quite effectively by the EU as conditional aid in other regions. This was much lamented by TACIS programmers (interview, Commission, April 2008). This new legal framework intersected with the general aid reforms. TACIS was programmed via the same CSPs and NIPs as the Mediterranean implemented via annual 'Action Programmes' (equivalent to the National Finance Plans for MEDA).

Recalling the basic interpretation of EU policy as a drive to cultivate its structural power, where does TACIS fit in? It is one form of the EU's agency in the region. It is potentially at least a more specific instrument than, for example, general trade agreements and it can be used to shape specific aspects of the partners institutions and economy. However aid in itself can't be expected to produce fundamental changes so it must be viewed in tandem with the other EU policies. The question at hand is whether TACIS has operated as an effective instrument for reform and integration (taken to be indicators of the EU's structural power) in the period after the 2000 regulation and the major EU aid reforms?

Under the reformed system, programming for TACIS was managed by Directorate E in the External Relations DG, while implementation (including annual TACIS Action Programmes) was handled by the Europeaid office and (when deconcentration came into place) the Delegations. The CSP format stipulated widespread consultation in drawing up the strategy papers but the legal regulation for TACIS did not require consultation of civil society actors. Studies of the Commission's quality support group of the writing of the 2001 CSPs show that Directorate E very much controlled the process (Commission 2002a, 8). In most TACIS countries evaluated, the Delegation did organise donor meetings to try and coordinate affairs (Ibid, 30). However member states were not always very involved, as they don't all have in-country agencies, and for this reason the member state Management Committee for TACIS discussed the CSPs in more detail than others (Ibid, 14) but all of them were passed. Non-state actors were given an input only in 1/3 of TACIS countries (Ibid, 10). The major external stakeholder in the process is the partner government, obviously. Where a PCA is in operation the CSPs could be said to be 'agreed' implicitly insofar as they support PCA objectives. Naturally there was consultation of different types but the documents are the Commissions (and the EU's) first and foremost. According to the official evaluation the fact that the EU's strategy is 'discussed but not negotiated with the partner country, reduces the effective partnership and dialogue approach' (Europeaid evaluation unit 2006, 10). According to the thesis of this book aid cannot be a genuine partnership, as it essentially promotes European interests and power. On the other hand, to be effective the aid strategy should have the basic support of the government and elements within society. The Commission has achieved a suitable balance for its purposes and the ENP method ensures more partner government ownership (while still serving EU objectives).

As with MEDA the Country Strategy Paper reforms and the common methodology were probably less than relevant for TACIS, as there already strong guidelines on what TACIS could be used for, regardless of the country analysis and stakeholder opinions. In fact one Commission official at the time felt the CSP format was least suitable for TACIS of all aid instruments, due to these preformed political priorities (interview, Commission, December 2002). Central Asia is a special case as they are classed as developing countries and have multilateral Poverty Reduction Strategy Papers which can inform the Commission's strategy. Unusually, the Central Asia countries were treated as a block with one strategy paper for the entire region, a clear indication of Commission priorities. For the other countries three-year Indicative programmes had been written in 2000 but were rewritten in 2001 (for the period 2002–2005) together with a 6 year CSP. There was one exception here, as mainstream aid to Belarus was frozen at the time a new CSP was felt to be superfluous. Certainly the CSPs did require a more comprehensive analysis of the partner country and the EU's interests than had been the practice before. The form of analysis varies somewhat. Also some of the Indicative Programmes are less precise than others (some specify the precise allocation for each project others only the allocation for each 'objective'). Categorizations differ somewhat, the Tempus educational support and exchange programme is sometimes described as aid for institutional reform and sometimes as socio-economic support. Of course in a long-term perspective aid for education can lead to reform, but the primary role of Tempus and the proximate objective is more directly related to socio-economic support and this is how it is classified here. The quality support group noted that the use of performance indicators was haphazard and that the Management Committee complained of 'substandard' or unclear conditionalities for specific projects. These problems are common throughout the EU or indeed any other aid donor's system and they spring from conflicting principles; the need for a rigorous versus a flexible qualitative approach. Nevertheless the documents could have been more impressive. The review of the CSP process in 2003 introduced some changes. A first CSP was written for Belarus with the hope that better cooperation with its government would be possible. A new CSP was written for Georgia due to the poor human rights record of the (soon to be overthrown) regime. The new aid strategy was exclusively geared towards political liberalisation and the rule of law. Also a new CSP was written for Moldova to account for the new European Neighbourhood Policy and its Action Plans. This was not felt necessary for other countries in the ENP. These changes do show a degree of flexibility on the Commissions part. The quality support group noted that there were continued problems with the use of indicators and that programmers (for TACIS and elsewhere) had failed to adopt the Commission's own assessment method for 'governance' (Commission 2005a, 14–16).

As one might have expected from the unprecedented emphasis on concentration and targeting of funds in the regulation, Table 4.2 shows that the funds made available to TACIS were allocated in line with the reform and integration agenda, and other political objectives. (Note that some type three activities also have an element of reform, such as Tempus or health and social policy reform). Type 1 projects include a public administration reform project in Russia worth €25 million in 2004. This involves technical assistance to further delineate the competencies

Table 4.2   Programming allocations per category, including Central Asia, from 2002–2006 (€ millions)

		% of total
1. Institutional and Legal Reform	545	41%
2. Support to the private sector	156	12%
3. Socio-economic support	473	36%
4. Other	155	11%
Total	1329	100

Source: Indicative Programmes

of federal regional and local authorities in the giant state, especially regarding budgetary issues (Europeaid 2004a). This is illustrative of EU efforts to tackle technical governance issues, hoping to promote reform insulted from political vicissitudes. Multiple rule of law programmes have been launched for unstable countries such as Georgia. A €7.8 million project agreed in 2006 involves technical aid to reform the Ministry of Justice (including developing its IT systems) with a special focus on improving the capacity to align with international legal frameworks (Europeaid 2006a). As in the Mediterranean, technical assistance projects to further implementation of the ENP and the Partnership and Cooperation agreements are common. These involve assistance on redrafting legislation and awareness sessions with political and economic elites. Aid to development of the private sector is concentrated in Russia and the Ukraine. One example is a 2005 project combining technical assistance to the Ministry of Finance to align regulation of the insurance sector with international standards and support the insurance sector directly via the Russian National Insurance Association (Europeaid 2005a). The 'other' category includes some political activities distinct from the structural power agenda. For example, a substantial part of the Russian IP was for the Kaliningrad region bordering the EU, and for general cooperation in security and border issues with the Russian government.

Beyond the national strategies, there were complementary region wide programmes, as in the Mediterranean, designed to reinforce reform through networking and to further integrate the region with Europe, socially and economically. The Commission outlined 'broader regional considerations' in 2001 and then upgraded this to a more detailed Regional Strategy Paper in 2003. The three themes focused on were Justice and Home Affairs, sustainable development and promoting trade and investment flows. The latter was supported through aid to share information and best practice on reforming telecommunications policy; minor investments to support private sector involvement in transport and energy infrastructure and to help leverage outside investments; and technical assistance to develop the use of information technology in the societies of the region (Commission 2003b). In addition to this there are the small scale TACIS instruments such as Bistro, designed to offer rapid, short-term and small-scale

Table 4.3   TACIS commitments 2000–2006 (excluding Nuclear Safety funding) (€ millions)

A. ENP states and Russia	2000	2001	2002	2003	2004	2005	2006	TOTAL
Armenia	7.8		10		10		17	**44.8**
Azerbaijan	21.6		14		15		22	**72.6**
Belarus				5		8	4.5	**17.5**
Georgia		4	14		27		20	**65**
Moldova		19.5		25		42		**86.5**
Russia	53	80	90	105	94	80	57	**559**
Ukraine	63.5	63	67	50	70	88	100	**501.5**
Regional Programmes (and cross border cooperation)	214.4	142	104.9	116.5	109.8	135.6	139	**962.2**
Total for these states	**360.3**	**308.5**	**299.9**	**301.5**	**325.8**	**353.6**	**359.5**	**2309.1**

B. Central Asia	2000	2001	2002	2003	2004	2005	2006	TOTAL
Kazakhstan	0,0	15,0	0,0	6,6	7,0	3,4	NA	**32.00**
Kyrgyzstan	0,0	10,0	0,0	4,5	6,2	15,25	NA	**35.95**
Tajikistan	0,0	0,0	0,0	3,7	9,6	17,35	NA	**30.65**
Turkmenistan	0,0	0,0	0,0	1,5	2,2	5,75	NA	**9.43**
Uzbekistan	15,0	0,0	0,0	8,7	11,0	9,25	NA	**43.95**
Central Asia as a block			50,0	26,7	14,0	15,0	NA	**105.7**
Total for Central Asia	**15.00**	**25.00**	**50.00**	**51.70**	**50.00**	**66.00**	**NA**	**257.7**

Source: Internal Commission factsheet 2008, and Commission 2007g for part B

assistance, (worth €100,000 or less), to public and private bodies in the region. From different legal bases, and different parts of the Commission, there were other aid instruments; most notably the European Initiative for Democracy and Human Rights was active, as discussed in the section on Ukraine.

Allocative conditionality?

As with MEDA, TACIS was legally supposed to reward countries pursuing political and economic reforms, but there was less of an emphasis on TACIS as an incentive-based instrument. In any case, as with MEDA, the EU's analysis was not really precise enough to offer clarity on how this would operate. Clearly if these were the only criteria for conditionality then it has not been applied, as Russia has received the largest share of the funding, see table 4.3, and it has hardly been a star reformer. Other criteria, cited in the previous chapter, were geopolitical importance, and willingness to cooperate with the EU. Another factor that should be noted is geoeconomic importance and market size, which also explains Russia's leading role. There are some cases, such as Belarus that (apart from being a neighbour) do not fulfil any of the criteria as the government is not reformist in any way and does not show interest in the EU's projects. Moldova and Georgia which are cooperative and enthusiastic with the EU, have had reformist governments and are in the near abroad receive relatively high commitments per capita. In regard to Azerbaijan and Armenia in the Trans-Caucusus, the relatively high allocations for the former could be explained by its geoeconomic importance combined with proximity. Ukraine is the largest per capita recipient and certainly has geopolitical importance; also it has had governments committed to economic reform (at least rhetorically) and political reform at certain periods (pre 2001 and post 2004) and is highly favourable to EU integration. If TACIS was a development instrument the countries of Central Asia would have received the bulk of funding. As it stands they have received a small proportion, this is explained by their distance from the EU (although they do have geoeconomic importance). On the whole it is fair to say that reform has not been the major factor behind country funding. To the extent that conditionality operates it is related to the quality of political relations, geopolitical importance to Europe and indeed economic interest and market size. The funding is not sufficient to act as a major incentive in any case.

4.4 Country Case Study: Ukraine

Both Ukraine and Russia owe their historical origins to medieval kingdoms based around Kyiv, and Ukraine has been historically linked to its larger neighbour. Although a strong sense of Ukrainian national identity emerged in the 19th century it was only in the first half of the 20th century that the current territory of the Ukraine became a coherent political and administrative entity

(Yekelchyk 2007). Previously, contemporary Ukraine was divided between the Russian empire and Western powers. The geographical and ethnic divisions in the country remain salient. Under the USSR it was allocated a role as producer of heavy industrial goods and talk of national identity was subsumed by Soviet communist ideology. Yet nationalist feelings never disappeared and once the USSR began to weaken the Ukraine was in the vanguard of the secessionist republics. Many Ukrainians and outside analysts felt that the Ukraine would prosper as an independent country due to its strategic location as a conduit between east and west and its large well-educated population (Motyl 1993, 2). However, as with the rest of the NIS the challenges of independence and reform would prove overwhelming.

Ukraine in the 1990s

In understanding the trajectory of the Ukraine in the 1990s it is crucial to note that there was hardly a revolution in terms of the transfer of power. The Communist elite saw which way the wind was blowing in 1990 and formed an alliance with the democratic and nationalist forces (Kubicek 1999, 58). A new autonomous political system was established and inevitably there were massive economic changes, but there was no radical reform. A strong Presidential republic emerged, which was consolidated in the new constitution of 1996. The first two Presidents (Kravchuk 1992–1994 and Kuchma 1994–2004) were ex-Communists. Although the rudiments of a democratic system did exist, from the start there was an authoritarian mode to political governance (Motyl 1993, 15). The new leaders had the task of state building for a divided country, which many in Russia and Europe did not see as sustainable. The historical division between West and East was still relevant in terms of religious and cultural affairs, and a large minority of ethnic Russian speakers existed in the industrial Donbas province of the East and the Crimea. This region was 'always an exceptional region within the former USSR' whose elites tended to interact with Moscow more than the state capital (Kuzio 1997, 83).[6] In fact the feared meltdown never happened and the Ukrainian state achieved a basic legitimacy, although these different elements still have a defining influence on the politics and political economy of the country. In regard to wider international relations the new state emphasised its European identity and leaders spoke of a 'return to Europe' (Yekelchyk 2006, 199), partly as a means of defining itself against, and balancing the power of, Russia.

Ukraine's initial approach to the new economic dispensation was far from 'shock therapy'. The reaction of the new government to the end of the Soviet pricing and production system was cautious and ambivalent. An early analysis that 'post-totalitarian elites lack the political economic and social institutions and resources necessary for determined and consistent policy making' would prove

---

6   There was also the question of the Crimea, which was traditionally a part of Russia and contained ethnic Russians and another potential separatist group, the Tatars.

accurate (Motyl 1993, 52). Understandably stability was the major concern of the regime. President Kuchma would take some steps from 1994 on towards privatising the massive state-owned sector. These reforms had a rather distorted effect however and to understand this we must understand the power blocks and interest groups in the new political economy of the country. Kubicek argues strongly that the defining factor in the early years was the absence of any 'civil society' (in the economic sense) autonomous from political power (Kubicek 1999). State elites dominate official and unofficial interest intermediation. The major business grouping, the USPP (Union of Industrialists and Entrepreneurs) was dominated by either conservative state owned companies or as time progressed by former state directors seeking limited reforms which they could benefit from. This was both influential and influenced by the government and parliament. Some sectors such as the heavy defence industry blocks (centred in the Donbas) had much to lose from liberal reforms (Motyl 1993, 54). The major labour union was also controlled by the state and later by the clans. Although groups such as the miners would flex their muscles (Harassymiw 2002, 374) this was more at the behest of rival elites than organised labour (Kubicek 1999, 58). On a general level the pressure of the economic crisis prevented consensus and encouraged infighting (Bojcun 2004).

As elsewhere, one fundamental task for the new state was to develop the public administration. Under the Soviet system the role of the peripheral administrations had been limited, 'the ministry of finance is merely a collection of clerks used to taking orders from Moscow and nothing else' (Motyl 1993, 137). There was not real tradition of a civil service and Ukraine was the first NIS to establish a civil service code, based essentially on the French and Spanish models (Krawchenko 1999). There was still left more discretion to individual ministries (political fiefdoms) than many would have wished (Ibid, 141). Generally Ukranian public administration was highly criticised. Corruption was endemic, with high profile cases – such as the downfall of Prime Minister Lazarenko in 1997 – being merely the tip of the iceberg. Despite over 20 laws passed, systemic problems persisted (Harasymmiw 2002, 195). Even outside of the shadow economy, tax collection was very problematic, which is always symptomatic of deeper governance problems.

Properly begun in 1994, the privatization process had a stop-start quality as interest groups in the parliament clashed with the government. Initially only small entities were privatised – such was the chaotic state of affairs that some of their directors had already begun to privatize them personally. Gradually, larger projects were undergone including sectors like consumer energy supply, and the collectivised farms also began to be privatized in 1999. Although the state sector was still large (especially for judged strategic sectors) by the end of the 1990s substantial privatizations had taken place. However, as elsewhere, this did not necessarily signify the development of a liberal capitalist economy. This was privatization under 'hybrid conditions' (Bojcun 2001, 7) or 'privatization without market discipline' (Derrer 2005, 141). The process involved handing over valuable state assets to powerful rent seekers, and as such did not encourage competition or efficiency (Harasymmiw 2002, 355–356).

Foreign capital played little role in these privatizations. Their shady nature and the restrictions on foreigners' role made them highly unattractive (Derrer 2005, 142). Accordingly government efforts such as the law of 1993 to encourage FDI had little impact. Nevertheless the global economy and the international community did play a significant role in this period. The government was forced to turn to the IMF for financing of the national deficit in 1994. A loan of $ 1.96 billion was agreed in 1995 although disbursement was staccato due to failures on the government's part to achieve the criteria (Kuzio 1997, 169). There was some flexibility shown on the IMF's behalf (Ibid). The government of a country as important as the Ukraine was not without bargaining power. It withdrew from reliance on the IMF in 1999 (Bojcun 2004, 56–59) only to return two years later. Clearly the government had a desire for policy autonomy if it could secure alternative financing. The World Bank was also deeply engaged in attempting to shape policy. In 1999 its country strategy postulated loaning from $100 to $800 million depending on the government's policies (Harasymiw 2002). Russia remained the greatest single trading partner but trade with the rest of the world increased substantially, and thus in this sense integration into the global economy did take place. Apart from its trade agreement with the EU, the government applied to join the WTO.

Ukraine's foreign policy and economic diplomacy struck a delicate balance between the West and with Russia. In this regard Russia's 'oil and gas whip' (Bukvoll 1997, 81) must be noted. From the Soviet era the Ukraine was totally dependent on Russia's energy supplies and post-1991 it had to pay for them. This left Ukraine in significant debt and vulnerable to economic coercion. Thus although Ukraine was keen not to allow the CIS become a powerful supranational economic institution (Solychank 2001, 77) it had to retain good relations with Russia. Fortunately other factors ensured that the more ambitious CIS plans were not implemented. While it signed a cooperation treaty in 1997 it did not join the union with Belarus and refused Russian offers to 'coordinate' WTO accession (Hayoz et al. 2005, 189). Undoubtedly some Westernizers see Russia as a link with Ukraine's problematic governance and want to escape from it to the West if possible. General public opinion is favourable towards cooperation with Russia (Hayoz et al. 2005, 170) but even the Russian speakers do not want reunion. Many of the oligarchs have tight links with Russia but even the most pro-Russian (although they favour close economic links) must be aware that real economic integration with Russia would open them to encroachment from their larger Russian counterparts. All in all very little was resolved in Ukraine in the 1990s, while national income and human development levels plummeted more sharply than any other of the NIS (Popov, 2007). Only in 1999 would the economy start growing again.

Conceptualizing the Ukrainian system

Variance in academics' understanding of certain aspects of Ukraine rests on the question of whether the state is weak or strong, which in turn rests upon what one includes in the definition of the state. Kubicek (1997) described the situation in the Ukraine as authoritarian corporatism (state elites controlling all of the interest groups) but accepted that the situation was developing into a more diffuse form of clientelism, too anarchic to be considered part of the state. There is a consensus about the existence of oligarchies, or highly concentrated blocks of financial, industrial, political and media power (Harasymiw 2002, 388). Such are the resources of these individuals and their groups that they can offer substantial patronage (or indeed exert coercion) to a greater extent than other institutions. These private business groupings are capitalist in their desire to make profits but not in ideology (Ibid). I would argue that they should be considered distinct from the state. What is clear is that official government institutions are weak. Less clear but crucial is whether the oligarchic system so deforms the public institutions as to render them incapable of reform (and relatively autonomous public policy). The oligarchic system gives rise to what Derrer calls the 'neo-feudal post-communist socio-economic structure' outlined in table 4.4 (Derrer 2005, 157). He emphasises that this is not just a stage but a working system of governance, it will not necessarily change (Ibid, 159).

Table 4.4   Derrer's schematization of Ukraine's deviation from liberal capitalism

A. An ideal type of liberal capitalism	B. The Ukrainian system
Large elite, value creation, meritocracy, basic trust in the system.	Small elite, clan structures, mistrust, survival.
Open, predictable	'Rule by uncertainty,' foreigners and smaller businesses 'crowded out'
Common, transparent accountancy standards and corporate governance	Particular accountancy standards and corporate governance
Rule of law, strong judiciary, clear taxation system	Weak judiciary, weak public administration in general
	High nominal taxes (weak collection).

Source: Taken from (Derrer, 2005, 155-158)

The EU's Ukraine policy in the 1990s

The Ukraine's importance to Europe encompasses geopolitical, geoeconomic and soft security concerns. Geopolitically, the alignment of Ukraine will help determine the future of Russia and the balance of power in wider Europe (Bukvoll 1997, 1-2). It is a transit country in many respects; it has served as a conduit for trafficking of people and contraband and is a transit country for Russian and Central Asian energy supplies to Europe. Ukraine is also a potentially large market and useful economic partner for the EU. On the Ukrainian side it had declared its interest in 'rejoining' Europe. This was related to political and cultural identity but also to economic necessity. Europe was seen as the Ukraine's path to prosperity (Harasymmiw 2002, 377). Accordingly the Ukraine signed a Partnership and Cooperation Agreement with the EU in 1994. This bound the Ukraine into comprehensive dialogue and institutionalised the EU-Ukraine relationship. Ukraine was given most-favoured nation trading status by the EU, it would reciprocate and provisions were made for harmonisation of Ukrainian legislation and standards with the EU. The economic provisions were swiftly ratified in an interim agreement while the slow process of ratifying the broader PCA was underway. Implementation proved awkward as

Table 4.5   TACIS spending in Ukraine 1991–2001 (€ millions) and 2001–2006

Tacis national programme	464
Other Programmes: regional, nuclear safety, science and technology ...	608

Source: Commission 2001e Annex 3

the Ukrainian government was accused of protectionism and obstructing trade in goods. On its side the EU refused to give the Ukraine 'market-economy' status – due to the unreformed nature of its economy – which meant that it was highly vulnerable to protectionist measures such as anti-dumping penalties. The under-institutionalised nature of the Ukraine made it a very awkward partner for the EU (Bojcun 2001, 7). On the more optimistic side, it could be argued that the EU was thus the ideal partner for it to develop laws and institutions. Most argue that the Ukrainian state did not have the capacity to implement the PCA, regardless of political will (Ibid 55–56; Gallina 2005, 202). A chicken and egg conundrum emerges in that the PCA was designed to help reform but lack of reform made it hard to implement. This is precisely where financial and technical assistance should fit in.

The operation of TACIS in the Ukraine suffered initially from the same problems as elsewhere and the task at hand was far beyond that of a modest technical assistance programme. The signing of the PCA did give a clear guidance to TACIS and the 1996 changes to the legal basis hoped to develop a more orderly instrument but it was still very broad and vague in terms of the purpose of EU finance. Indeed, far from helping diplomacy aid emerged as one of the bones of contention between both parties. The Ukranian government was not happy with the small amount and technical assistance focus of the instrument, it understandably wanted more 'tangible investments' (Bojcun 2001, 17). As table 4.5 shows the figures for Ukraine were not large, if you take away nuclear safety. The national TACIS programme funded advice on how to reform, the major focus being the Ukraine-Europe Policy and Legal Advice Centre (UEPLAC). It also funded several projects to develop civil society and democratic values supplemented by global TACIS facilities such as Lien[7] and the separate TACIS democracy/ EIDHR instrument. In terms of the private sector support to SMEs and corporate restructuring in general was a major focus. Other EU aid to the Ukraine consisted of macro-financial assistance (loans) of €435 million and a euratom loan for nuclear safety (Commission 2001e, 12).

An official evaluation of the operation of TACIS in Ukraine in the late 1990s concluded that aid had 'increasingly contributed to systemic change' (Europeaid evaluation unit 2003b, 20) but that there were major problems. The UEPLAC centre had suffered from a lack of continuity and clear direction. It noted that TACIS focused on promoting EU models, to the extent of ignoring national realities and other international models (Ibid 19). It argued that training in general had been effective. It pointed out major problems in judicial and public administration reform projects due to the slippery and changeable domestic environment. As to wider institutional change, it argued that civil society support needed to be a more coherent part of the overall programme. (The EIDHR was praised for its numerous micro projects). There were some successful projects to cushion the pain of transition, including support to social insurance and the pensions system, although the meagre funding means that the long term problem of finance for social welfare was not solved. Aid to SMEs had been ineffective due to the focus on start-ups and the lack of continuity of the aid projects. Aid for corporate restructuring had been (predictably) ineffective given the widespread corruption and rent seeking. The evaluators concluded that 'Dialogue on policy-making is often poor' even after the ratification of the PCA in 1999 (Ibid, 68). A major problem here was the incoherence of the Ukrainian government; there was good communication with the National Coordination Unit for TACIS aid but this was not enough. Clearly, TACIS as it was working was of limited use in supporting either EU objectives or Ukrainian development.

Although rhetorically Ukraine's political elites were for integration with Europe, EU-Ukraine relations were not close during the 1990s. Elites were less than enthusiastic about the dependence economic integration might foster (Bojcun 2001, 55), as the PCA implementation problems testify. The EU was preoccupied with Eastern European candidate states and also may have been wary of offending

---

7   Which linked Ukrainian and European NGOs.

Russia through making too many overtures to the Ukraine (Bojcun 2002, 56). Despite lukewarm relations the EU became the major non-CIS trading partner of the Ukraine, whose external trade in general increased substantially in this decade. That Harasymmiw could write in 2002 that Ukraine was now 'a trading state' (2002, 379) was in no small measure due to the EU. Yet the internal economic and institutional system was a barrier to greater EU penetration and conducive to continued substantial Russian influence. From the EU's point of view the object is to develop liberal economic policies with clear transparent laws and regulations, allowing the gravitational pull of the EU to work.

EU interventions in the Ukraine post-2000

From 1999 on, Prime Minister Yushchenko showed a willingness to reform and tackle corruption, including revising previous corrupt privatizations and dealing with the notorious energy sector. An ambitious privatization programme announced in 2000 planned for up to $3 billion worth of new privatizations, in a more transparent and legal manner (Harasymmiw 2002, 358). The Yushchenko government ran up against powerful opposition and he was dismissed in 2001. Along with former minister Tymoschenko he formed the 'Our Ukraine' party which articulated liberal interests (including some powerful businessmen more sympathetic to reform). In the meantime President Kuchma's democratic credibility had been badly damaged through various scandals. General Russian investment in the Ukraine increased enormously from 1999 on and Kuchma began to move closer to Russia although still keeping a certain distance. He accepted to further develop infrastructure links as a part of a deal on energy debt but resisted Russia's ongoing proposals to give Gazprom shares in Ukranian transport companies as a part of this. In brief a certain pattern emerged of relatively liberal forces struggling against political and economic networks that resisted liberal models. To label the former as pro-Western and the latter as pro-Russian would be a simplification, but this does describe their leanings. This conflict peaked, but did not conclude, in the Presidential election and the Orange revolution of 2004-2005 that brought Yushchenko to power as President.

Impending enlargement (which would make the Ukraine a neighbour) and already existing soft security threats revitalised EU interest in the country. A Common Strategy devoted to the country in 1999 signified the importance of the Ukraine. A Justice and Home Affairs Action Plan in 2001 would result in more concrete cooperation, and also affect aid policy. In March 2003 the EU agreed Ukraine's entry into the WTO and launched the ENP the same year. The latter was designed particularly with border countries like the Ukraine in mind and it was among the first to sign an Action Plan in December 2004 (Commission 2005c). In its case much of the Action Plan was devoted to implementing or building on issues in the original PCA but included the possibility of a future free trade agreement. The latter included substantial sections on general security and foreign policy cooperation but most of it referred to reform of political and economic governance. On the political side Ukraine agreed to ensure probity in future elections and to allow freedom of the media. It agrees cooperation with the Council of Europe and UN human rights bodies (and ratification of international human rights conventions). On the economic governance side it agrees to further work on harmonising its rules with Europe, to reduce non-tariff barriers to trade and to improve the investment climate through regulatory reform in consultation with domestic and foreign business interests. This is reinforcing and specifying the PCA and is monitored by the PCA institutions.

This text was negotiated and signed during a period of political turmoil in the Ukraine. Kuchma had continued his dual foreign policy in agreeing a common economic space with Russia, Belarus and Kazakstan the previous year while creating a new 'higher council' to support European integration (Hayoz 2005, 187). After the apparent victory of the Our Ukraine block the EU signed a further ten point plan with Yushchenko in 2005 agreeing to increase aid, allow European investment bank loans and move more quickly towards a free trade area. It was hardly the path to accession many had hoped. Gallina argues that the ENP is positive in that it allows for more contacts at all levels, and that even a vague prospect of accession can act as a psychological motive for reform (Gallina 2005, 208-210). In the meantime aid policy is a crucial instrument to encourage the reforms the EU wants, and it can develop the context within which deeper integration of the Ukraine becomes more realistic.

The TACIS national programme 2002-2006

The Commission had already begun to reform TACIS to address some of the earlier criticisms. The regulation of 2000 provided for direct investment in socio-economic development and tried to ensure more a specific focus for each country. An indicative programme was written in 2000 but this was replaced by the CSP and NIP written in 2001. This new format did allow for a more long-term strategic approach by the Commission, one drawback being that the national context was still very much in flux. The analysis of this document did reflect a frank approach to get grips with the political realities of reform in the Ukraine. It directly cites the oligarchs (Commission 2001e, 5, 8) as a major stumbling block to reform, although its solution to this problem (see below) is nothing original. It does not take the rhetoric of the government for granted and notes that the trajectory of Ukraine is still unclear (Ibid 5). In regard to the Government's reform programme it points out the incoherence of the various legal reforms (Ibid, 7). It is explicit about Kuchma's democratic shortcomings although it also worries that the elections of 2002 may put a block on economic reform (Ibid, 5). There is also a degree of honesty in discussing stumbling blocks to attracting further investment, these include poor governance but also poor physical assets, for example deteriorating infrastructure. The solution of the Commission is to focus on the former (which is cheaper). Generally the analysis is not rigorous in terms of using quantitative methodology; apart from basic socio-economic indicators none are used.

The CSP cites the PCA as the overarching guiding policy. In discussing problems in implementing this it argues that the problem is not just one of capacity (the common verdict) but also a question of political will. Generally it notes that Ukraine's internal political and economic problems are hindering the EU's broader goals and thus aid policy is of prime importance. It also stresses that these problems 'expose the country to Russian political and economic influence' (Ibid 3), articulating the competition between both parties. In contrast, institutions of global governance such as the WTO and the IMF are very much seen as partners (Ibid 8). Overall the writers of this document are highly conscious of the broader structural foreign policy of the EU. Statements such as 'with declining living standards affecting an increasing proportion of the population, there is a growing risk of rejection of market reform policies' (Ibid, 16), illustrate that programmers feel that they have to justify social support through EU objectives rather than ethical principles. The basic strategy to further the Europeanization of the Ukraine is not radically different from before. The document emphasises that deeper liberalization of politics must occur and the need for radical institutional reform accompanied by economic growth and social measures to cushion the pain. There are signs that it is addressing and learning from the problems of previous donors. It notes the decision of the World Bank to concentrate on systemic reform given repeated problems in working in specific sectors (Ibid, 9). It is perhaps overly positive about the impact of previous EU aid (Ibid, Annex 4), although it does accept the failure of efforts to promote SMEs, and posits new policies here. It admits that training of officials hadn't always had the multiplier effect needed and hopes to target more senior people for training. It emphasises that UEPLAC (the policy advice centre) will be given more continuity. It notes that TACIS has been effective in guiding and reforming selected large commercial banks and hopes to use this experience to further mould the banking sector.

The resulting National Indicative Programme (see table 4.6) is not entirely 'systemic', like the World Bank's approach but combines broad reforms with specific sectors where there is a certain momentum for change (in particular trade policy because of the PCA and WTO changes). The three priority areas chosen (as per the regulation of 2000) are the three primary categories used in this book. Of course there is always a degree of flexibility in using such nomenclature. The Commission categorises the 'border management programme' as institutional reform, which I do not agree with as it is really a specific security and policing programme. The overall funding is modest but there is a large proportion of this devoted to the agenda described above. As to the comprehensiveness and rigour of the plans, the indicators for the trade facilitation element were rigorously worked out via the joint PCA committee. Others were less so. There is an explicit admission of political risk for the reforms and a lack of faith in the government as a reforming partner. Therefore the principle of conditionality is made clear for each project (that the money is not automatic), but the specific

Table 4.6   National indicative programmes for Ukraine (€ millions)

2002–2003	
Legal, judicial and administrative reform	21
Business trade and investment promotion	20
Fuel gap/ energy support	20
Civil Society	16
Border Management	22
Social Reform	16
Total for this period	**115**
2004–2006	
Legal and administrative reform	15
JHA	60
'Civil Society' Media and Democracy	10
Training and education	*25*
Assistance to enterprise development	25
Dev of financial markets	8
Local development	*15*
Support to energy sector reform	*12*
Support to the health sector reform	18
Support to development of social assistance policy	24
Total for this period	**212**

Source: National Indicative Programmes

criteria are less clear. There is also a general statement about cooperation being dependent on Ukraine's support for democratic principles and PCA rules. Given that EU cooperation had continued in the preceding period (when neither were adhered to) this is a weak admonition. On the other hand this vagueness gives the Commission the flexibility and autonomy to use the aid politically. For increased leverage the World Bank method of having explicit scenarios with different funding rates would be useful.

Box 4.1   UEPLAC Stage 4 (TACIS Action Programme 2003)

The Ukraine-Europe Policy and Legal Advice Centre has been a consistent element of TACIS efforts to promote reform and alignment with Europe. Stage four of UEPLAC (granted €4.5 Million) was launched in 2006. The centre's steering committee includes the major concerned government ministries and units as well as Commission officials, to help ensure smoother cooperation. This phase is almost exclusively focused on legal approximation as there is a basic framework to work within and an official plan for harmonizing of legislation. It also tries to promote implementation and foster EU norms through training and networking seminars. Apparently this socialization is mutual as the centre appears to have taken on the worst elements of (alleged) Ukrainian administrative practices in regard to dealing with outside interest. Nevertheless it is vigorous and effective in commenting on Ukrainian legislative approximation plans and assisting in preparing the specific legislation. UEPLAC is a primary example of how the EU inserts itself into the Ukrainian system, with moderate finance but a powerful policy framework, and extends the European legal order.

Box 4.2   Taxation reform (TACIS Action Programme 2003)

An efficient taxation system is obviously crucial both to the development of a market economy and to the rule of law more generally. Ukraine's inefficient and confusing tax system has played a major role in the general corruption of the state. This €1.5 million project supported support tax reform from 2005-2007, in coordination with a broader World Bank programme. Specifically it funded experts to offer assistance on drafting legislation and advice on reform of the tax administration. Again it also involved harmonisation with European standards (Commission Delegation, internal project document, 2005). International experts note substantial improvements in the taxation framework, with continued misgivings as to the administration (IMF 2007a; World Bank 2005).

The second NIP was written after the ENP had been announced but not implemented, and Kuchma had lost all credibility. The Commission did not alter its strategy but declared it would 'leave a sufficient margin of flexibility for action programmes to respond to changing priorities and need' (Commission 2003d, 6). There is another generic support for institutional reform project. This again was focused on legislative harmonisation. There were some recent successes to note here such as the conclusion of the EU-Ukraine bilateral market access protocol. Also the Parliament had adopted the Law on National

Box 4.3   Civil society development (TACIS Action Programme 2004)

> A new approach to civil society report aims to set up 'grass roots NGO ca-
> pacity-building in the field of economical governance' and in particular con-
> sumer rights hopefully 'providing citizens with access to relevant information
> enabling them to lobby for good economic governance'. It is a small part of
> a 31 million euro package for institutional reform. Modest in approach this
> is evidence of the effort to link the economic and political reform agendas.
> Consumer rights organisations are emblematic of the kind of economic civil
> society, which makes a market economy sustainable. It is an embryonic ver-
> sion of the kind of social engineering the Commission would like to engage
> in, had it the resources.

Box 4.4   Coal sector policy support (Action Programme 2005)

> Coal is a hot political sector due with militant labour unions, and much coal
> mining is located in the 'special' Donbas area with its Russian speaking
> population. The coal sector is also intrinsic to the heavy industry oligarchs the
> EU wishes to sideline. The Commission is convinced that many coal concerns
> will have to close. This €10 million project is to help the government design
> a comprehensive strategy for starting this process and mitigating the political
> and social impact. The AP states that 'the European Union itself has much
> experience in this area and the project will gain from this experience'. EU
> states also had much more resources to mitigate the pain. This project will
> offer advice on designing compensation measures, but not finance for these
> measures.

Programme of Approximation of Ukrainian legislation to the EU legislation in
2000 (Commission 2003d, 7) and a scoreboard was being developed in the PCA
committees to monitor progress. Other elements of this 'institutional reform'
package were to continue support to judicial reform and a new legal framework
for SMEs. Civil Society and democracy support included a new focus on the
media. Private sector development includes developing financial markets (the
banking and insurance sector), which could have a major impact on society
and economics but the funds involved are modest. Social support is given more
funding and there is more cash allocated per annum. Again it is noted that
specific projects, like the SME and financial sector support are dependent on
ongoing systemic reforms, without going into detail.

     Other small-scale TACIS facilities supported the national programme in this
period. Many of these are relevant to promoting civil society and good governance
such as the Institution Building Partnership Programme (IBPP) for NGOs.
This supports partnerships with European NGOs for organisations involved in
development social welfare, environmental issues or indeed trade unions and

Table 4.7   TACIS commitments in Ukraine 2001–2006 (€ million). This includes estimated Ukrainian benefits from regional, cross-border and nuclear safety budget 2001–2006 lines

2001	2002	2003	2004	2005	2006
147	122	105.6	113.3	143.1	144.3

Source: Commission CSP 2007,30

chambers of commerce. Also the Cross Border Cooperation 'small projects' were particularly relevant to the Ukraine due to its lengthy European border.[8] These also indirectly address governance issues, although this is not the direct aim of this instrument. Then there is the Regional Cooperation programme. This is a little complex as the EU does not want Ukraine integrating with Russia but does want it integrating with other cooperative countries such as Georgia, Moldova and Azerbaijan. Projects here were concerned with supporting elite cooperation (with each other and the EU) mostly in the areas of transport, energy and JHA issues. Thus in this chaotic period the EU managed a mix of programmed national aid projects and other TACIS interventions in Ukraine. TACIS was still modest in terms of funds committed, see table 4.7, and there was not a massive increase after the Orange revolution.

Beyond TACIS budget lines, Ukraine received a macro-financial loan of €110 million in 2002. Such assistance has not been needed since and the EU is fading out its activities here anyway. There were other small budget lines that are not discussed in detail here. The most interesting non-TACIS aid instrument was the European Initiative for Democracy and Human Rights initiative. This is hardly an instrument of structural power in its own right (it includes many purely ethical goals such as abolishing the death penalty and rehabilitating torture victims) but its efforts to promote democracy and good governance may reinforce the efforts of structural instruments such as TACIS. Ukraine was chosen as a 'focus country' for 2002–2004 (countries were selected for their strategic importance and receptiveness to aid). NGOs were funded to implement projects related to training security and legal forces in human rights, countering torture, improving legal conditions and supporting an independent media (Commission 2001d, 67). From 2004 on Ukraine still received substantial funding under the new method's category 1 (rule of law and access to justice) and category 3 promoting democratic processes. In all 5.95 million was committed under the EIDHR from 2001-2006 (Commission 2007d, 30). A large proportion of this were micro projects, very small grants (averaging approximately 100,000) to support local organisations for specific projects with over 3.6 million allocated for the period 2001-2006. These are a cheap and effective way to support local organisations. Examples

---

8   Followed up by Neighbourhood Projects, started in this period.

of these are a 92,000 grant to a Kyiv based organisation to improve the rural population's knowledge of the legal system and 70,000 to a regional organisation to train Ukrainian human rights NGOs. These two link in with the broader TACIS reform project (which includes developing civil society and the rule of law) but this is relatively rate, most of the other projects do not, and are more concerned with ethical objectives and/or EU visibility.

As to international aid more generally; from the beginning Ukraine was second only to Russia as a recipient of aid in the region. In the first decade of independence, financially significant assistance was given by EU member states also, in particular from Germany, the UK and the Netherlands. In this period, by far the greatest single donor was the US, which invested heavily in this strategically important country. In the post-2001 period the US has remained the largest single donor, although EU aid is almost as high. Germany is the only other donor which grants relatively sizeable funding. As to priorities, the US has evolved somewhat, from a bottom up focus, due to disillusionment with the government, to more government-led aid in the ensuing period (USAID 2002). The US was also distinguished by highly politicized democracy support funding from 2001-2004. Unlike the case of Morocco, discussed in the previous chapter, member states are also engaged in all of the core reform areas, especially Germany, France, the UK and the Netherlands. They are also heavily involved in private sector development activities (Commission 2003d, annex 3; Commission 2007d, 26-27). Conversely there is no division of labour; the various European donors are not specialising in specific areas. Multilaterals such as the World Bank are equally involved in support for reform as well as directly investing in development projects. As with the Mediterranean there is close cooperation between the EU and the Bank, which revised its assistance strategy 'to provide a more realistic and focused set of outcomes that are consistent with the EU Action Plan, yielding an opportunity for joint monitoring by the government, the EU and the Bank' (World Bank 2005, 12).

The impact of the EU's reform project in the Ukraine

The political and economic trajectory of the Ukraine was not settled in 2007 although it had moved in the direction European policy-makers wanted. Ukraine's alignment with the EU's foreign policy is 'excellent' (Commission 2006b), but its domestic structures are out of kilter with the EU's vision. The Orange Revolution in 2004–2005 seemed to signify a liberal victory and certainly signified the emergence of a dynamic civil (and political) society movement. As noted, the EU had been engaged in supporting civil society, although the PORA youth movement, widely regarded as the most influential and partisan movement involved in the protests, was supported primarily through American funds. At the critical juncture when the regime may have been tempted to repress the protests the EU played (again along with the US) a crucial role in refusing to recognise the elections, and in mediating. Yet deeper change would prove more difficult. Yushchenko's pragmatic decision to work with some of the oligarchs alienated

Table 4.8   The Worlds Bank Institute's measurement and rankings of governance in Ukraine

		Score	Governance (-2.5 to +2.5)
Measurement of regulatory quality	2006	-0.47	
	2000	-0.73	
Measurement of Control of Corruption	2006	-0.67	
	2000	-1	
Measurement of Government Effectiveness	2006	-0.57	
	2000	-0.66	

Source: World Bank Institute

part of his following led by Tymoshenko, who soon left the government. Such discord and voter disillusionment allowed a comeback for Tymoschenko in the parliamentary elections of 2006 who became Prime Minister as leader of the largest party, leading to a hostile and uncertain cohabitation between the rival parties. In 2007 the spectre of some kind of armed conflict between different elements of the security forces loyal to different branches of government again reared its head, although the situation was calmed down and new parliamentary elections announced. These led to a new government with a re-formed Orange coalition of Timoshenko and Yushchenko. Political stability aside there has undoubtedly been significant political liberalization (Flikke 2008).

It is not postulated that aid could play a major role in 'regime change' and the thrust of the EU's aid policy was on more quotidian governance and economic policy issues. Here there is tangible progress as noted by the Commission's progress report on Ukraine's Action Plan. In terms of achievements it notes the new law on competition, which would play a major role in altering the oligarchic structure of the economy over time if implemented, and the liberalising of trade policy (Commission 2006b). Other international organisations and research institutes are in accord with the Commission's verdict. The IMF outlines, more systematically than the Commission, a reform progress table citing areas of improvement (IMF 2007a, 37). This notes that over 5,000 business regulations have been amended or repealed, that the tax benefits offered to specific groups have been repealed and that there were promising examples of large transparent privatizations. It also notes the Ukraine's achievement of market economy status from the EU and the US, progress towards WTO membership and particular reforms of the energy sector. A World Bank review in 2005 agrees that there has been an improvement in climate and government since its country strategy was written (2003) though not enough to change the highly conditional nature of Bank assistance (World Bank, 2005). The US government signalled its

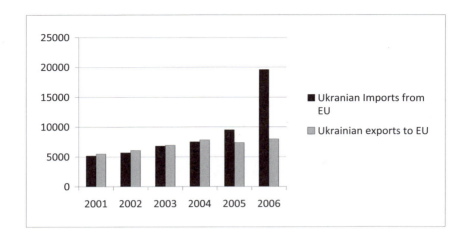

Source: DG Trade 2007b, 4

Figure 4.1   Ukraine's trade in goods with the EU (25) from 2001-2006 (€ millions)

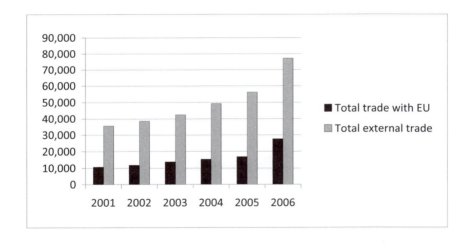

Source: DG Trade 2007b, 4

Figure 4.2   Ukraine's external trade 2001-2006 (€ millions)

approval by moving it to the threshold level for receiving Millenium Challenge Account aid, a special development fund given to countries deemed (based on a series of indicators) to be democratic and adopting the right economic policies. Corruption was the major reason that it wasn't over the threshold. The World Bank Institute's measurement and rankings of governance, shows a clear trajectory of improvement regarding four key policy and governance variables, although the Ukraine is still on the negative side of the median.

As implied above, the situation is not wholly in line with liberal hopes. Ongoing corruption, despite more extensive high level reforms, is emblematic of the illiberal nature of Ukraine. The Commission report cited notes that the investment climate and economic governance is still poor overall. Societal, normative and economic structures are always going to be slow to change but there are also still problems with the legislative framework. Also state institutions (executive and judicial) are still highly criticised despite much aid to this area. The IMF's country report criticised the continuing problematic investment climate even in comparison with other transition countries (IMF 2007a, 35). It evaluated the general institutional framework as 'not pro-market', citing a lack of financial development (stock markets) as a major block; this is partly due to poor corporate governance – an area TACIS had been involved in trying to improve (Ibid). Reform legislation in this area is ongoing.

Returning to Derrer's table one could argue that the Ukraine has removed some of the regulatory features which are anti-capitalist, but the key socio-economic characteristics and many of the 'particular' regulatory features remain. The macro-economic and the macro-political situation will be fundamental forces helping or hindering reform. Neither of these are easy to predict. This period has seen major economic growth for the Ukrainian economy, which has filtered down to improved living standards for the population (World Bank, 2005, 1). Despite impressive recent growth, international experts are agreed that the Ukrainian economy remains 'highly vulnerable to external shocks' (Commission 2006b), partly due to its reliance on key sectors such as steel.

How have these developments affected the EU's economic presence in the Ukraine? Trade had already more than doubled from 1995 to 2001 (Eurostat 2006, 36-37) and figures 4.1 and 4.2 show Ukraine's trade with the EU has continued increasing in this period and the trade balance has become more favourable for the EU. Ukraine's trade with the rest of the world has increased at a comparable rate. The proportion of Ukraine's imports being supplied by the EU has increased dramatically in 2005. The proportion of Ukraine's exports going to the EU has decreased (although overall exports have increased). The EU was by 2006 the greatest trading partner of the Ukraine, with 35 % of its total trade, ten % more than Russia (Trade DG 2007b, 6). Ukrainian FDI has quadrupled since 2000 (IMF 2007a, 33), although this is from a very low base. Statistics on the source of Ukrainian FDI are sketchy; Russian FDI is generally underestimated as it may take place through Ukrainian registered companies or through companies from other sources (ICEGEC 2006, 13–15). What is clear is that, led by Germany, EU investment has increased dramatically since 2004 (Ibid, 15). The EU invested €5.5 billion in 2005 (Trade DG 2007b, 1), and has become by far the greatest single source of FDI.

In summary, Ukraine is more integrated into the global economy than before and the EU's economic presence has increased significantly. Although incomplete there have been substantial changes to the regulatory and official institutional system. Many of these are particularly geared towards the EU and short of some kind of radical regime change these legal and institutional structures will tie the Ukraine into Europe. This is illustrated by the fact that both of the major political blocks officially favour European integration, albeit one much more sincerely than the other. It would be premature to say that the EU has achieved the full degree of structural power postulated, due to limited societal and economic changes and continuing Russian power. The deeper economic oligarchic structures (although the EU and other donors mention them less in recent reports) still remain. Another hoped for structural change that did not occur was to lessen Ukraine's dependence on Russian energy. This leaves it vulnerable to influence of Putin's Russia, which is a more forceful and coherent economic actor than the EU but lacks the latter's attractiveness. However legalistic, bureaucratic and selfish the EU may appear to Ukrainians, its *modus operandi* makes it much less threatening than Russia. These very different forces interact with the major centres of power within Ukrainian economy and society, with no sign of a definitive outcome. However, the EU's policies have given it greater influence and leverage than before.

What has been the precise role of TACIS in this? Arguably the European Commission has practically inserted itself into the Ukrainian administration (which is a fragmented entity in any case) through its persistent and multilevel technical assistance. The persistent focus on reforming legislation and practices related to international commerce has helped the emergence of a more open economy. It is also engaging with civil society and attempting to liberalize the Ukrainian policy at several levels, here it is supplemented by the EIDHR and other international donors. There are of course limits to its impact. This kind of aid is perennially under pressure to evolve and adapt to the political and economic frameworks. There is an impression of the Commission feeling its way, trying out pilot programmes, learning from experience and where possible leveraging its finance with those of other donors. The effect of the limited financial resources of TACIS is most noticeable in the social support dimension, where know-how and policy advice can only go so far if the government lacks the revenue to provide substantial social welfare programmes. It also means that TACIS cannot be considered as a significant force in promoting economic development as opposed to institutional and regulatory models. Yet the possibility of institutional reform in the Ukraine will to a large extent be determined by its economic development, including whether the economy can diversify (and provide new jobs for victims of restructuring) and develop more diffuse patterns of economic power.

Conclusion

TACIS has been used to exploit the space created by the fall of the Soviet block to promote European rules and norms. Within its funding constraints it evolved into a useful tool – which became much more coherent, focused and relatively effective – for the EU's structural objectives. This is due to alterations to its legal basis, organizational improvements and a stronger policy framework in general. Despite these adaptations, TACIS is regarded as having been a relatively inflexible instrument, and the European Neighbourhood and Partnership Instrument which replaces it, is quite different (see chapter 7). TACIS was useful for legal reform and approximation, but as in the Mediterranean, the full implementation of reform is harder to influence. In regard to Ukraine, aid policy has been unable yet to alter the deeper neo-feudal or neo-patrimonial structures. Aside from political and social norms, these are rooted in the low level of economic development and the oligarchic structure of the economy. Yet it is unclear how the EU can influence these fundamentals without offering 'structural funds' type financing (massive increases in aid geared to economic development) or the prospect of joining the EU. Thus it is widely believed that Ukraine can only really be transformed if offered a path to accession (Karber Stiftung 2005). The essential strategy of the ENP is to reform and integrate Ukraine without full accession, but this seems a very optimistic scenario.

Yet Ukraine, like other friendly states such as Georgia, remains at least a feasible prospect for Europeanization, unlike states with politically recalcitrant leaderships such as Belarus and Russia itself. The salient fact in the history of European and Western engagement in the NIS is the inability to reform Russia and its re-emergence as a rival autonomous configuration of political and economic, as well as military, power. This in itself precludes the more ambitious project of reforming and integrating the ex-Soviet Union and is likely to be noted as a historic failure. TACIS will only be a footnote in the story of how Russia was lost. The scale of the country would always have required a quantum leap in resources offered by Europe and the West if they wanted to shape its evolution. The current situation is one in which deep economic interaction persists between the EU and Russia while they struggle for structural power within the region, a struggle epitomised by the rival regional integration schemes established.[9] As a form of power projection, the EU's gradualist aid and trade approach has much to recommend it in comparison with Russia's cruder use of economic coercion. Its major weakness is its energy dependency and its lack of high level political cohesion among member states to support the Commission-led policies. In this context, as in the Mediterranean

---

9   The Russian effort is less comprehensive than the EU. In fact such is the crudeness of Russia's approach to countries such as Ukraine, Belarus and Georgia that it lends weight to the argument that the reintegration of the ex-Soviet space was not a major objective of Putin (Sakwa 2008, 294). However, it is undoubtedly true that Russia is seeking structural power in key sectors, such as energy.

region, the achievements of aid in supporting the European interest are hostage to other developments.

Chapter 5

The European Development Fund in Africa

In EU geography, Sub-Saharan Africa is linked with certain Caribbean and Pacific states to form the 'ACP' group. These disparate regions are grouped together based on colonial heritage and a common peripheral status in the international system (Kahler 1982). As outlined in chapter 2, Sub-Saharan Africa (henceforth referred to as Africa for simplicities sake) was the setting for the first EU external aid policy, the European Development Fund, in 1958. Notwithstanding the many changes since then, the EDF remains only half-Europeanized as it is funded by member states outside of the EU budget. More importantly, Africa remains the location of most of the poorest and underdeveloped states in the world. EU aid policy here differs from that of the regions previously discussed in that a more explicitly developmental instrument and more tightly linked with the international development community, for whom Africa is the primary focus. Yet here also the EU is pushing for deeper economic and institutional integration, in a manner not fundamentally different from its policies in other areas. The actual importance of Africa to Europe has ebbed and flowed through the years, but it has always been an area of influence which it has intended to maintain. Marginalized in the 1990s, Africa has risen in importance – for better or worse – since the turn of the century (Michel 2006). In this context EU aid policy is understood as an effort to support western dominated global governance (in contrast to rising powers such as China) as much as specific EU interests. This has led it on a divergent path from European civil society, and the wider European public, which is concerned with an ethics-based development effort. Ghana is chosen as the case study country, although there are more obvious examples to demonstrate the linkages between EU aid and structural power. South Africa in particular is a locus of economic and geopolitical power. The EU has an extensive aid policy there and a vigorously pursued free trade agenda. In many ways this is quite similar to the cases discussed in the previous chapters. Yet this is a different budget line to the EDF, which as the largest single aid instrument deserves to be covered. Nigeria is a state of major geoeconomic and geopolitical importance and the EDF supports an extensive governance reform programme. Yet it would not be a typical example of the EDF, most of which goes to states lacking obvious strategic importance. Ghana is more representative of the nature of the EU development project in Sub-Saharan Africa.

5.1 Africa in the International System

Given its colonial history and its continuing weak and dependent role in the global political economy, Africa's evolution has clearly been shaped by exogenous structures and actors to an exceptional degree. Yet Bayart argues trenchantly against a deterministic, structuralist approach to Africa (Bayart 1992), maintaining that, notwithstanding external influence, indigenous institutions and actors have shaped its future to a large extent. Also one should obviously be wary of generalising about such a large and diverse continent, that includes major economies such as South Africa, and states admired for their governance such as Botswana. Vast amounts have been written about the states that emerged from decolonization. Most would admit that the nature of the colonial state had a massive impact on the structure of the newly independent states, hence the term post-colonial state. The new elites adopted the modernizing machinery of the late colonial administrations but this interacted with indigenous institutions and powers. (Youngs 2004, 27-28). It was the African state that inspired the concept of the neo-patrimonial regime (Erdmann and Engel 2006), with political patrimonialism and economies driven by clientelism and rent-seeking. Official state structures were generally weaker than those peripheral states in the EU's near abroad. There were many different political regimes (nationalist one party regimes, military regimes and allegedly communist regimes) and there were vastly different types of states in terms of geographical location, material resources and ethnic make-up. Logically, these would take different trajectories over time. In the early years this form of governance often coexisted with comprehensive statist efforts (Davidson 1992; Crawford 2004), although such states never attained anything like the integration of communist/radical states in other regions (Bayart 1993). Africa's new leadership attempted statist development policies, but within the context of deep economic links with the developed world, and Europe in particular. The EU would dissuade them, via the carrots of Yaoundé and Lomé, from seeking a radical break with this pattern. There were numerous attempts at regional integration with the hope of promoting investment and economies of scale, supporting pan-African autonomy and reducing dependence on Europe (Lancaster 1995, 192). Apart from institutions set up by White South Africa or France, regional integration failed (Bach 1999), mainly due to economic weakness and political systems unsuited to structured legalized cooperation (Kahler 2000). As with efforts at regional integration, the development project in general disappointed immensely, due to a multitude of factors including a lack of internal and geopolitical stability. Decreasing terms of trade and rising interest rates led to financial crises in the 1980s. Given the resulting attenuation of state resources the role of private networks of power and distribution would accentuate. In some cases this combined with internal ethnic conflict would lead to collapsed states and a reversion to pure patrimonialism or warlordism (Somalia, Sierra Leone, Liberia). In other cases the state retained (although still shot through with patronage) significant strength, using donor resources to bolster its power (Mwenda and Tangri 2005). The era of globalization certainly had a massive impact on Africa in that the accompanying neo-liberal ideology would form international development policy. Yet economic globalization, in terms of the transnational private sector, did not actually directly impact a great deal on Africa as it was excluded from the new circuits of commerce and production (Duffield 2001; Hoogvelt 2001; Hirst and Thompson 1999).

Bilateral and multilateral donors, as well as the third sector, have been intimately involved in African development from the beginning of the independence era. As they were unable to borrow from private capital markets, African governments had to borrow from governments and public institutions to secure the kind of finance that every state needs. The influence implicit in this context grew enormously as the IFIs responded to the financial crisis of the 1980s with much more comprehensive interventions in the economic and political systems. The much maligned stabilization and structural adjustment programmes required macro-economic reforms, deeper changes to the regulatory system and the nature of the economy. The World Bank went beyond economic policy to include 'governance' in Africa in its remit (World Bank 1981, 1989, 1992). After 1989 this agenda would expand to include democracy itself. These policies certainly had a major impact, although the power of the IFIs should not be overestimated as structural adjustment was rarely fully implemented (Mosley et al. 1991). Regarding governance reform, local powers managed to warp the reforms and quite literally 'adjusted' the patronage system rather than inducing structural change, yet the discourse and macroeconomic policies of neo-liberalism were triumphant (Hibou 2002).

The 1990s saw a more sophisticated and consensual effort to spread free market capitalism, with more attention towards social development (Callaghy 2001). New schemes, such as the IFI sponsored Poverty Reduction Strategy Process in chronically indebted countries, were allegedly focused on helping the poor. These were linked to Highly Indebted Poor Country Initiatives (HIPC 1 and 2) offering graduated debt relief for the poorest countries. PRSPs and Comprehensive Development Frameworks (for less poor developing countries) were supposed to be country owned and country led. Civil society participation was also a part of this process (Callaghy 2001, 141). They also involved greater donor coordination and the essential conditionality was still enforced (Development Initiatives 2002). Given the above, and the vigour of African elites in pushing neo-liberal solutions (Taylor and Nei 2003), this could be seen as a deepening of international hegemony over Africa. Certainly Sub-Saharan Africa is the world region most dependent on aid, debt relief and this makes it in many ways the primary site for global governance in general (note the activity of the International Criminal Court in Africa as opposed to other regions). Yet indigenous institutions and regimes are not merely passive actors to be moulded by outsiders, and the 21st century has not seen the triumph of liberal capitalist globalization foretold. In Africa, China is pursuing its own structural foreign policy for political and economic influence, and it offers enormous financial support without strings attached (Taylor 2005). In this context the EU sought to consolidate both Western-orientated global models and norms, and further expand its own influence.

5.2 The EU's Policy Framework

When the Treaty of Rome was signed in 1957 France was attempting to preserve its African empire via a French Union which offered autonomy moderated by supranational integration (Martin 1995, 165). This was related to the long-standing French vision of a Franco-African Partnership or '*Eur-Afrique*' which stressed the interdependence (and logical division of labour) between both areas (Lister 1988). As the French Union faded France promoted a structured relationship between its ex-colonies and the EU as a part (and only one part) of its continued influence. The overlap between the origins of EU development policy and European colonial projects gives ready ammunition to critics of the EU's role in Africa, but this historical conjuncture is not in itself proof of neo-imperialism. The Yaoundé aid and trade arrangements of 1963 and 1969 were greatly expanded with the Lomé Convention of 1974. Lomé included nearly all of independent Sub–Saharan Africa and ex-British and French island colonies in the Caribbean and the Pacific, creating the rather awkward ACP 'group'. The motives for this particular membership of this group have been questioned; it didn't include all ex-colonies (powerful nations such as India) for example. Neither did it include all of the poorest countries in the world. Rather it was a grouping of poor countries in set regions, whose economies were no threat to Europe (Kahler 1982). In particular Lomé was carving out a relationship between the EU and Africa. This was not just a French project. Europe more generally had an interest in ensuring access to supplies of valuable materials such as lead, copper, zinc and uranium. This was an era of rising third world power, 'the height of commodity power' (Gibb 2000). There was also a geopolitical component in preventing the spread of communism in Africa. This was blatantly illustrated by then Director General of the Commission's Development DG comment, in the 1990s, that 1989 had made Lomé 'irrelevant' (Lister 1997, 137). Why would this be the case if Lomé was primarily about development?

The relatively generous provisions reflected the relative power of third world countries at the time (Gibb 2000). Free access to Europe for most industrial products was guaranteed, partner states did not have to reciprocate. EDF aid was a legal commitment on the EU's behalf. Partner countries could choose the projects for which they wanted funding. New kinds of aid instruments were established to relieve the asymmetries and uncertainties of international markets. It is striking that even this – by our contemporary standards generous – arrangement was criticised as European power projection. Lister noted that control over cash disbursement gave the Europeans a lever of power (Lister 1988). While the institutional set up of Lomé reflected aspects of European integration with the establishment of joint institutions at various levels, the ACP group was a weak negotiator, and the leadership of Nigeria in negotiating the first Convention would not be repeated (Lancaster 1995, 196–203). Others argued that these selected underdeveloped countries were being locked into complementary and exploitative trading patterns and alternative development strategies were being pre-empted (Kahler 1982, 201). Kahler also noted that safeguards in the trade clauses meant that the EU reserved the right to impose barriers if needed. For this and other reasons Galtung saw Yaoundé/Lomé as an example of neo-imperialism through structural domination (Galtung 1973).

These asymmetries would become more apparent as the financial meltdown shattered most ACP states. The EU began to take a more explicit interest in the internal make-up of its partner states. Policy dialogue was established in this decade and would inevitably be one-sided. Hopes that the EU would add weight to the 'alternative development discourse' supported by UN bodies, as opposed to the neo-liberal project, proved misplaced (Lister 1997; Therien 1999). Lomé IV in 1989 was a major watershed. This had some of the old flavour with aspirations for a New International Economic Order but this was now supplemented by the goal of inserting ACP states into the global economy. It launched explicit human rights and democracy conditionality, as well as structural adjustment.

As the 1990s progressed EU policy further developed. The new South Africa could have been a powerful interlocutor for Africa but the EU took care to treat South Africa separately, signing a separate bilateral Trade agreement and establishing a separate –well funded – aid programme.[1] Worldwide the EU was pushing for global trade liberalization hoping for access to dynamic developing markets, an objective which the Lomé relationship was cramping (Babarinde 2004). Thus it began to try and normalise its relations with Africa. Even France was normalising affairs (Martin 1995, 165), although while reducing its direct aid it increased funding for the EDF as part of the Europeanization of its policies (Chafer 2002). Europe still wanted a relationship with Africa, but one more in line with globalization and with new security concerns (Sub-Saharan Africa was a major source of migration and general instability). The Commission's new approach was based on the argument that the trade concessions had failed to promote development. This was undoubtedly true although whether this was because they were too generous or not generous enough was not explored. The Commission noted that 'the post-colonial era is over', as in that particular considerations and sensitivities in the EU's ACP policy were obsolete (Commission 1997, 3). Although lip service was still played to the principles of 'contractualism, security and predictability' (Ibid, 4), the major role of the EU in 'development' would be to support partners to engage in liberal economic reforms, through aid conditionality and free trade. Concurrently the Commission envisaged 'creating a new trading dynamic and strengthening Europe's presence in the ACP countries by enabling EU business to tap into these countries comparative advantages' (Ibid, 22).

This new approach was incarnated in the Cotonou agreement (2000), which as a framework agreement involved considerable less specific legal commitments than before (Babarinde 2004, 35). There is a degree of flexibility– to the point of insouciance at times – but a strong insistence on the key principles. Economically,

---

1   South Africa was granted €885.5 million for 2000–2006 (Official Journal, 2000) .

the major principle was a move towards reciprocity and an end to the special Lomé trade preferences. This was presented as a necessary imposition of WTO rules, although the EU itself had helped shape these rules, (Gibb 2000, 13). Lomé's preferential trade terms would be extended only for eight years. After this the least developed countries (LDCs) could gain access to the EU market via the 'Everything but Arms Initiative' while the non-LDCs could avail of the EU's General System of Preferences which offers some concessions to other developing countries (Babarinde 2004: 40). Neither of these are contractual though (Ibid). If African states wanted full, contractual EU access, the EU proposed free trade Economic Partnership Agreements with 6 ACP regions (4 African). Said regions should complete their own economic integration prior to this, although in fact they sit uneasily alongside existing regional structures. The EU had already imposed on the formation of regional integration in Southern Africa through its free trade area with South Africa (Gibb 2000, 475–476). The EPAs also cut across the LDC– non LDC divide, as the proposed regional units include both. The push for EPAs was accompanied by an altered aid instrument which was to be much more conditional. Civil society participation was legally enshrined in regard to the general relationship and in aid policy, although the EU had already rigidly formed the boundaries of what is possible. Cotonou also had provisions for heightened political dialogue, in accordance with EU wishes to expand its role in 'high politics'. In general the EU's policy towards Africa has developed from post-colonial patronage to a more extensive effort to integrate and reform its partners. As the Commissioner for Development admits, the EU's interest in Africa has revitalised somewhat due to concerns over energy, migration, security and rivalry; 'there is now no denying that Africa has become a sought-after continent in a short space of time, thanks to its strategic importance. Today, Africa really matters.' (Michel 2006). Recent policies such as the EU's Africa strategy (2005) aim to coordinate member states activities more.

The Commission was given a mandate to begin EPA negotiations in 2002, they are essentially free trade instruments similar to ones the EU has signed with relatively developed countries, albeit with more flexibility on timescale. They include free trade in goods, services and provisions on protecting EU investors. Commission leaders strike a moderate tone and insist that their motive is developmental: 'What we want in exchange is not commercial I have no European business leaders knocking at my door demanding greater access to ACP markets – but a commitment to improving the business climate in your countries, for your benefit' (Mandelson 2004).

When pressed Commission officials, including the director general of the Trade DG, admit that the only development element is that reciprocity is 'useful medication', i.e. that the EPAs will force reform (Third World Network 2006). The EU is also pushing for common rules for national procurement systems and competition policy, which it tried and failed to push for in the WTO (Wilkinson 2006, 123). Given the feelings of the European public, the harshness of the EPAs is astonishing. It is strikingly illustrative of the EU's tendency to promote its own structural power above other considerations. Unsurprisingly the EPAs have aroused fierce opposition from European and African civil society (EPA Watch 2007). One African NGO network declared that

> These agreements are set to be even more restrictive of the policy choices and opportunities available to our governments, and even more severe in their impacts than the World Bank/IMF structural adjustment policies as well as the WTO agreements (Africa Trade Network 2006).

The same statement deplored the weakness of African governments which could only bargain within the agenda set by the EU (a typical example of structural power). African governments are less vocal but constantly bemoan the lack of 'flexibility' in practice (African Union Trade Ministers 2007). Officials and politicians from EU member states have expressed concern at the Commission's approach (Collingworth 2006), but it is the member states who gave it this mandate. In fact the Commission is performing its classic role as an agent of the European interest, leaving the member states at one remove from a not very palatable policy.

In summary, Africa is less strategically important than the near abroad and EU is acting as an agent of globalization to a large extent but still includes a drive for structural power. The EU's objectives would lead to operational structural power in that they involve giving EU policy-makers greater purchase over the form of development and regional integration in Africa, while a deep free trade area would strengthen its negotiating power in the WTO. In terms of passive long-term structural power the following could be postulated. It will have locked in liberal capitalism with regional integration and with the EU itself. If these policies do engender development Africa would develop in a primarily *Eur-Afrique* context, with structural advantages for European business. China's much trumpeted role in Africa would seem rather one-dimensional in comparison. Certainly the EPAs would bolster EU trade with Africa, where it is still by far the greatest trading partner (WTO 2007, 9). In Africa in particular, the greater significance of EU success would be in terms of deeper passive long-term structural power for the future, as Africa is still under-developed at the present time. The EU clearly already has a degree of structural power which it is using to further its goals, but it also needs more specific instruments.

5.3 The Role of the European Development Fund

The EDF is distinctive in that its conditions, objectives and procedures are outlined in agreement with the EU's partner states as a part of the contractual nature of the Lomé /Cotonou relationship. They are detailed in the core text and annexes/protocols to the Conventions, and apply for a set period of time (five to six years). The fact that it is negotiated may imply that it is less of a foreign policy instrument than MEDA or TACIS, but it would be naive to suppose that EU money does not operate for EU objectives, and as discussed earlier the formal equality of the EU-ACP relationship is misleading. The following sections argue that the role of the EDF is different but essentially comparable to other EU aid instruments, in particular since its emphasis on reform has been heightened.

The EDF from Lomé I to Cotonou: an evolving instrument

Original EDF assistance was in the form of funding for, usually quite large, development projects. The aim here, as well as actually promoting development, was to secure good relations with African states and keep them locked into the Lomé relationship. Aid was to be predictable and secure, although the member states had final say on disbursement. Apart from the EDF Lomé involved a new aid fund called Stabex to compensate for fluctuations in the prices of agricultural commodities exported by partner states. Later Sysmin was established for minerals. These were indeed radical in conception as 'market-correcting' instruments in line with ideas of a New International Economic Order. As things evolved aid would focus more on correcting countries to align them with international markets. New aid forms, more in accordance with evolving international norms, emerged with later EDFs, such as the risk capital facility managed by the EIB, to offer reimbursable finance to commercial companies and efforts to develop 'decentralised cooperation' between European and African NGOs.

With Lomé IV in 1989, human rights and democratic principles were made more central to the EU-ACP relationship. This was used to suspend aid to several countries, although in fact the legal justification for this was unclear (Crawford 1996, 506). The agreement actually offered limited increases in funding, see table 5.1. As the then President of the ACP Council of Ministers put it; 'the Lomé IV volume of financial resources of ECU 12 billions remain much less than either the ACPs' legitimate expectations or the Convention scope and objective requirements call for ~ or indeed the Community means permit' (Selafi 1990). Selafi did appreciate the fact that most aid was in grant form, unlike other donors (Ibid). For example, the new EU structural adjustment support facility was, in contrast to the World Bank, non-reimbursable. Yet in defining the criteria for granting such aid a prior agreement with the IFIs was a pre-requisite (Article 246). And so the EU was essentially supporting the same radically pro-market agenda albeit in a more palatable manner. The revised Lomé IV in 1995 reinforced the fact that aid was now conditional. The importance of democracy, human rights and the vague concept of good governance was further highlighted (Article 5), and it introduced the idea of performance based funding. It also allowed, at the behest of new democracies in the region, the use of development aid to support democratization. Trade was also given greater prominence as was regional integration (which had always been an element of Lomé, rhetorically at least). In summary, while Sysmin and Stabex still existed and Lomé IV still stipulated that aid would be based on the strategies of ACP states on a 'predictable and continuous basis' (Article 221),

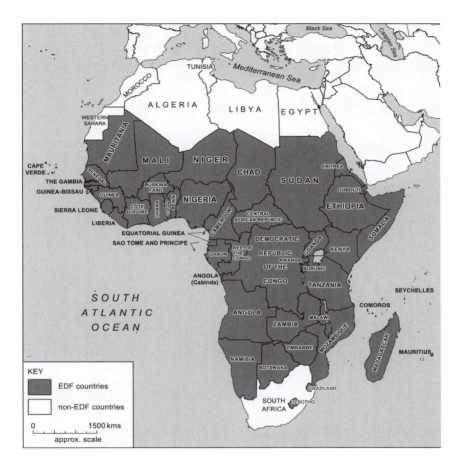

Map 5.1   EDF Recipients

the EDF had become more of a political instrument, working for the EU's norms and interests. By 1994 only a minority of EDF aid was for traditional development projects (Lister 1997, 126), the rest going to technical assistance and conditional budgetary support.

The major criticism of the EDF has been the low disbursement of aid commitments, due to awkward procedures. There was over 20 billion euro outstanding in unpaid commitments by 1999 and the situation was actually worsening (Raffer 2000, 5).[2] There have been suggestions that this was partly

---

2   Unused EDF funds could be diverted to other aid funds, or carried on. From EDF 9 they have to be at least committed within the set time period.

Table 5.1   EDF budgets (for ACP countries) since 1985 (€/Ecu millions)

	Total EDF package*	Grants	Special loans & risk capital
EDF 6 Lomé III	7,400	4,860 + 1,340 for stabex and sysmin	1,200
EDF 7 Lomé IV Part 1	10,800	7,995+1,980 stabex and sysmin =	825
EDF 8 Lomé IV Part 2	12,967	9,592 + 2,375 for stabex and sysmin	1,000
EDF 9 Cotonou	13,500	11,300	2,200

Source: The Lomé and Cotonou Conventions

*   Not including EIB own resources.

deliberate (Ibid) but this is hardly credible as it would not be in the Commission's interests to withhold cash that was not part of the Community budget. Evaluators noted a lack of cohesion at all levels (Europeaid evaluation unit 1998, 45–52). Specialised forms of assistance were also criticised. An evaluation of a trade development mechanism stated bluntly that it had failed, due to inflexibility and a failure to engage with the private sector (Evaluation Partnership 1998). All of these problems do not just affect the use of aid to relieve poverty and support development but detract from the other political and strategic uses of aid. In the case of low disbursement this even affects the crude use of aid as a diplomatic sweetener.

Accordingly, in looking at EDF 9 in the Cotonou era we need to look at whether (as had occurred with the other aid instruments) these basic features have improved. The Cotonou Convention did change the context for aid in several respects. In line with the new regime, there is more prominence given to regional integration (Article 29) and aid could be used to develop 'measures and actions which help to create and maintain a predictable and secure investment climate' (Article 75). As to the form of financial aid, programmed budgetary support aid is given more prominence, in accordance with general trends. Above all there is a heightened form of aid conditionality (which had remained relatively underdeveloped compared to instruments such as MEDA). Aid levels are now purely indicative and based on 'needs and performance' (Annex VI). They can be revised at mid-term and end of term reviews. Performance would be assessed based on:

> Progress in implementing institutional reforms, country performance in the use of resources, effective implementation of current operations, poverty alleviation or reduction, sustainable development measures and macroeconomic and sectoral policy performance (Ibid).

One notes the inclusion of poverty and environmental concerns but the major focus is on institutional, policy reform and general governance. Regional aid can also be upgraded or downgraded in the course of the aid period. Thus the 9th EDF accentuated existing trends towards heightened conditionality and a focus on reform. It was still less obviously an instrument of structural power than TACIS or MEDA which are explicitly designed to reform and integrate strategically important countries. Rather it is best described as more standard development aid, tweaked toward European interests and influence. It still functions in its original role as a diplomatic sweetener (to go with the Cotonou medicine) although the new design is less suitable for this purpose. Its purpose is to promote poverty reduction and economic growth, which should enable regional integration and the EPAs. It is also geared at institutional and policy reform, including democracy promotion.[3] It is to support this through specific interventions and through general conditionality. These reforms would again further regional integration and the EPA process, and more generally promote liberal economic institutions amenable to Europe. Lastly it directly supports regional integration and the EPAs through technical assistance. As outlined in the previous section its success here would further and deepen the EU's already substantial structural power. To judge its effectiveness here we need to investigate whether the Commission and the member states have succeeded in giving the instrument more cohesion than before, managing it more efficiently than before, operating conditionality in practice and focusing the finance and expertise to unlock economic growth and institutional change.

The management of EDF programming: an open system or an EU instrument?

Under the particular EDF arrangements the member states keep tighter control over the Commission's use of funds than other EU aid instruments. For EDF the member state committee (the EDF Committee) had to give its approval for any project over 8 million. This was still a loosening of the system compared to what had been before. Aid was programmed according to the Common Strategy Paper format with a single five-year Indicative Programme (2002–2007) but a mid-term review to make changes. Programming is managed by the Development DG of the European Commission. As discussed in chapter 2, this DG has been regarded as less geared to EU interests than others. Is this apparent from its steering of the EDF? Or is it pursuing EU objectives in a slightly different context with less blunt strategic imperatives?

Programming of the Country Strategies was less politically controlled from Brussels headquarters than was the case for MEDA and TACIS. In-house surveys noted that the Country Delegations played more of a leading role in formulating the strategy than Brussels (Commission 2002a, 8). It also implied, and this is evident from the papers themselves, that they fitted more into international and

---

3   The EU is less ambivalent towards democracies in more distant regions which have less direct impact on its security.

multilateral donor efforts like the Poverty Reduction Strategy Paper process. In that sense the programming process could be said to be more open. EDF programming is also explicitly supposed to be based on the partner governments own strategy (unlike other aid instruments which say that this is desirable but not a necessity). Yet these development strategies are already to a large extent pre-determined in any case. In reality national input into the Country Strategy is hardly greater than other areas studied. Another novel feature was the explicit role for non-state actors in aid management, including programming. This is interesting as providing the actors in question were supportive of the EUs agenda and strategy their involvement would greatly strengthen the aid strategy. If they are hostile to aspects of the EU's policies, as they would be in terms of certain reforms and the EPA project, then giving them a serious input would signify the EU loosening its control over the use of funds and the EDF could hardly be called an instrument of structural power. Numerous studies have been done of the role of civil society groups in programming. Official Commission reports note that the role of these groups was more than in other aid programmes and lists examples of seminars and other fora (Commission 2002a, 2005a). The view from the other side is much more sceptical. Even an admittedly superficial NGO report – based on what was reported in the CSPs – found no evidence of civil society having any real power over programming (APRODEV 2002). In depth country studies led by Eurostep also argue that the civil society role was – if not entirely tokenistic – more consultative than anything else (Takam 2003). Even allowing for the fact that civil society groups would rarely declare themselves entirely satisfied with the attention given to them the evidence is overwhelming that they have not had a major role in programming. In conclusion the slightly more pluralistic procedures of the EDF does not mean that the EU and the Commission have greatly loosened their control over the instrument. The reasons for this are not just care to prevent misuse of funds (this is really a separate and quite technical issue) but because it has its own interests and ideology to promote.

The EU's strategy and methodology for EDF country aid

It is difficult to generalise about such a large number of Strategy Papers and Indicative Programmes for countries of many shapes and sizes. Strategic objectives are, naturally, couched more in terms of the EU's development policy objectives and the Cotonou agreement than EU interests, although the later are included, for examples the Nigerian paper discusses the EPA agenda and the CFSP common position on Nigeria. The country analysis for ACP states has more of a focus on poverty and government policies regarding this than for other areas. There is still a substantial focus on institutional and policy reform, analysed with no more or no less rigor and detail than other regions. As with other regions, analysis of the political context and the governance of the country more generally is haphazard in terms of methodology (Commission 2005a, 15). In other respects the ACP documents are more rigorous, for example there is a comprehensive 'intervention framework' for each action, outlining objectives, results and indicators. All in all these are more development documents than the CSPs for other areas. In many ways the CSP framework is most suited to the EDF as it is primarily a development instrument. Yet EU trade policy objectives still find their way into the targets for reform programmes.

EDF funding priorities are also distinct from the other instruments. This is unsurprising as Africa includes a greater proportion of extremely underdeveloped or failed states than the other regions covered. Country funding is divided into an 'A' envelope for programmable aid and a separate 'B' envelope earmarked for contingency purposes. This can be used for issues such as conflict resolution, emergency food or humanitarian aid, stabex/sysmin. Its funds can be transferred to the 'A' envelope or to other EU or international aid instruments. Table 5.2 shows the funding priorities according to the Indicative Programmes for this period, including the changes made in the mid-term review. The 'other' category includes B funds (except those transferred for activities 1-3 in the A envelope). The usual methodological disclaimers apply and absolute precision for each heading is not possible. Most striking is that, there are no specific private sector support projects at the country level. (There are some projects which have an element of private sector support and there is aid at the regional and ACP-level through the Centre for the Development of Enterprise, which aids companies and business associations, it was allocated €90 million for this period).[4] There is more devoted to standard development and social support than in other programmes, as one would have expected. Yet there is still a large proportion devoted to policy and institutional reform, although the large figures for 'reform' also include changes allegedly geared primarily to poverty reduction.

On the whole, the EDF is used for a broader range of purposes and uses a wider range of modalities than other instruments. For the federal state of Nigeria for example the Commission decided to devote all its funding (apart from the 'B' reserve) to the state and local levels of government and picked 6 focal states. In Somalia aid has been devoted to basic state building and emergency measures. One commonality with other EU aid is that conditional direct budgetary support is used increasingly; up to 1/5th of EDF 9 is in this form (ECA 2005, Annex 1). This is for reasons already discussed in previous chapters. It is easier to disburse and it gives the Commission and other donors an entrée into the budgetary decision-making process in the partner country. The European Court of Auditors had severely criticised how this aid was operated, but in 2005 it noted (while still critical) that the Commission's methodology and practice for monitoring compliance was more precise and effective (Ibid, 75-82). As with other areas direct budget support improved EDF disbursement rates significantly, with a rate of 78% in 2006 (Europeaid 2006b, 66).

---

4   Also there are concessional loans from the EIB.

Table 5.2   Thematic priorities of the indicative programmes 2002–2007 and (€ millions) (including changes made in the mid-term review)

Reform	3599	38%
Socio-economic Support	4215	44%
Other	1700	18%
Total	9514	

Source: Country Strategy Papers and mid-term review document

Other forms of EDF aid and other instruments

The major other form of EDF funding is via regional level aid. This is given to the four 'regions' outlined by the EU to form EPAs. Regional assistance takes similar forms in all cases, mainly focused on technical assistance to facilitate trade integration and investment in infrastructure to upgrade regional interconnections, with advice on improving transport policy. There is also aid for conflict prevention schemes and other issues but the main effort is on boosting regional integration. This faces considerable challenges as regional integration has been a perennial disappointment in Africa but it is working in line with massive pressure from the EU in support of the EPA vision. As well as this the sysmin and stabex system still exists although downgraded in importance (funds from channel 'B' of the country allocation may be used for this purpose). There are other more 'global' funds such as the Africa Peace Facility and Water Facility (Commission AR 2007, 64). Outside of the EDF Africa is also a major recipient of humanitarian aid (ECHO), democracy aid (EIDHR) and NGO-cofinancing.

Conditionality in practice

The performance-based funding heralded in Cotonou could potentially have quite an impact as aid forms a very large part of many African government's revenue. EDF 9 allocations per country are outlined in table 5.3. It is, again, hard to pinpoint what the key factors are as both Given the range of needs and performance criteria taken into account, as well as unofficial factors related strategic and geoeconomic importance. The EU operates pre-emptive conditionality in not agreeing Country Strategies with dictatorial or anarchic countries. In the case of Mugabe's Zimbabwe – an international if not a regional pariah – and conflict ridden Eritrea CSPs were presented to the EDF Committee but blocked (Commission 2002a, 14).[5] The other countries which did not have a CSP/indicative programme agreed in 2001 were.[6]

- The Ivory Coast: It had descended into anarchy and conflict with French peacekeepers. A CSP was signed for 2003
- Sudan: Eventually agreed a CSP in 2005 due to the peace agreement to end its North South civil war.
- Togo: Consultations still ongoing in 2007.
- Guinea: Signed in 2002.
- Equatorial Guinea: A highly repressive dictatorship, eventually a CSP with minuscule funding was signed in 2005.
- Liberia: Initially aid was pre-empted because of human rights violations, then because of the civil war. A CSP was agreed in 2006.

EDF 9 aid was refused or delayed mainly due to hostile political relations, chaos and/or egregiously autocratic rule. Disagreements over economic policy are not punished so dramatically. The Commission outlines the indicative allocation to make clear to countries what they are missing. For example, Ivory Coast was made aware that it was losing out on €243.4 million due its non–signature of a CSP. Countries (or civil society) can receive other EU aid forms and in some cases ad-hoc EDF funding so there is a degree of flexibility.

The mid-term review was designed specifically to ensure that there was an opportunity to revise and refocus aid if necessary and to implement more subtle forms of conditionality. In most cases there was an automatic increase in funding as uncommitted funds from previous EDFs were transferred over. Apart from that there are various changes, which are summarised in an in–house review of the process (Commission 2005a). The Democratic Republic of Congo, which was (hopefully) emerging from years of conflict and is an area of interest for EU foreign policy, was given €270 million euro extra. This can hardly have been based on its general governance record although the Commission approved of how the government managed the aid given hitherto. The only country seriously 'punished' was Cameroon which had its allocation reduced by €95.8 million due to perceived problems with its budgetary procedures and failure to launch transport reforms. Other countries such as Lesotho and Nigeria had their direct budgetary aid suspended and funding switched to different projects but their overall allocations were not damaged. The Republic of the Congo also had implementation problems leading to a change in aid focus, but its overall allocation was not reduced. More technical problems in implementing aid projects were also a common reason for alterations. While unused funds from the B envelope were often transferred to the A envelope, for some countries with poor absorption capacity (such as

---

5   Eritrea's was later approved in 2002.

6   Somalia had a special strategy drawn up as there was no actual government to deal with.

Table 5.3   **Country allocations of EDF 9 (€ millions, including some uncommitted funds from previous EDFs)**

	The original NIP allocation	After mid-term review
Angola	146	NA
Botswana	91	96
Benin	275	303
Burkina Faso	351	448
Burundi	172	229
Cameroon	230	139
Cape Verde	39	52
Central African Republic	107	105
Chad	273	247
Comoros	27	27
Congo (Republic of the)	50	109
Democratic Republic of Congo	205	493
Djibouti	35	35
Equatorial Guinea	5	NA
Eritrea	97	152
Ethiopia	538	523
Gabon	79	72
Gambia the	51	59
Ghana	311	329
Guinea	81	NA
Guinea-Bisseau	81	83
Ivory Coast	264	264
Kenya	225	320
Lesotho	110	118
Liberia	118	NA
Madagascar	334	434
Malawi	345	303
Mali	375	446
Mauritania	191	192
Mauritius	35	50
Mozambique	324	511
Namibia	91	96
Niger	346	401
Nigeria	596	563
Rwanda	186	186
Sao Tomé and Principe	13	NA
Senegal	291	323
Sierra Leone	220	231
Somalia	149	149
Sudan	190	NA
Swaziland	43	39
Tanzania	355	404
Uganda	363	320
Zambia	351	376

Source: Country Strategy Papers and mid-term review documents

Malawi) a portion of the B envelope was simply deleted. There are also signs of the Commission attempting to use performance-based funding to stir competition within the different sectors and geographical areas of countries. Reforming states in Nigeria could compete to gain access to some of the €200 million plus funds the EU made available. In Gabon the Commission withdrew 5 million allocated to the transport sector due to frustration with the relevant ministry and switched it to the education ministry.

5.4 Country Case Study: Ghana

Although a small country – its current population is approximately 21 million – Ghana has been a bellwether state in Africa. It led the African decolonization movement, and then became an example of successful neo-liberal reforms and a favoured recipient of international aid. The country is in a sense a colonial construction of Britain and has a very diverse make up, with up to a hundred tribal identities and a variety of religions including Christianity, Islam and indigenous forms; but the state has not experienced serious centrifugal forces or intense ethnic politics (Nugent 2001, 21–23). Historically, Ghana has interacted systematically with European powers since the 16th century due to its role as a locus of slave and gold trading. The latter inspired the name Gold Coast which the British gave to the contemporary area of Ghana. Parts of this area had a highly developed political culture and economy. Davidson recounts how the Asante confederacy had attempted to reform and develop while retaining independence (Davidson 1992, 67–70), but the British had attained full sovereignty by the end of the 19th century.

From colony to best pupil: Ghana in the 20th century

Ghana was in a good position by independence in 1957, with relatively strong financial reserves and some successful economic sectors (Herbst 1993, 17). There was widespread belief that the British distorted and exploited Ghana's economy, hence independence leader Thomas Nkrumah's famous maxim 'seek ye first the political kingdom and all else will follow'. In reality, development, and real sovereignty, would prove elusive and Ghana became a symbol of Africa's economic underachievement. The politically ambitious Nkrumah pushed for over-ambitious industrialization projects funded by the profitable but neglected cocoa industry (Frimpong-Ansah 1991). As a part of his statist ideology Nkrumah greatly enlarged the underachieving state bureaucracy, which together with parastatal enterprises provided benefits to regime supporters (Ibid 97–98). On the political level this drive for power and progress led to a one-party state (1964). All of the above led to budget deficits and mounting debts which were not sustainable without extra financial resources, which the various (unstable) governments in ensuing years attempted to achieve. Failure to get loans from bilateral creditors, led to reluctant and staccato engagement with the IFIs (Ibid). The 1970s would see a harsher economic situation with negative terms of trade leading to another series of coups until the Provisional National Defence Council (PNDC) took power under Flight Lieutenant Rawlings (1981/1982). The PNDC was radical in ideology but efforts to secure finance from the Soviets proved fruitless (Hutchful 2002, 39) and thus it ended up implementing structural adjustment in cooperation with the IFIs. Toye argued that it was also aware of its need for technical assistance from this source (Toye 1991, 158). The economic recovery programmes were devised by the government with IFI assistance and monitoring. They involved macro-economic stabilisation – led by the IMF – and later broader economic liberalization led by the Bank. In return the government got up to $1 billion of finance from 1983 to 1986 alone (Herbst 1993, 119). Aid increases from European and other bilateral donors followed in due course. The 1980s programmes are deemed to have achieved a high degree of compliance with the IFIs conditions (Toye 1991). The authoritarian PNDC were able to force through reforms that were painful for previous elements of the regime coalition such as the trade unions, which signified a substantial power shift (Herbst 1993, 62). Herbst described Ghana as 'the paradigmatic soft state', open to be moulded by global economic governance (Ibid, 4). Other perspectives suggest that this too is going too far as compliance was limited, especially regarding public sector reform (Tangri 1990). The regime actually wanted to improve the role of the state in the economy rather than implement a neo-liberal model (Hutchful 2002, 164–165). However the scope of reforms was such that the adjustment could not be understood as a Lenin-style tactical readjustment (Ray 1986, 118), they amounted to a new direction.

Clearly there were complex dynamics at play and these would further evolve in the following decades with political liberalization (free elections in 1992 and a transition of government in 2000) but economic disappointment. Generally, although growth and improvements in living standards continued, economic progress was not what might have been hoped for from an alleged 'best pupil'. Patronage politics and a symbiosis between business and political interests continued (Nugent 2001, 419). This was partly due to democratization allowing new politico-economic networks to take advantage of the previous regimes weak regulatory framework and donor funds (Hutchings 2002, 220-226). Democracy was also partly responsible for government overspending (Ibid, 215). Over 1999 and 2000 the government was unable to meet the IMF's criteria for assistance despite some leniency by the IMF (Commission 2001h, 12). Ghana's debts made it eligible to join the HIPC initiative but because of this non-compliance it could not join until 2003. All in all, Ghana has been a beacon of stability in a troubled post-cold war West African region, and is on a liberalization trajectory, but one cannot assume success or that government policy can be moulded at will.

The EU's policies towards Ghana

As a part of his economic and political nationalism, Nkrumah rejected the idea of association with the EU. He argued that the inevitable division of labour would relegate Africans to 'hewers of wood and drawers of water' (Sargent, 1963). However Ghana did join the Lomé Convention, for reasons already discussed. The country is not in itself of major importance to the EU and has not been singled out for special initiatives and relationships. It has interacted with the EU via the Commission and the multilateral ACP institutions. Amongst member states, the UK as the ex-colonial power has a significant presence in the country, as does France as a part of its general interest in West Africa. The EU was Ghana's single greatest trading partner but it also had substantial dealings with other capitalist regions and the Soviet block (Ray 1986, 2). Lomé did ensure tariff free access for Ghana's key products, timber and cocoa, although cocoa processing was done in Europe. The CAP did not directly affect Ghana's trade with Europe, but Ghana did feel the indirect negative effects of EU agricultural subsidies (Europeaid evaluation unit 2005b, 69-70). Stabex was of interest to Ghana but that instrument did not have enough funding to compensate for the extent of commodity fluctuations. As the EU itself was not itself a creditor it did not have much leverage in the 1970s and 1980s, apart from its trade and aid policies, which were not highly conditional at this time.

Ghana was affected by the growing interventionism of Lomé IV, but this was a sideline to its broader reform efforts. As the EU's development policy evolved, Ghana, although not economically or strategically important, became more significant as a 'star reformer' in Africa. As a cooperative country it offers the EU a space to demonstrate what its role could be as a development partner. It is also one of the more advanced countries in ECOWAS, a grouping with substantial population and energy resources, and potentially of security relevance. The EU's new Cotonou regime was aiming to further lock-in reforms in progressive states such as Ghana. As a non-LDC, Ghana had to open up to the EU to get full EU market access, or it could opt to maintain its tariffs and go for the Generalised System of Preferences. Yet as the Commission Delegation publicly warned Ghanaians in 2006, this is not as comprehensive or reliable as an EPA (or the old arrangement). The reciprocal element of this, the dropping of tariffs on EU imports would, quite apart from the problems created for local industry, have an effect on the revenue of the government. Ghana has been singled out as likely to suffer considerable financial loss due to the large proportion of government expenditure funded by duties on imports (Busse et al. 2004, 12).

The EU is clearly engaged in developing and consolidating liberal capitalist institutions in Ghana, in line with other international actors, and particularly supporting the integration of the ECOWAS region. This effort may be best described as developing the structural power of neo-liberal global governance, while noting that the EU is itself a major locus of global governance. Also, such a process is likely to increase its presence as it is the major economic partner.

The EPA project itself is a specifically European power-play. There is clearly a potential conflict in that harsh trade policies may damage the development that is necessary to consolidate reform. This is apparent in all EU external relations but especially relevant for underdeveloped states in Africa. Yet the EU is determined to link both agendas. The importance of the EDF in this scenario, as a symbol of European solidarity and a tool to encourage reform and free trade, cannot be underestimated.

The EDF in Ghana

After 1989, the EU began to devote EDF aid more towards reform, to consolidate the changes already made. Ghana was granted structural adjustment grants from EDF 7 and 8 with total commitments of over €105 million (Europeaid evaluation unit, annex 3: 3–5), 85% of which was actually paid out. There was also over €93 million in general budgetary support (Ibid). Most of these were in the latter part of the 1990s when Ghana's fiscal situation became problematic and threatened its reform programme. The non-reimbursable nature of this was especially valuable to the debt laden government. A large part of EDF funding still went to rural development and infrastructure. Smaller funds were also devoted to the private sector and trade promotion. Disbursement and speed of delivery were not high. In the aggregate, the EDF funds allocated were quite large for its population but not enough to establish that Ghana was being rewarded for its reforms. As a cooperative emerging democracy Ghana was an ideal venue for the European Initiative for Human Rights which supported various projects.

Table 5.4   EDF allocations for Ghana (€/Ecu millions)

7th EDF	256.7
8th EDF	248.7
9TH EDF NIP 2002-2007	311.0
A envelope Rural Development Transport Macroeconomic support/reform Other	80 70 60 21
B envelope Contingency	80

Source: (Europeaid evaluation unit, 2005, 19-20; Commission 2001h)

To support the EU's agenda the 9th EDF had to finance activities likely to sustain growth and development to keep Ghana on track. It had to combine this with continued pushes for governance and policy reform and link this with its broader agenda of intra-regional economic integration. Ideally there should be a high degree of local ownership to ensure success. In fact the government's own strategy had already been effectively integrated with the broader international community agenda. To avail of the HIPC initiative Ghana had developed an Interim Poverty Reduction Strategy paper in coordination with international donors (including the EU). The ten key points in the PRSP were entirely commensurate with the EU's objectives. They included reinforcing democratic institutions, promoting regional integration, good economic governance and creating 'an open and liberal market economy' (Commission 2001h, 12). Thus it was not difficult for the EU's Country Strategy Paper to be aligned with the national policy. There was also consultation of civil society – already involved with the PRSP – and five seminars were organised. As with other countries it hard to see what, if any, impact this had on aid policy.

Ideally the EDF should offer sufficient financial resources to act as a carrot in itself. In fact Ghana's EDF allocation was substantially increased, see table 5.4. The A allocation (which is the portion the country can plan for, and which is pretty much guaranteed barring major disagreements) was increased by €102 million. The CSP does not imply any heightened political or geoeconomic agenda on the part of the EU. The analysis of Ghana is standard with no particular focus on EU objectives and interests – apart from development. The analysis of governance and public administration is particularly poor and superficial given its importance in this context. The intervention strategy and allocation of funding is not substantially different from before. As table 5.4 shows the bulk of funding goes to rural development and transport. The former includes microprojects and broader agricultural development in the North of the country. It has minor governance related issues relating to continued decentralization. Transport mostly involves investment in the road infrastructure with some technical assistance for the Ministry of Transport. Both of these are coordinated with other donor activities but not to the same degree as the macroeconomic support which involves direct budget aid dependent on a variety of conditions related to public administration and expenditure policy, see box 5.1 for more details. This builds on previous EU technical assistance. The other smaller projects related to health issues and good governance. There was no direct private sector support unlike in previous strategies. There is also, again surprisingly, no linkage with the revitalised regional integration agenda. This is in sharp contrast to Mediterranean aid where there is overlapping technical assistance. Transport infrastructure support, also building ongoing EDF projects, should further Ghana's links with its Western neighbours (Europeaid evaluation unit 2005b, 38). The mid-term review did not alter the general strategy of the CSP and was generally complementary to the government. 32 million from the B envelope was added to the core activities programmed, the rest had been used to support the mining sector and for multilateral aid. This

Table 5.5   EDF spending in Ghana in 2006 (€ millions)

	Commitments	Disbursements
7th EDF	3.361104	.551416
8th EDF	2.810722	20.520404
9th EDF	74.495801	35.978472

Source: Internal Report of the Commission Delegation to Ghana

transfer could be seen as a minor bonus. Previous EDFs have been still active in this period as table 5.5 illustrates.

Of other EDF programmes which affect Ghana, the most important is the regional aid programme for West Africa, allocated €235 million for this period (Commission 2002e). The main focus is on intra-regional transport networks and economic/commercial integration. The latter essentially involves technical assistance to develop a Customs Union at the ECOWAS level. Ironically ECOWAS was founded partly to increase the power of West African states vis a vis the developed world (Francis 2005, 132-136), but the developed world now supports it to further its own penetration of the region. There are still enormous challenges to regional integration at the ECOWAS level, not least the political instability of several countries, as well as the prior existence of an already highly integrated grouping of Francophone states in West Africa. The aid includes institutional support for both organizations and also involves TA for promoting the movement of people and technical harmonization measures. A joint committee of both regional organizations and the Commission is established as a part of this process. In regard to other EU budget lines, neither the EIDHR nor other NGO financing arrangements have been active in recent years. There are of course, as already recounted in box 5.1, many other donors active in Ghana. The UK increased its aid levels markedly in the new millennium and is (along with the World Bank) the largest single donor. This is followed by the Netherlands and Japan. The EU is at the mid-level in terms of financial disbursements with France, Germany and the US. Although the degree of coordination for multi donor budgetary support is exceptional Ghana is one of those areas where there is substantial harmony within the donor community. This has culminated in the launch of a multi donor Ghana Joint Assistance Strategy (DFID 2007) for Ghana in 2007, an important step to move cooperation to the strategic level. This cooperation is international rather than specifically European.

The impact of the EU's policies

The EU needs economic and social development, partly as an end in itself but also to support further economic and institutional reforms and develop Ghana's relations with the EU. In the period from 2000-2007 Ghana has had healthy

Box 5.1   The EU and Ghana's budget: macroeconomic support via budgetary aid

EU finance here forms a part of a Multi-Donor Budget Support (MDBS) programme to reform Ghana's budgetary process and policies. Macroeconomic slippages, or the desire to go beyond financing constraints, have been a source of conflict with the international community ever since the 1960s. The EU was instrumental in starting the MDBS.* Launch of the MDBS was dependent on Ghana fulfilling other multilateral criteria for debt relief (HIPC). The aims of this finance are manifold. It intends to help reduce the budget deficit, develop more efficient and accountable public management and ensure increased targeting of the most vulnerable (CSP cite). It involves comprehensive policy dialogue and intricate micro-conditionalities based on an agreed 'performance assessment framework'.

A 2007 evaluation by British and Ghanaian researchers gives a comprehensive account of the operation and impact (ODI et al. 2007). The conditions for this are outlined in depth. There are triggers, (required policies of quantitative conditions in all of the areas above) which must be achieved for a base payment and then an extra conditionality in the form of targets (Ibid, 34-37). Triggers release a base rate of payment while targets must be achieved for an extra performance payment. Controversially, but based on EU practice, targets may involve policy changes as well as expenditure (Ibid, 37). The evaluation's relevant conclusions were as follows (Ibid 128-131):

- It has been an efficient and cheap way to provide funding. An average of $300 million has been provided in this period.
- This is not enough to directly shape the macroeconomic situation but is substantial. The macroeconomic situation has improved in line with the agreed objectives (there were other factors here, most notably favourable economic growth).
- The basic conditionality and policy dialogue was effective although the extra performance targets led to an unnecessary level of bargaining and arguing and actually detracted from the overall vision.

The MDBS is emblematic of recent aid policy which includes softer pro-poor elements but also deeper systemic donor input into policy and governance. It is a prime example of the EU leveraging its funding with other donors for maximum impact.

* which has also involved 4 member states, 2 other bilateral donors and the IFIs over a 4 year period

economic growth and it is on course to achieve key millennium development goals such as halving poverty, but not other ones related to living standards, such as access to water (IMFb 2007, 14). In a similar vein the joint aid strategy paper notes that beyond the GDP growth Ghana's human development index has not improved (DFID 2007). Growth itself is crucial for the EU agenda, as it helps ensure macroeconomic stability and directly affects the ability of the government to reduce tariffs and liberalize in general. The role of the EDF in this growth is relatively minor. An official evaluation of the 8th and 9th EDF in Ghana gave a positive verdict of its contribution to poverty reduction and economic growth. The evaluators conclude that rural development aid has had an impact in terms of poverty reduction rather than economic growth, while the reverse is true for transport aid. It also notes the positive poverty reduction affects of other policies (Evaluation Unit 2005b, 48). Most would agree that the crucial external 'aid' has been the multilateral debt relief. The EU has not been a major player in this process but individual member states have played a lead role (Callaghy 2001).   In terms of the progress of reform in this period, Ghana is generally ranked highly in terms of its democratic institutions which have further consolidated in this period. The World Bank Institute does not show any changes in the various governance criteria discussed for other case study countries. In the case of a developing country like Ghana institutional 'reform' is more akin to institutional development. The IMF argues that vital liberal institutions such as financial markets are progressing in tandem with real changes (IMF 2007b, 18-19). Generally, the backsliding which may have been feared from the rhetoric of the governing party while in opposition (Hutchings 2002) has not taken place, but even a relatively weak state such as Ghana shows again that the international community's ability to impose *specific* reforms is limited. For example, little progress has been made on the form of public sector reform desired (DFID 2007, 14).

Ghana has been engaging and supportive of the neo-liberal turn in pan Africanism and within ECOWAS. In 2003 ECOWAS was the first ACP grouping to open negotiations for an EPA with the EU. Or as a civil society publication put it 'Ecowas Ruptures Unity of ACP countries' (Third World Network-Africa 2003). Nigeria allegedly opposed the launching of negotiations but could not find sufficient support. This move was undoubtedly of enormous strategic benefit to the EU in attempting to build momentum towards the signing of EPAs. In regard to EU's presence in Ghana's economy, it must be noted that Ghana is not important in any conventional economic sense, unlike the ECOWAS grouping as a whole. UNCTAD figures show that FDI inflows have remained constant and meagre at $156 millions in 2006. This is less than a tenth of aid in that year and a little under a tenth of private remittances from its diaspora (DFID 2007, 7). The EU is still by far the largest trading partner of Ghana, with 33.8 % of its total trade, far ahead of Nigeria (12.1%) and then China and the USA (Trade DG 2007c, 6). Trade patterns have not changed markedly, Ghana exports commodities and imports manufactured goods. This is illustrative of the fact that the structure of the economy as a whole has not changed markedly despite the economic growth

(DFID 2007, 13). The ECOWAS region as a whole remains highly dependent on the EU, which receives almost two thirds of its exports and supplies over half of its imports (Cline-Cole 2005, 11).

Summary of the role of the EDF in Ghana

Like most other areas of the developing world the economic and political nationalism of Ghana's elites have been long superseded by neo-liberal imperatives. The major international form of structural power was the financial leverage of the international community. The EU institutions always had leverage via trade and aid but the core work of building liberal capitalist policies and institutions in Ghana was done by the IFIs. This ongoing liberalizing project in Ghana also furthers the EU's own agenda of a Ghana integrated in an open West African region, tightly linked to the EU through an economic partnership agreement. The actual role of the EDF here is to support the Cotonou agenda in three ways: through acting as a carrot and helping development in general, supporting general liberal reforms and directly supporting the precise changes needed for an EPA. In practice the EDF in Ghana has operated for the first two. There is little aid specifically for EPAs (apart from at the regional level). Increased allocations have 'rewarded' the government for its general compliance. Its development dimension has focused on two major themes, for which sufficient funding can be had to have an impact. The budgetary support for all-encompassing macroeconomic reform is an effective vehicle for systemic influence over public administration and economic policy. The country evaluation notes that cross-cutting ethical issues, like gender and environment are under addressed. This actually tallies with the hypothesis that the EDF is geared to supporting structural EU interests. Despite these efforts the underdeveloped nature of the economy and the lack of a powerful private sector pose serious barriers to the liberalization track desired. Yet, as in the other cases, the amount of finance limits the impact that the EDF can have here.

Conclusion

The EDF is a long-running instrument that has always served the EU's interests, regardless of the rhetoric of partnership. It has been refined in recent years and while it still serves as a diplomatic sweetener, its main function is as a structural intervention to promote economic development and liberalization. Apart from the excessive role of the member state Committee and some other idiosyncrasies, there is little evidence that the anomalous status of the EDF actually had a negative bearing on its use in this period. As in other cases, efficiency has improved and the EDF is an effective form of EU agency in the region, where it works in combination with the broader international community. Both punitive and rewards based conditionality have been implemented although the latter is pretty moderate. EU aid conditionality is of slight importance relative to general IFI-led HIPC conditionality. Unlike aid to the near abroad, EU conditionality in Africa is not directly linked to the signing of free trade agreements. It does seek to encourage governments along the desired trajectory. Relatively developed countries such as Ghana are less amenable to conditionality but more capable of developing along the desired lines. Whereas weaker conflict–torn states need the money more, and thus there is more leverage, but the context is not right for the EU's kind of structural interventions. Eventually the EU's timetable for signing regional EPAs was not met. For the EDF to be more directly effective in supporting EPAs it would require a radical increase in funds, to show that the EU was prepared to invest to cushion the effects of free trade. This has not occurred. In any case the EU has achieved interim free trade agreements with many of the most important countries. Whether this degree of legal and commercial penetration is worth the bad feeling the EU seems to engendering is a moot point. As discussed in chapter 7, there is increasing disgruntlement not just with EU trade policy but with its aid strategy. Africa itself has experienced relatively healthy economic growth in this period, although it remains far from the millennium development goals, while instability, and the specter of global warming, threatens even these modest gains. Although the EDF is more directly attuned to development than the other aid instruments discussed, it still plays only a marginal role in dealing with these challenges, due to its competing role as a tool for EU interests.

Chapter 6

'Gentle Commerce' or Structural Power? EU Aid to Emerging Markets in Latin America and Asia

This wide-ranging chapter looks at the EU's aid to geographically diverse countries and regions. Many will baulk at the notion of grouping together the countries of Latin America, and South and East Asia; however the EU does this with its aid policy. These areas have little in common save for the fact that they include dynamic developing economies which offer strong commercial opportunities, and are potential new axes of power. From the European perspective they also share the fact that they are at a remove from the EU's core security concerns. Furthermore, although there are colonial linkages with these regions there has been a much less intimate post-colonial relationship than has been the case for the Africa, Caribbean, Pacific countries. The EU used a generic aid instrument for all of these distant partners, based on the Asia and Latin America aid regulation of 1992. There is no rigorously accepted definition of an 'emerging market'. The countries focused on here are the 'newly industrialising countries' countries (that have achieved rapid growth and significant foreign investment) within these vast regions, which are ranked in the IMF's 50 largest national economies (as measured by GDP). These are

- Mexico, Venezuela, Chile, Argentina and Brazil in Latin America
- Indonesia, Malaysia, Thailand and Vietnam in South East Asia
- China
- India

The last two are dealt with relatively briefly as there is already substantial material devoted to their implications for the West (Smith 2007), and their sheer size means that aid is always going to be limited in impact. This chapter offers an opportunity to look more directly at the role of EU aid in promoting its influence in the context of economic globalization. One core aspect of this is the EU's role in shaping regional integration in dynamic world regions, and the case study is of Mercosur in South America.

6.1 The ALA

Grilli's comprehensive study of EU development policy in 1993 had two chapters on these areas entitled 'Latin America: The Periphery' and 'EC and Asia: Growing Further Apart'. This neatly summarises the prevailing feeling about the EU's lack of engagement with these regions. It did have its Generalised System of Preferences for developing countries outside of Africa and the Mediterranean, but this was widely regarded as an inferior trade relationship. As globalization intensified, the EU has upgraded its policies here accordingly. These work in tandem with multilateral trade negotiations, but also act as a form of insurance should the multilateral path break down (Aggarwal, 2004). The EU's activities in these regions would not surprise anyone with any knowledge of global business and economics. Arguably, EU policy can be understood simply in terms of commercial interest without recourse to political concepts. Yet this method of promoting long-term commercial interest has clear political and power implications, as outlined in the following pages.

The legal framework for aid in the period in question was established by the ALA regulation of 1991 (Official Journal 1991). As with TACIS and MEDA, the regulation made clear the geoeconomic as well as developmental purpose of aid. It did this by explicitly separating assistance into two forms: financial and technical assistance for development and 'mutually advantageous economic cooperation' (Ibid, preamble). Trade promotion was a major goal of the latter. In fact some types of the former aid could also work directly for geoeconomic and structural power objectives with support for regional cooperation and strengthening institutions listed as objectives. Accordingly this distinction is not focused on here. The aid was managed by different DGs within the Commission until the creation of the External Relations DG in 1999, a fact which tangibly illustrated the heterogeneous nature of the area in question. Since then, Latin America is handled by directorate G and developing Asia by directorate F. Even in the post-1999 period there were differences in that aid to Latin America had one indicative programme for the period 2002–2006 whereas aid in Asia had two IPs over this period. The following sections will further explore the EU's structural power motivations, and how aid has been used for these. Do the framework laws, planning documents and funding priorities reflect these proposed objectives? How has it balanced its use of funds between purely developmental work and the strategic self-interest dimension? And how effective has it been in either case?

6.2 EU Aid to Latin America: Keeping it 'Onside'?

Latin America has long been a beacon for anti-establishment forces. Its dramatic inequality, ethnic divisions and often vigorous but staccato economic development have made it a a politically volatile region (Anderson 2007, 9). Yet in recent history Latin America seemed emblematic of the end of the history and the dominance of global neo-liberalism. All of the core states in question experienced a controlled democratization and the implementation of neoliberal economic models. Mexico's incorporation into the North American Free Area in 1994 (which lacked any of the social democratic pretensions of the EU) may have been the zenith of this process. The Common Market of the South (Mercosur)[1] launched in 1991 was also a part of this, although its approach to neoliberal globalization was more nuanced. Hope for a Free Trade Area of the Americas was dashed in the context of a dramatic shift to the left throughout the continent. This has been based on the perceived failure of neoliberal development policies to reduce poverty or achieve significant economic growth (Hershberg and Rosen 2006; Damian and Boltvinik 2006). The Chavez regime in Venezuela has used its resource power to vigorously promote a socialist, anti-American and anti-capitalist globalization model, and regional integration based on these principles. In ending his and other countries relationship with the IMF, and supporting the renationalization of resources in the region, Chavez has become a text book example of the kind of leadership that the EU and other global actors have sought to preempt. While most of the other core countries have also moved to the left they are much less radical (Regalado 2007, 227–228). Argentina was a case study of neoliberal development but recurring financial crises led to a collapse of this model. Its recovery has been led by leftist governments and much more radical popular movements. Aided by Venezuela, it has repaid the IMF and effectively ended its relationship with that institution. Less dramatically, in Brazil Lula's Workers Party has tried to implement social reforms within an essentially liberal policy framework. Chile also has a moderate social democratic government since 2006.

Generally the EU's interests in this region are similar to those of the US. It wants to protect its investments (the EU is the greatest source of FDI in these countries, apart from Mexico) and ensure that the region remains open to the global economy both because of its commercial importance and because of the role a Chavista style Latin America could play in the third world. Europeans also want to extend their economic presence in this dynamic region. Mexico is a large economy which also offers an entrée into NAFTA for the Europeans, in particular low cost labour within the free trade area. Chile is regarded practically as a developing country and with which a reciprocal economic partnership could be reached. The Mercosur countries are dealt with more in the case study section, Brazil in particular is a massive emerging market. There are also some broader political and security interests in the region including, the prevention of drug trafficking. In many ways the region represents an opportunity for the EU, which has been viewed with less hostility than the US, and there is a natural partnership with local powers eager to counterbalance America. EU leaders can also put associate the EU with the European 'model' of a social market economy, calculated to appeal more to Latin American elites. As the former Trade Commissioner put it on a Mexican visit 'I

---

1   Mercosur includes Argentina, Brazil, Paraguay and Uruguay. (Venezuela is in the process of joining and Chile and Bolivia have associate membership.

do not believe that allocation of resources can just be left to the markets, or that any interference in market mechanisms is bound to be counterproductive. I believe that global markets are important; but I also think global markets need global institutions to sustain and regulate them' (Lamy 2002).

Serious EU-level engagement here came later than for Africa and the Mediterranean, partly because of the region's dominance by authoritarian protectionist powers up until the 1980s. The EU's increased interest was to some extent a result of the accession of Portugal and Spain but would have occurred anyway due to globalization. It signed a framework agreement with Mexico in 1991, followed by a broader economic and political cooperation agreement in 1997 (swift on the heels of the entry into force of NAFTA). This envisaged a free trade area which was rapidly agreed (by 1999), leading to a dramatic increase in trade after a slump during the 1990s; 'we have re-established the "proper" weight of our trade relationship with you by neutralising the distorting impact of NAFTA' (Lamy 2002). Another expansive FTA was signed with Chile in 2002, with similar results. There are no major agreements with Venezuela. EU relations with the other Mercosur countries are conducted to a large extent on the interregional level. It has 'framework cooperation agreements' with Brazil and Argentina. These provide for cooperative institutions and do not amount to serious integration. The EU is working on upgrading bilateral relations but for the moment the EU-Mercosur dialogue is the main track. Regional dialogue (with the entire 'Latin American' region and the Caribbean) occurs through the 'Rio Group' ministerial dialogue and the Latin American summit between heads of state.[2]

Aid to Latin America in the 1990s suffered from similar organizational and methodological defects as the other regions already studied (Europeaid evaluation unit 2002, 2). Funding for this region was much lower although it did increase substantially in the 1990s. The official evaluation of 1999 argued that EU aid had improved from being almost totally ad-hoc to being more programmed with some degree of consultation (Europeaid evaluation unit 1999a, III). Yet the process was still regarded as not being comprehensively planned (Europeaid evaluation unit 2002, 2). The latter evaluation did note that 'more recent country strategy papers have grown in comprehensiveness and accuracy to become an important reference framework for the improvement of both aid programming and global cooperation' (Ibid, 2). Table 6.1 shows the breakdown of aid allocations for the major countries. Regarding thematic priorities, reform and private sector support gets a large proportion, although in this case the figures are so small as to preclude much extrapolation, see table 6.3. Argentina is the only country whose allocation was changed at the mid-term review (Commission 2004f). More funding is given to social development sectors to help relieve the effects of the financial crash. Some trade concessions were also given and there is funding for trade related technical assistance and, optimistically, funding for implementing the EU-

---

2   The EU also has specific arrangements with Central American countries which are not covered here.

Table 6.1   Aid allocations for the major economies of Latin America (2002–2006)

Argentina	55.8
Brazil	51
Mexico	56.2
Chile	34.4
Venezuela	38.5

Mercosur association agreement, which has yet to be signed. The EU was the one world region for which Argentinean exports increased during its crisis period (Ibid). Brazil, Mexico and Chile also have a substantial portion of aid devoted to economic and trade policy reform and private sector support. Venezuela, which is wealthy but has a relatively underdeveloped economy, receives development and reconstruction aid. Unlike ACP and Mediterranean aid, direct budgetary support mechanisms have not been used.

Regional level aid (for Latin America) takes up a significant amount of overall funding.[3] These horizontal programmes promote cooperation within the region and with Europe. The major ones are AL-Invest, ALFA and Urb-AL which support linkages with European companies, educational linkages and collaboration on urban development. The 2002 evaluation found that the large emphasis given to these type of bottom-up aid projects made programming difficult. It also found that these 'do not favour the involvement of the least progressed organizations/ enterprises, thus increasing instead of reducing the development gap' (Europeaid evaluation unit 2002, 62). This may not be a major problem from a selfish point of view as the EU wants to develop relations with the more dynamic sectors and regions. A Regional Strategy Paper was introduced in 2002 to try to improve planning. This was only for Latin America wide horizontal programmes and not for 'sub-regional' cooperation. A recent evaluation argues that no real 'strategy' can be discerned for these instruments (Europeaid evaluation unit 2005c, 6). However this did judge the horizontal programmes as successful in reinforcing relations between Europe and the region, if not in reducing the inequality between these regions (Ibid 40–41).

6.3 EU Aid to the ASEAN Tigers

The Association of South East Asian Nations (ASEAN) is not an integrated block in economic terms.[4] It is not a Customs Union and has (after many false starts) only made serious strides towards a free trade area this century. It was initially established in 1967 as a diplomatic/security community and this has always

---

3   13.5% of ALA funds in 2003 (Europeaid evaluation unit 2005c, 28).
4   ASEAN also includes Singapore, Laos, Burma and Cambodia.

been a major sphere of activity. Indonesia, Malaysia and Thailand are among the Asian tigers whose astonishing growth since the 1960s challenged development paradigms on the right and the left. Vietnam is at a lower stage of development but has also had some success and is considered a newly industrializing country. This success has enabled these states to exert some autonomy regarding the universalist pretensions of global governance, including the democracy and human rights agenda. The financial crash of 1997 and the recourse to the IMF for Indonesia and Thailand (but not Malaysia) decreased faith in global economic governance (Sitglitz 2002) and since then there has been a reinvigoration of regionalism via the ASEAN framework and other projects.

The importance of these countries cannot be understood separately from their role within ASEAN and the broader Asia-Pacific area, generally perceived as the most dynamic economic region in the world (Commission 2003f, 8). The ASEAN block has long had significance as a source of manufactured goods and a destination for FDI for European multinationals. EU investment in ASEAN is second only to Japan (Ibid, 10). Again the increased geoeconomic competition post-1989 led to renewed interest on the EU's part: 'Most of Europe's main economic partners and competitors are currently forging economic partnerships and alliances with the region/and or its individual members, which could challenge EU interests in the region' (Ibid). The EU's broader interests include security/anti-terrorism cooperation in the case of Indonesia, democracy promotion and general alliance forging on global issues.

From the early days the EU has adopted a proactive approach towards ASEAN, far beyond what the actual role of this regional organization merited. Political dialogue was established in 1978 and a legal agreement was signed in 1980. This agreement was the first of its kind and arguably this external recognition played a role in legitimating ASEAN in its region (Robles 2004). However, as Robles recounts, the relationship was not without friction. The Europeans found ASEAN a frustrating negotiating partner in regard to commerce, due to the block's failure to integrate or even develop a consensus position. On the other hand the ASEAN members were perturbed at the EU's willingness to impose punitive trade measures, having developed a degree of dependency (Ibid). Disagreements over the role of human rights in the relationship have also been a barrier (Reiterer 2006, 237). The Commission admits that intensive institutional cooperation and dialogue has led to relatively little in terms of concrete cooperation and integration thus far (Commission 2003f, 7). Negotiations for a free trade area began in 2007 but there is little reason to believe this will be achieved in the short-term.

The EU also engages with ASEAN via the Asia-Europe Meeting (ASEM) which includes the real economic heavyweights in East Asia (China, Japan and South Korea). This is standard EU style diplomacy promoting various political, administrative civil society and business linkages to promote Europe's presence in this economic hub. Interestingly bilateral relations are relatively underdeveloped. Only the poorest country in this quartet (Vietnam) has signed a legal cooperation agreement, with the usual human rights conditions. It is significant that the richer countries have not felt compelled to sacrifice their preference for informal arrangements, and hard not to agree that 'this different approach reflects the relative distribution of power' (Reiterer 2006, 237).

EU development assistance has played a role in the EU-ASEAN relationship from the beginning. There were few other means of interaction due to the lack of integration of the former, and EU aid was 'one tangible proof of the value of regional cooperation and of the organization's ability to procure benefits for its members by joint action vis a vis the rest of the world' (Robles 2004, 40). The focus was mostly on rural development and overall funding was small but ASEAN countries did receive a higher per capita level of commitments than other parts of Asian and Latin America (Ibid, 45). EU assistance failed to encourage further ASEAN integration, as did much greater Japanese aid, offered for a similar purpose. Thus EU aid has been mostly bilateral, but has still attempted to engage on the regional level. Since 2000 there have been several regional projects worth €75,181,684 in total, 27% of which has gone towards technical assistance for economic integration and the harmonization of business regulation and standards (Commission 2004i, Annex 3).

As table 6.2 shows the vast majority of aid for this period went to Vietnam and Indonesia, the more populous states with the greatest developmental and political challenges. The relatively large proportion of funding for socio-economic development is down to large development programmes for these countries. Indonesia does have the added factor of security relevance and fears about the countries internal stability. The reform element of EU aid here includes aid to the judiciary and to local government as well the trade and investment framework. After 2004 there is more funding allocated to the rule of law and to public finance management reform. This also incorporates direct European commercial interests, in a convoluted manner, as the objective is to ' increase the participation and visibility of the European business community in the interventions that translate public finance management improvement into sustainable growth through more intense investment flows' (Commission 2004g, 14). The bulk of Indonesia's funding is allocated to direct development and environmental support (which also has crosscutting governance elements). For Vietnam there are similar priorities. The first NIP for Vietnam was modified to add a small projects facility and some

Table 6.2   Allocations for the ASEAN emerging markets 2002–2006 (€ millions)

Indonesia	216
Malaysia	5.6
Thailand	13.2
Vietnam	162

Table 6.3   The thematic funding priorities of NIPs for the relevant countries of Latin American and ASEAN

	Latin America (5)		ASEAN (4)	
	€ millions	% of total for this group	€ millions	% of total for this group
1. Institutional and Economic Reform	65.85	28%	94	24%
2. Support to the private sector	28.73	12%	16	4%
3.Socio-economic support	92.2	39%	242	61%
4.Other	49.71	21%	44.8	11%
Total	236.49	100%	396.8	100%

Source: National Indicative Programmes

alterations in geographical focus. Overall most aid goes to direct socio-economic support but there is a not negligible amount devoted to economic interaction and reform. There is little mention of democracy and no evidence of democratic conditionality. [5]

There are also ALA Asia-wide aid programmes quite similar to those in Latin America, which can apply to ASEAN governments, businesses and civil society (as well as other parts of Asia including India and China). Asia-Invest and the EU-Asia technology and information communications programmes focus on connecting small to medium sized enterprises in both regions. A 2002 evaluation of the EU argued that 'Asia-Invest seems less relevant than its brother-programme in Latin America, since the EU-Asia linkages among the enterprises are more volatile' (Europeaid evaluation unit 2002, 49). The major changes that have been made since then are to facilitate the participation of countries in poorer regions.

6.4 EU Aid to China and India

China's phenomenal growth in the global economy could be construed as either the ultimate triumph of neoliberal globalization or its nemesis. Its success has been based on the liberalization of its economy but this has been carefully

---

5   There have not been any evaluations of EU aid to these countries in this period.

circumscribed thus far (without even mentioning the political framework). The Chinese regime has managed to reconfigure state power, its elites being conscious of the need to avoid the chaotic Russian experience of the 1990s (Yongnian 2004, 165). Not only has it led the developing world in attracting FDI, despite its governance problems and the numerous restrictions the government places (Chow 2007, 334–335) but its power has enabled it to glean much more technological transfer from FDI than most other countries (Smith 2007, 233). Europe's interests in China are hard to overestimate. It is one of the EU's greatest trading partners, in fact many sectors of the European economy are dependent on China, which is also a fearsome competitor for European companies. European business wants to increase its own investment in China as it develops into the largest market in history. Again having a less confrontational relationship with China than the US may facilitate this. As the Chinese government's official EU strategy paper put it 'There is no fundamental conflict of interest between China and the EU and neither side poses a threat to the other' (Government of China 2003, 2). More generally the liberalization of China is one of the greatest stages in the development of a liberal truly global economy. Accordingly Europe has a vital stake in continued liberalization, including developing the rule of law. The Commission listed EU priority actions as to 'ensure success of the Doha development agenda, monitor and assist China's compliance with its WTO commitments, and monitor new regional agreements to ensure WTO compatibility' (Commission 2003e, 4). The latter reflects the unspoken fear that developing regionalism in East and South East Asia may not take the 'open' (uncritically pro-globalization) turn that the rest of the international community would like. China could be seen as a new kind of strategic 'developmental state' which succeeds without democracy through retaining strategic political control over the economy. It could serve as a model for those who reject the reforms of the EU and its allies. It also has the capability to compete with the EU for influence in the developing world. On China's part, it wants the EU to:

> step up economic and trade regulatory policy dialogue; give attention to updating the Trade and Economic Cooperation Agreement Between China and the European Union at an appropriate time; properly address irrational restrictions and technical barriers, ease restrictions on high-tech exports and tap the enormous potential of technological cooperation and trade in line with the WTO rules; grant China a full market economy status at an early date, reduce and abolish anti-dumping and other discriminatory policies and practices against China (Government of China, 2003, 6).

The major economic objective is to be given Market Economy Status from the EU, which would make it more difficult for Europeans to slap punitive measures on Chinese companies without more proof of the alleged offences.

As one would expect there has been a plethora of dialogues and joint institutions established between the EU and China. The legal framework remains modest; the key document is a perfunctory Cooperation agreement from 1985, which established Most Favoured Nation trading relations between the parties. The relationship is not all sweetness and light. The EU retains an arms embargo on China (since Tiananmen Square). In 2004 the EU appeared ready to drop the embargo, a major symbolic issue for Beijing, but under pressure from the Bush administration it reneged. In 2007 talks started on a Partnership and Cooperation Agreement but as trade disputes have escalated in recent years this is likely to a tortuous process .

That China, which is itself a major financial backer of other developing countries, receives development assistance may surprise many. Yet when one accepts that aid serves self-interest calculations it is not surprising that China has been a major recipient in recent years, receiving over $5 billion per annum in grants and special loans (Commission 2002g, 19). Established powers want to help steer China's development and promote their presence within China (also it does have vast poor regions in the hinterland in genuine need of development aid). Although the EU is not the major donor it has been highly active here. The Chinese government has clear preferences regarding the type of aid it wants: 'China welcomes more EU development aid, especially in such fields as the environmental protection, poverty-alleviation, public health and hygiene and education. China also welcomes a stronger and more active role of the EU in human resources development' (Chinese government 2003, 5–6). However EU aid more reflects its own economic and strategic interests, although worked out in agreement with the government (Commission 2002g, 19–20). Since 1996 EU aid had moved away from projects to broader support for the 'reform process' (Ibid). The CSP for 2002–2006 does not explicitly discuss the EU's self-interest considerations but the funding priorities outlined in table 6.4 make this clear. The document is unusual in the length of detail about the input of various member states to the aid strategy. The relatively high level of interest on their part reflects the importance of the recipient. Said importance is also reflected in the relative detail and rigor of the analysis of the country context.

For the first NIP (2002–2004) the bulk of funding went for what could be termed structural power considerations. This included a WTO accession assistance package (continuing on a previous one) which involved the usual forms of technical assistance. A project to develop the 'Information society' also served EU interests as it included legislative reform and business links between Chinese and European IT companies. Aid to promote civil society was also envisaged as well as technical assistance and cooperation to prevent illegal migration. The mid-term review reduced the allocation for both of these projects (by 50 and 90% respectively) and gave them to the reform and sustainable development track (Commission 2004h, 7–9). This was because of difficulties in getting whole-hearted cooperation from the government for the kind of projects the EU envisaged. The following NIP has a large programme to protect intellectual property rights, vital to Europe's major companies and a major element of contemporary capitalist norms. 25 million is allocated for capacity building and governance support. There is also an educational cooperation project which again has a strong self-interest dimension in that it will promote European universities. 5 million is allocated for sectoral dialogue. There is no serious element of democracy conditionality in the EU's aid to China, even the mid-term review changes involved reallocating aid rather than attempting to 'punish' the government. A comprehensive evaluation of EU aid to China was completed in 2007 (Europeaid evaluation unit, 2007a). This noted that EU efforts in the trade and reform spheres were less than successful in addressing poverty. However, it did give a favourable verdict on the commercial and institutional impact of this aid. There were two caveats here. As always it was hard to tell how much of this was due to EU assistance and pressure as opposed to that of other international actors. Perhaps more importantly the success was in getting the government to adopt legislation while implementation remained in question (Ibid, 24–26). The evaluators also noted the perennial dispute over the type of aid, the recipient wanting investment funds and the donor favouring technical assistance.

In the 1990s India made major steps from being a statist economy to a market-based one (Jenkins 1999). It has taken advantage of globalization to position itself as a technology (in particular software) powerhouse and a giant on the global stage, second only to China as an emerging player. As with China its sheer size and population resources make it impossible to ignore. It has always been more open than China; it was a founder member of the GATT and a functioning democracy. Whether its democracy is a help or a hindrance to economic development is openly debated, as the impoverished masses, if they vote, can derail the economic strategy. The Congress party regained power in 2004 with a mandate to restrain

Table 6.4   Thematic funding priorities for China and India 2001–2006

	€ millions	% of country total	€ millions	% of country total
	China[*]		**India**	
1.Institutional and economic Reform	105	40%	18	8%
2.Support to the private sector	26.2	10%		
3.Socio-economic support	65	25%	158	70%
4. Other	66	25%	49	22%
Total	262.2		225	

*   The China figures incorporate changes made in the mid-term review to the first indicative programme, when good governance financing was reduced by 19 million and other sectors increased.

the prevailing free-market policies, although it is fair to say that in practice it has not done this. Although India is a member of the South Asian Association for Regional Cooperation (SAARC, which also includes, Afghanistan Bangladesh, Bhutan, India, Maldives, Nepal, Pakistan and Sri Lanka), the EU's relationship with India is totally bilateral, as SAARC is not a coherent entity.

The EU and the West in general has a keen interest in India's development. As a democracy it is much closer to the model of development the EU wants to promote than China (to whom it may act as a counterweight). More specifically to the EU, it has the same interests in India as in any other massive economic block. India is a major trading partner; it is now a massive market in its own right that European companies could access. India is also an influential player in World Trade talks and is a valuable collaborator on scientific and technological issues. India signed a basic economic agreement with the EU in 1973. Their 1993 cooperation agreement was more comprehensive, including political conditionality and stipulating EU assistance as a feature of the relationship. This did not provide for free trade however, and efforts to upgrade the economic relationship have intensified in recent years. At a summit in Deli in 2005 they produced an Action Plan, one stream of which was a free trade and investment area. The EU is pushing to include protection of intellectual property rights and a wide range of regulatory issues 'we both have an obligation to ensure that regulation and non-tariff barriers do not unnecessarily get in the way of trade' (Mandelson 2007b).

The Indian government, conscious of its emerging role as a great power has begun to phase out development aid and announced it would accept future aid only from a few important donors including the EU and also Russia, the US, the UK, Germany and Japan (Europeaid evaluation unit 2007b, 56). The country still has enormous social challenges and major developmental needs. EU assistance to India is shaped by these developmental challenges, although also clearly informed by economic and political opportunities. It is also determined by constraints and opportunities implicit in the fact that India is a federal democratic state of enormous size. The Commission's basic diagnosis in the CSP (Commission 2002h, 15–16) is to further growth through greater social support, generic governance reform and reform of economic policy in particular. As with China the EU had moved away from projects to broader programmes, in this case mostly concerned with poverty reduction, in the previous decade.

Activities funded from 2002–2006 included a trade and investment development programme (15 million) for this large, but potentially much larger, trading partner with 'a continued relatively high degree of protection' (Commission 2002h, 9). This was the usual package with assistance on highly technical regulatory issues, support for intellectual and media activity to 'drive the debate on economic reform in India', and support for EU investors including assistance for targeted dynamic states to facilitate EU investors (Commission 2002h, 11). A wide variety of quantitative indicators is suggested to measure this from trading flows to media coverage (Ibid 13). There is also 3 million for cooperation between EU and Indian economic think tanks. Yet as table 6.4 indicates by far the greatest focus is on social support with a large 'partnership for progress' project allocated 158 million. This is designed to work on health, education and sustainable development in a single state. The state in question would have to show reforming enthusiasm and would be selected in consultation with the federal government. It also has a large governance reform component in that it is intended also to aid transparency, devolution of power and decision-making (Commission 2002h, 26). This programme is included under development aid in the table as it is primarily about poverty reduction and it is not possible to unbundle it into sub-categories. Therefore the table 6.4 is slightly distorted but it does accurately reflect the EU's greater focus on traditional development issues, in contrast to China. This is a result of greater affinity with India, greater need on India's part and slightly less urgency in regard to economic power.

As in the case of China, divining the impact of EU aid on India is highly problematic. An official evaluation of 2007 was praiseworthy as to the overall alignment of the EU's aid strategy with the Indian government (Europeaid evaluation unit 2007b, 28). Such alignment is relatively rare (apart from the poorest countries whose development strategies have been co-written with the international community). In this case it is possible because of the EU's willingness to focus on poverty reduction and its interest in good relations with the government. In regard to these programmes the evaluation was positive as to the impact (limited though it necessarily was) of the EU's efforts in the spheres of education and health. The evaluators were also complementary as to the design and evaluation of the Commission's trade and investment support programmes; however they argued that these play a negligible role in shaping economic relations compared to the trade policies of both actors (Ibid, 57–58). They also found the networking projects between business and other elites to be a cost effective and useful means of developing the EU relationship. There was little evidence supplied for this particular conclusion. A recent study has shown that the EU is viewed rather negatively by Indian elites, as a relentless pursuer of commercial interest (Fioramonti, 2007). Ineffective aid highlighted was in the sphere of governance reform where they argued that the EU had not contributed to the goals of decentralization and devolution of power (to the local level) and that the governance reform elements of individual EU programmes are not coherent (Evaluation unit, 2007, 52-53).

6.5 Regional Focus: EU Aid to Mercosur, Aiding Regional Integration?

The Mercosur project has been an important experiment in regional integration in the post-cold war era and the EU has been attempting to insert itself into this process from the beginning. As the EU is the *primus inter pares* of regional organizations in terms of size, history and depth of integration, EU policy makers feel uniquely qualified to advise and assist other regional entities. However this is a very challenging task, due primarily to the ambivalent and changeable nature of Mercosur and the turbulent changes in the political economy of the region in recent years. EU aid policy in this case is a fascinating example of an effort to develop regional integration and inter-regional integration in a context of flux. This is very much a long-term endeavour.

The Mercosur context

Mercosur was one example of the new wave of regionalism after 1989, closely associated with globalization (Higgot 2000). This has generally been described as 'open regionalism', seen as a facilitator of global governance and/or the American-led world order (Katzenstein 2005; Doctor 2007). Regionalism may be perceived as a stage of globalization if, as with the North American Free Trade Area, it involves facilitating free trade and investment without a common external face or any public interventionism. On the other hand if it involves a customs union and proactive development policies it may be understood as a reconfiguration of public power, which attempts to mould globalization and mediate its effects. Apart from this distinction the different institutional forms of regionalism have complex power implications. Legalization is an importance factor; whether regionalism is primarily based on formal legal rules or, as is often the case, on relatively informal norms (Kahler, 2000). Such informal regionalism is less facilitative of global governance and interaction with the EU. Whether regionalism is based on intergovernmental or supranational institutions also has a bearing. Hypothetically, a supranational closed region would be a powerful rival player to the EU, but a supranational open region would be ideal for the development of structured relations.

Regarding Mercosur two statements can be made with relative confidence. Firstly it has always been ambivalent towards globalization as two contrasting models have obtained; one in line with neoliberalism the other much more interventionist (Carranza 2006). Secondly and related to the first point, it has always had an explicit power dimension in terms of both political foreign policy issues and economic power, it is what Carranza calls an 'autonomous project of strategic regionalism' (Ibid; Phillips 2001; Klom 2003). A brief overview of its historical development will illustrate the interest it holds for the EU and the challenges it poses to it.

Mercosur was launched by the Treaty of Asunción in 1991 signed by Argentina, Uruguay, Brazil and Paraguay. Brazil was and is the dominant state within this grouping in terms of economic size, trading weight and population. Argentina and Brazil together are on a different level in terms of capability and size from the others and indeed 1991 followed on from previous bilateral arrangements between this pair. This integration took place in the context of profound transformations within both countries. Following on from years of statist, import substitution policies and limited liberal economic reforms under authoritarian regimes they were navigating new development policies under democratic systems and the tutelage of the international financial institutions (Gwynne and Cristóbal 2004). Asunción

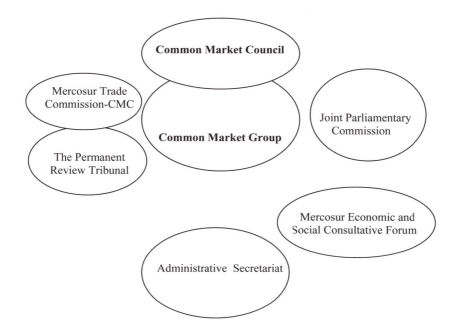

Figure 6.1   The Mercosur institutions

outlined the goal of a common market, while the later protocol of Ouro Preto outlined a Customs Union (still incomplete) and clarified the institutional make-up. In this respect it followed the EU model of economic integration, and it was also similar in that while being primarily economic it involved broader political and strategic goals. What was dissimilar was the intergovernment make-up of the institutions (see figure 6.1). The main decision-making bodies are the Common Market Council, which consists of the foreign ministers and economic ministers of the member states and the Common Market Group (consisting of representatives of both bodies) which handles quotidian affairs. Given the imbalances of the member states already discussed this intergovernmental structure further accentuates the asymmetric nature of Mercosur.

The economic impact of Mercosur was substantial, with major increases in trade within the region and commercial expansion beyond. This success was signified by the joining of Chile and Bolivia as associate members in 1996. These are part of the free trade area but not the common external tariff. Yet the commercial success did not greatly aid the acute poverty and inequality of the region, which many argue had been exacerbated during the period of liberal economic reforms (Chen and Ravillion 2004). This situation led to serious interruptions to the integration process in the 90s which were overcome only by the efforts of the highest political leadership. The first crisis was Brazil's devaluation of its currency which distorted trade flows and led to a mini trade war with Argentina. In response there was a renewed call from Brazilian president Cardoso to broaden the agenda of Mercosur to include monetary policy, support regional infrastructure and more scientific, cultural and educational cooperation (Phillips 2001, 565 – 572). He also called for more proactive development of regional infrastructure (Ibid 572), which signified an interest in more of a public role in development policy. The crisis and these announcements were overshadowed by the melt down of the Argentinean economy in 2000–2001. This necessitated a temporary suspension of Argentina's participation in the Customs Union. When the dust had cleared from this period there was a new political framework within the core countries. The left leaning Presidents Lula and Kirchner were keen to reinvigorate Mercosur as a means to enable interventionist development policies and to ensure autonomy from the United States (Carranza 2006, 805–807). Since then the staccato integration process has continued, with further protocols developing the institutional framework.

The EU's interests

From the beginning the EU took a keen interest in Mercosur and an Inter-institutional cooperation agreement was signed in 1992. After the block showed its durability an interregional framework cooperation agreement was signed in 1995 whose main aim was 'to prepare the conditions enabling an interregional association to be created' (Official Journal 1996b, Title 1). This also established structured channels for dialogue along the usual lines. Negotiations on a free trade area were begun in 1999. The EU negotiating stance has been very much in tandem with the multilateral WTO trade rounds (Aggarval 2004). Progress here has been quite tortuous as there are serious vested interests on both sides which have much to lose. Obviously the European agricultural sector has much to fear from Brazilian and Argentinean agro-exports and has been unequivocally hostile to the free trade project, while Brazilian domestic industry is equally fearful of European competition (Klom 2003). Efforts to bring together businesses from both regions via the Mercosur European Business Forum have not yet overcome these tendencies towards inertia. Negotiations continue, although overshadowed by multilateral trade issues and arguably the internal problems within Mercosur have made reaching a full free trade agreement impossible at this stage.

The very fact that the EU has opened negotiations despite the strong opposition of European agriculture is testimony to the interests at stake. In the 1990s Mercosur was the most promising emerging market for the EU (Doctor 2007, 298). European companies had benefited greatly from the privatizations in the finance and telecoms sectors (Ibid, 301). As a Commission paper put it: 'Between 1990 and 1996, exports increased by 250% and direct investment reached ECU 6500 million. Today, the EU is Mercosur's largest trading partner, and European firms hold 43% of the total of foreign capital invested in the region. This shows that what Europe has at stake in its relations with Mercosur is substantial' (Commission 1998, 1). Competition with the US was also a factor here, Doctor argued that 'peaks in EU negotiating seriousness tended to coincide with peaks in perceived US influence in the region' (Doctor 2007, 290).

The EU has consistently privileged dealing with Mercosur as an entity rather than individual member states although for purely commercial considerations it may have been better to concentrate on the two core countries. As discussed in the case of ASEAN, the EU has a broader interest in encouraging regional integration. If the Mercosur develops successfully along the EU model of supranational integration this helps the promotion of the EU model worldwide. Also if this model was adopted this could moderate the domination of Brazil and the role of protectionist Brazilian interests. The Commission's diagnosis of Mercosur's failings in 2002 privileged this analysis: 'The lack of appropriate supranational institutions has impeded progress towards deeper integration. The absence of a strong technical body vested with the power to propose and implement laws at the Mercosur level has been a major obstacle to moving forward' (Commission 2002i, 17). It is particularly beneficial for the EU to insert itself into the process in its early stages: this would ensure 'open regionalism' (which is no means a foregone conclusion in Latin America) specifically linked to Europe. EU support for 'open regionalism' can be understood the same way Katzenstein and Lundestadt viewed US support for European regionalism (Katzenstein 2005; Lundestadt 2001); as a means of locking in governance systems in accordance with its models, values and interests and thereby facilitating its own penetration of the region. If it is effective in these efforts it has an influence on the evolution of these regions far beyond that of a simply commercial partner.

The role of aid

The EU began specific regional integration aid soon after the establishment of Mercosur. This was supplementary to bilateral country aid and Latin America wide horizontal programmes (which the Mercosur countries took a large slice of). What financial and technical assistance can do to promote regional integration is unclear, but it has been one of the few instruments available to the EU to get some purchase over the Mercosur process. At least the EU could call on the considerable experience and expertise on all aspects of regional integration within its own institutions. The major focus of aid was on trade (technical standards and customs) and economic integration, including support to the development and harmonization of statistical methods and broader policies. Notably the line between support for intra-regional integration (Mercosur itself) and inter-regional integration (EU-Mercosur) is constantly blurred. There was a relatively small amount devoted to assisting the embryonic institutions of Mercosur, in particular the secretariat, see table 6.5.

An official evaluation specifically of EU aid for regional integration in Mercosur was produced in 2002, (5 months before the regional strategy paper for 2002–2006). The statistical development projects are regarded as very useful and influential for the integration of the block (Europeaid evaluation unit 2004,

Table 6.5   EU aid to Mercosur, commitments 1992–2002 (€)

Economic integration and intra-regional cooperation	Trade	Institutional support	Total
19,462,262	21,465,000	8,389,223	49,316,495

Source: Europeaid evaluation unit 2004, 22

31). Apart from the usual (at that time) procedural problems with EU aid the evaluation came up with some resonant criticisms. It noted that EU aid policy was not always in line with the Mercosur model of integration and suggested that the EU was trying to impose its own ideas: 'The EC has been, at times, disinclined in its strategy to recognize the intergovernmental and operational structures chosen by Mercosur and explicit emphasis was placed on creating and building supranational institutions as the only vehicle suitable for the integration process' (Ibid 39). This is in line with the above supposition that the EU would seek to replicate its own model to develop its own structural power. But it clearly affected the sense of ownership of the partner (Ibid 53) and was probably unrealistic in the circumstances. In regard to how the EU managed the aid it noted the particular coordination problems for aid of this sort, and recommended better coordination structures within the Commission. Regional integration aid is at a nexus of aid policy, trade policy and political relations. Probably the most important point was that the major barrier to integration was the asymmetries in development between its member states (Ibid 55). Yet for EU aid to tackle this directly would take much more funding for direct investment in the poorer countries and regions.

The regional strategy paper of 2002 took on some but not all of these recommendations. The year in question was a time of crisis in Mercosur and the success of the aid strategy was always going to be contingent on indigenous political developments. As things transpired these were not unfavourable to further

Table 6.6   Regional indicative programme 2002–2006 (€ millions)

Support to the completion of the internal market	12.50
Support to Mercosur Institutionalization	21.00
Developing a Mercosur Civil Society	14.50
Total	48.00

Source: Commission, 2002i, 27-31

integration but not especially favourable to inter-regional integration with Europe. The major challenges the EU saw for Mercosur were to complete the internal market, strengthen its institutions and further integration into the global economy with the establishment of a 'single investment space' (Commission 2002i, 19–20). The basic EU aid priorities had already been jointly agreed in a memorandum of understanding in 2001. These are outlined in table 6.6 (funding is not significantly increased from before). As before there is seamless link between supporting Mercosur and the EU's relationship with Mercosur. Stream 1 involves further technical work on harmonising regulations and standards and also Mercosur wide support for SMEs. For stream 2 the Commission notes that the nature of Mercosur's institutions are a 'sovereign right' of its member states and 'our cooperation in this area has to be particularly sensitive, respectful and always at the request of Mercosur' (Ibid 26). Aid here includes support to the new Legal Tribunal and the proposed monetary institute, improvement of the IT capacity and resources of the secretariat and also EU-Mercosur parliamentary dialogue and EU Mercosur economic agreements (the latter are not best described as institutionalization). Technical assistance is the form that the assistance takes. These streams are in line with country programmes on trade facilitation already discussed but there is no evidence of detailed strategic complementarity between the country and regional levels. The Civil Society support is a new emphasis focused on trade unions and other interest groups, academics and NGOs. Again this relates to both intra-Mercosur and EU-Mercosur. Underlying all of this the negotiation of an inter-regional association agreement is the 'unquestionable priority' (Ibid, 26).

These projects have been implemented as planned, although the traditional implementation delays remain. There are some other donors involved here to a small degree (Japan) but there is no other entity engaged on anything like the same level as the EU. Writing in 2007 the Commission is still discussing the ongoing problem of a lack of ownership on the Mercosur side and the time taken to identify the implementing partners on the Mercosur side as there are few Mercosur institutions to deal with per se (Commission 2007f, 1). It has since settled on the Common Market Group as the default partner for aid projects (Interview, Commission, April 2008). The Commission's aid strategy has continued support along the previous lines. Evaluating the impact of this form of EU aid is especially problematic as the scale is even larger than bilateral aid and the number of intervening variables is vast. EU aid has certainly facilitated the gradual institutionalization process. The Permanent Review Tribunal, although its operation has been criticised, has implanted an embryonic supranational element. Obviously, whether this seed grows will depend on the political will of the Mercosur governments, but the EU has helped ensure the possibility of supranational regionalism. More generally, it is fair to say that the governments, domestic policies and general discourse of the region are further to the left than the Europeans would like, and the entry of Venezuela and its bombastic President introduces a new and highly unpredictable factor. However, after some fluctuations the EU's economic presence within Mercosur is growing again and it is certainly better placed than the United States

Box 6.1   **Samples of EU support for institutionalization**

Support to the Mercosur Administrative Secretariat 900,000 € (2002–2004)

As already implied, Mercosur's secretariat is nothing like the European Commission. Its official role is limited and it has no autonomous power. Yet it is the original supranational, Mercosur institution, and its role has been increased with the Protocol of Olivos (2002). This project upgraded its IT systems and human skills to increase its capacity to act as a force for integration. It was also intended to lead to 'increased information flow within the region and between the region and the EU'.

Support to the Mercosur Joint Parliamentary Commission 917,175 € (2002–2004)

The Joint Parliamentary Commission (JPC) is a potential means of deepening Mercosur beyond economic and governmental elites. This project supported the JPCs links with other Mercosur institutions, national parliaments and the European Parliament. It specifically supported the JPC's own secretariat, and helped it develop a documentation centre to further Mercosur's institutional memory.

Improving the Mercosur Dispute Settlement System 283,253 € (2003–2004)

As discussed above, legalization is a key element of regionalism and a core feature of the EU's activities in general. Dispute settlement is obviously crucial for any meaningful regional integration. This modest project involved a study of the Dispute Settlement System and proposals for its improvement. The Mercosur method had involved ad-hoc tribunals (open only to governments) on a case per case basic; this is just about the least degree of legalization and institutionalization possible. The establishment of the Permanent Review Tribunal (outlined in the Protocol of Olivos, 2002), was a step along the lines the Commission had hoped for, towards more institutionalized dispute resolution. This study also explored ways of involving the private sector, which would be a further deepening of Mercosur.

Source: Commission Delegation to Uruguay

---

to expand this. The free trade area is not dead, although it has not yet been agreed, and its aid policy has helped it become a privileged and unique partner of Mercosur (despite considerable conflicts of interest in trade issues).

Conclusion

Grouping Asia and Latin America into one aid instrument has left an awkward framework for aid policy-makers and implementers, and implies that less importance is given to these regions. Constant discussions about a new aid regulation were not followed up until the end of the period in question (see the next chapter). ALA aid policy also has had to serve a balancing act between purely developmental objectives and those linked more to reform, commercial interaction and structural power. This is not different in kind from aid to the near abroad and sub-Saharan Africa but it has had a less institutionalized macro-political framework to operate in. It has also had even less funding than these other instruments. Thus, even more so than for other areas, the lack of hard cash limits the impact, particularly as the countries discussed are large and avail of significant autonomous resources. Allocative conditionality is not feasible as governments such as India, China, Indonesia or Mexico are hardly likely to consider the funds available from the EU in their calculations (although market access is a different matter). Similarly the impact that such modest amounts of aid can hope to have on vast economies and polities such as India and China is sharply limited. With Mercosur the EU cannot directly impact the development asymmetries (a major barrier to the regional and interregional integration desired) as the resources are not available. Notwithstanding these limitations the EU could well be considered as getting very good value for money from its assistance programmes. These have given it a core involvement in shaping the reforms of China. They have helped it sweeten its relations with India, and helped to deal with the poverty-barrier to fuller liberalization. Likewise they have helped the EU insert itself into the dynamic ASEAN economies, and facilitated the development of a special relationship with Mercosur. In that sense EU policy-makers have performed the balancing act successfully to further the EU's influence, although to say that the EU is achieving structural power within most of these regions would be an exaggeration.

Chapter 7

New Instruments, New Trajectories? The Ongoing Evolution of the EU's Aid Policy

All aid agencies must work in an environment of flux, and this applies to their own organizational framework as well as the context in the developing world. Such mutability is especially marked for EU aid policy-makers as the Union itself is still evolving, reforming and mutating. Changes related to the global environment, European integration and EU external relations policies have all lead to ongoing pressure to further reform aid policy. The new vision was first proposed by the European Commission in 2004 (Commission 2004j). Buoyed on by the relative success of its recent reforms, the Commission called for the radical consolidation of EU aid instruments, based on geographical lines. Consolidation did occur in 2006 with new legislation for a reduced number of instruments; however the changes were not exactly those sought by the Commission. This chapter analyses the thinking behind the reforms and to what extent they are geared to facilitate the use of aid for structural power. It also studies to what extent the changes will address shortcomings highlighted previously. As always the reality is complex and there are contradictory tendencies. There are substantial pressures from global institutions and European civil society to increase the purely developmental focus of EU aid. Yet the power projection element of aid policy is still prominent, although it is mediated through new policy frameworks and linked with other objectives.

7.1 The Reforms of 2006

The major events in European integration in this period were the enlargements and the Lisbon Treaty on reforming the institutions. Neither of these had a direct bearing on aid policy, although the new mostly Eastern European countries could be presumed to lean more towards a global development and aid policy than towards special post-colonial relationships. On the global level, the first decade of the new millennium saw, contrary to previous signs of donor fatigue, an unprecedented rise in public engagement in developed countries with development issues and third world debt. This in turn led to renewed international initiatives for development, albeit ones linked to a neo-liberal consensus. These new pressures for development and poverty reduction policies found expression in the European

- A European Neighbourhood and Partnership Instrument for the ENP countries.

- A Development and Economic Cooperation Instrument for the rest of the world.

- The European Development Fund.

- An Economic Cooperation Instrument.

- An Instrument for Stability designed specifically for crises and unstable countries, with suitably flexible procedures.

- A European Instrument for Democracy and Human Rights.

- A Humanitarian aid instrument.

- A Macro-financial stability instrument.

- An Instrument for Nuclear Safety.

Figure 7.1   The post-2007 EU aid instruments

Consensus on Development in 2005, a document which related to member state aid policy as well as EU-level aid (Council 2005). This involved commitments (or rather re-commitments) on the states' part to devote .7% of GDP to aid by 2015, to coordinate more in international organizations such as the World Bank and generally to use aid for poverty reduction objectives, in particular the millennium development goals. The document may prove a step towards the Europeanization of aid policy, in that it gave the Commission a voice regarding member state funding levels (Carbone 2007, 55–56). In regard to the policy content, the Consensus can be understood as a contrary tendency to the use of aid to support EU interests. Of course nothing in the global environment changed the basic argument that global actors are in ongoing competition for structural power and new EU initiatives suggested a continued and accentuated use of aid for this purpose. For example the increased salience of energy security issues is likely to affect aid policy, as one of the instruments which might contribute to alleviating Europe's vulnerability. More generally, new competitor states such as Russia and China, and the rise in third world power as witnessed in harsher WTO negotiations, have increased the pressure on Europe to expand its own influence. Established Western powers such as the United States are refining their aid instruments for structural power and security purposes (USAID 2004).

With these contradictory pressures, and more prosaic organizational considerations, in mind the Commission produced its paper on EU aid policy in 2004. It argued, unsurprisingly, for the increased management of European aid at the European level, partly because only at the EU level could key common objectives related to security, migration, and the extension of EU standards and norms be conceived and implemented (Ibid 4). The weight of the EU en-masse was also relevant here; 'each euro spent at EU-level has greater *leverage* and consequently more impact than the equivalent spending at national level' (Ibid, Author's emphasis). This is because the EU 'has its hands on all operational levers at once' and 'can therefore ensure consistency and synergy between main external relations instruments: political dialogue, trade, aid, economic cooperation, external projection of internal policies' (Ibid). Although the aim was 'more Europe' in aid policy it was also to reduce the number of different aid instruments. The Commission argued that the vast number of horizontal instruments and the varying legal bases and procedures even for the primary economic aid instruments discussed affected the overall coherence and efficiency of EU aid. MEDA, TACIS and ALA had substantial similarities in that they were shaped in the post-1989 era and all mixed development with commercial and power interests but they did have heterogeneous frameworks and procedures. (While the EDF was substantially different). The streamlining the Commission advocated would improve coherence, efficiency and also allow for better programming and even better dialogue with recipient countries.

What the Commission proposed was a move to only five external aid instruments (excluding pre-accession aid) which would incorporate all of the previous horizontal instruments (Commission 2004j). The proposed instruments were as follows

1. A European Neighbourhood and Partnership Instrument for the ENP countries. This was a logical development for the highly specific relationship that the EU was intending to cultivate with its neighbours.
2. A Development and Economic Cooperation Instrument for the rest of the world. This would incorporate the ALA regulation for Latin American and Asia and also the European Development Fund for ACP countries. This would involve the budgetization of the latter (its full incorporation into the EU system), which has been a long-running goal of the Commission.
3. An Instrument for Stability which would be designed specifically for crises and highly unstable countries and would have suitably flexible procedures and modalities.
4. A humanitarian aid instrument which was unchanged.
5. A macro-financial stability aid instrument which was unchanged.

The first three were to cover all policy areas from reform to political development, environmental and security issues.

It is safe to assume that these reforms would have further increased the EU's ability to strategically use aid, but as events unfolded the Council and the European Parliament did not exactly follow the Commission's proposals. The politics and interests which had hitherto shaped the fragmented EU aid system blunted the Commission's efforts to unify and downsize it. The member states refused to fully Europeanize the European Development Fund, and its specific legal framework continues (while the Commission is still the primary programming and implementing agent). The proposed Development and Economic Cooperation Instrument was given a more purely developmental focus by the Parliament and renamed the Development Cooperation Instrument (Legislative observatory 2006). A separate Economic Cooperation with Industrialised countries instrument was created for the more directly commercial element of aid. A separate horizontal European Instrument for Democracy and Human Rights was maintained, partly because the Parliament has taken a particular interest in this instrument and partly because the publicity factor is greater for a specific democracy instrument than one incorporated into general aid policy. Other horizontal elements were incorporated into the DCI and ENPI. The resulting shape of EU external aid policy is outlined in figure 7.1.

7.2 A New Vision? The European Neighbourhood and Partnership Instrument

The ENPI replaced the MEDA and TACIS instruments in 2007. It is the instrument most directly linked to a broader EU policy (the ENP) and one would thus expect it to cohere tightly with political objectives. One would expect it to be directly linked to the ENP Action Plans which are a detailed list of reforms/actions for the partner governments. Aid is still programmed in six-year and three-year strategy and indicative papers. The Commission emphasises the innovative nature of this 'policy-driven' instrument (Commission 2004j). However in reality the change may be less than is supposed, as the EU has a tendency to exaggerate the 'newness' of new policies. As argued previously the former aid policies were already 'policy-driven', as opposed to development instruments. For the former TACIS countries there was a substantial change as the ENPI was a more flexible instrument in many ways; allowing direct budgetary support for example (interview, Commission, March 2008). For the Mediterranean there was less of a change but in both cases programming documents were more adaptable. Other innovations appear more cosmetic. There is a more explicit emphasis on cross-border cooperation (Official Journal 2006a Preamble, 13), border regions within the EU will be assisted by the European Regional Development Fund, and this is seen as a major development in terms of harmonising EU internal and external aid policy but its significance should not be overstated. There is no question of neighbouring countries getting access to EU regional funds. Multi-country intra-regional aid is also envisaged, this is nothing new except that there is now the possibility for Mediterranean and Eastern neighbours to engage in joint projects. It is hard to see how relevant this is apart from providing some tangible manifestation of the neighbourhood 'region' the EU has constructed. More fundamentally, the basic objective of the aid is to 'promote enhanced cooperation and progressive economic integration between the European Union and its neighbours' (Ibid 22) and this is not fundamentally different from before. The regulation was allocated €11.8 billion for the period 2007-2013, an increase in funding overall but significantly less than the Commission had hoped for.

How has the ENP been implemented in practice? Table 7.1 shows the country break down for 2007–2010. Mediterranean partners get the lions share of country funding, although many aspects of the ENP seem more geared towards the Eastern land borders of the Union. Generally the Country Strategy Papers are not as explicitly linked to the ENP and the Action Plans as one might have supposed. In the NIPs the specific projects planned are cross-referenced with the relevant points in the Action Plan, although sometimes this appears more of a bureaucratic formality. The impression that the ENPI was going to follow the model of pre-accession aid in being rigorously linked to agreed reform targets is not borne out by the reality, and indeed this is not surprising as the ENP is vaguer than the accession process. It should be noted that aid is not in fact the ENP's major mechanism. The primary (and somewhat indistinct) 'carrot' the EU is offering is greater access to the EU in various forms. Thus the aid element of the new policy is essentially similar to what had gone before. There are new facilities and policies such as EU-Neighbourhood cross-border cooperation. As well as this there are regional aid programmes for the Mediterranean and the Eastern regions as well as horizontal programmes which can apply to all or some countries from both

Table 7.1   ENPI country allocations 2007–2010*

Algeria	220	Armenia	98.4
Egypt	558	Azerbaijan	92
Israel	8	Belarus	20
Jordan	265	Georgia	120.4
Lebanon	187	Moldova	209.7
Libya	8	Ukraine	494
Morocco	654	Russia	120
Palestinian Authority	632		
Syria	130		
Tunisia	300		

Source: Commission 2007b

*There are also € millions 1504.7 allocated for ENPI thematic and country programmes.

regions. The latter includes direct assistance from a unit in the Commission's Enlargement DG to assist harmonization with EU legislation,[1] and a governance fund to reward countries in the vanguard of reform. Thus the range of aid activities is still complex but the fact that these are all within the ENPI framework does help the coherence of aid policy. In addition to the ENPI the EIDHR is still active in the region and some elements of the Development and Cooperation Instrument may apply.

In the Mediterranean region the zenith of international pressure for reform may well have passed, certainly in terms of democratization. The Iraq quagmire and the strategic dangers it poses have led America to retrench its support for friendly but authoritarian states. Ongoing terrorism, including a revival and transnationalization of terrorism in the Maghreb also reinforce this tendency of the US, and European governments, to settle for cooperation with the existing regimes. The EU is continuing its efforts, although democratization was never its immediate focus in any case. Morocco remains one of the bright spots in the region, but is still far being a liberal polity and economy. Its general election of 2007 was free and fair in itself, although the low turnout gives an indication of how much the population feel they are able to exert influence. Its greatest challenge remains its low human development and living standards, even relative to its income group, which obviously challenge both stability and the reform trajectory. Ongoing efforts to combat this include the National Human Development Initiative (NHDI) launched in 2005. Meanwhile the government continues its outward looking economic strategy and its liaison with the EU. A progress report in December 2006 is complementary regarding Morocco's progress in economic reform (Commission 2006a). In that year negotiations begun for an extended free trade agreement liberalizing trade in services and the right of establishment. The EU has continued to reward Morocco with the highest aid allocations of any other country. Interestingly its focus is more on social and developmental objectives than before with 79% of funding devoted to these issues. The reform projects that do exist include a continuation of the two previous public administration reform programmes. Social and development aid includes support for the health sector, transport infrastructure and 60 million to support the NHDI, although it notes worries over how this is working (Commission 2007c). Thus the current aid strategy can be understood as a recognition that Morocco is genuinely attempting to reform and integrate with the EU, and that the major task is to ensure that economic and social levels continue to improve so as not to derail this effort. EU aid in this context is more of an indirect instrument of structural power. This is manifestly not the case for the rest of the Mediterranean partners where direct reform aid plays a much greater role than in Morocco. Former 'support to Association Agreement' programmes are

---

1   The TAIEX (Technical Assistance and Information institutional Exchange Programme).

now supplemented by more comprehensive 'support to Action Plan' programmes in countries such as Egypt.

To the east of Europe, the Ukrainian political situation continues to oscillate while the institutional structures of the country continue their gradual reform. The strongly pro-European block is once more in the ascendance since the 2007 parliamentary elections. Yet the uncertainty and instability preceding the election, which drew warnings from the EU's leadership, indicate the fragility of democratic consolidation in the country. Meanwhile the vulnerability of Ukraine to Russia's economic power remains. The EU has certainly developed a rich institutional framework at this stage with the Action Plan buttressed by the ten points for further cooperation, including an envisaged free trade area, and also a separate memorandum of understanding on energy policy. The EU's CSP is quite bullish about what the EU can expect to achieve noting that Ukrainian officials 'have shown a greater level of commitment and ownership as a result of the clearer political framework provided by the ENP' (Commission 2007d, 11). It also argues that

> As the largest donor to Ukraine, the EU has the leverage necessary to make a major contribution to the reform process. In addition most donors recognise the special role of the EU due to Ukraine's European aspirations and are increasingly aligning their activities with the policy objectives set in the EU-Ukraine Action Plan (Ibid 13).

The majority of country funding for 2007-2010 is dedicated to reform (60%), the clear feeling being that Ukraine is still on the fence in terms of its direction and that the currently favourable political framework should be exploited to comprehensively reform the institutions of the country. An element of this is for democracy and human rights but most goes to reform of public administration, and the regulatory framework. The indicators and the precise implementation focus will be determined via dialogue within their joint institutions. The remainder of EU funding goes to public infrastructure development. Given its geographical position Ukraine is much more involved in cross-border cooperation than Morocco, participating in four programmes related to Poland, Romania, Moldova and the Black Sea region. Notwithstanding the opportunity that does exist for the EU, the reality of illiberal economic and political influence within the country is still a formidable obstacle.

To conclude this section, the ENPI is not as radically different from the previous instruments as was initially suggested. The ENP and Action Plans do offer a stronger overall framework for reform within which the EU's aid can work. The fundamental limitations of the MEDA and TACIS instruments still apply. Whether legislation can be translated into a real change in the recipients' institutions of partners is doubtful given the equivocal will to reform of many partner governments and the strong vested interests against liberalization. Although ENPI funding is slightly greater than before and is engaging with development and social issues, its investment element is not enough to have a direct substantial impact on economic development. Should a global downturn lead to reduced growth, the reform momentum is likely to slow dramatically. Geopolitical factors beyond the EU's control affect its structural policies. The lack of a coherent foreign policy on the EU's part means that Russia has a certain advantage when it comes to power politics and can use this to maintain or expand its presence. Indeed Russian influence is currently felt to be substantial even within certain EU member states (European Council on Foreign Relations, 2007). In a different sense, failure of the European's to moderate or offer a coherent alternative to US foreign policy in the Middle East, has negatively affected its broader role in the region, and the reform environment. Lastly, short-term security considerations continue to play a major role in EU policy and dilute its pressure for structural reform. Notwithstanding these limitations, the ENPI represents a further refinement of the EU's use of aid for structural power and, if the broader environment is propitious, could play a significant role in reshaping Europe's neighbourhood.

7.3 The Development Cooperation Instrument: A Reprioritization of Development?

This new instrument seems to involve a refocusing towards purely developmental objectives and this may imply a moderation of the use of aid for structural power. Unlike the ENPI or the previous ALA regulation it is based solely on the development articles of the EC Treaty (article 179). This was under pressure from civil society development networks (CONCORD 2006), supported by the Parliament (Legislative observatory 2006). The Council of Ministers accepted the Parliament's demands to make the regulation based solely on article 179, but rejected its efforts to guarantee levels of funding for specific social sectors. The text makes explicit that 'the primary and overarching objective of cooperation under this regulation shall be the eradication of poverty in partner countries' (Official Journal 2006b, Article 2), and there is an emphasis on complementing multilateral development policy, in particular the millennium development goals. Yet of the core objectives/activities outlined in the following article many are clearly compatible with EU structural objectives (in particular 1,3 and 4):

1. the promotion of democracy and the rule of law
2. sustainable development
3. 'encourage their smooth and gradual integration into the global economy'
4. 'strengthen the relationship between the Community and the partner countries and regions'
5. environmental protection

Thus again the change may not be so great in reality, and there is sufficient flexibility for aid also to be used for structural power. As this aid is destined for

Table 7.2   DCI indicative allocations for 2007–2013 (€ billions)

Latin America	2.690
Asia	5.187
Central Asia	.719
Middle East	.481
South Africa	.980
Thematic Programmes	5.596

Source: Annex IV of the regulation

numerous regions of enormous geoeconomic (and in some cases geopolitical) importance this is to be expected. The major geographical focus is on Latin America and Asia, but also included were Central Asia, the Middle East (beyond the Mediterranean) and South Africa. 5 horizontal thematic programmes with a global reach are also included including cooperation on migration and civil society participation in development.[2]

€16.987 billion euro has been allocated to this instrument for 2007–2013; the breakdown is in table 7.2. The DCI is harder to characterise than the ENPI because of the geographical diversity of recipients. The procedures for country programming are not changed except that the Parliament's Development Committee is starting to have more of a say in programming documents. One noteworthy change to how it operates in Latin America and Asia is that Sectorwide Adjustment Programmes are now possible, in line with general trends in EU aid policy. Yet SWAPs do not feature much in the current NIPs as for most countries the financing is too low to make direct budget support meaningful. In Asia a bewildering combination of regional and subregional aid programmes still exist as well as country programmes. For Latin America there is an essentially similar package of horizontal and country programmes obtains. The regulation prioritised regional integration as an objective and the Commission is maintaining its regional integration aid for Mercosur, undeterred by the difficulties in reaching a free trade agreement. Unusually the Commission actually blames both sides for failing to move far enough on trade concessions (Ibid 22). Its aid strategy for 2007–2010 continues along similar lines (Commission 2007f). 70% is to support Mercosur economic integration (and EU-Mercosur integration). A smaller portion is devoted to civil society participation and the EU's obsession with EU 'visibility'. There is a financially small but potentially significant basket of projects devoted to

---

2   The others were 'investing in people', (human development), environmental protection and food security. These can also apply to EDF and ENPI countries.

technical assistance for institutionalization. This includes aid to establish the Mercosur Parliament and legal assistance for the permanent tribunal and support for the secretariat to develop policies such as regional aid to improve the cohesion (and thus further the integration) of the Mercosur block. For maximum impact the Commission would provide investment funding itself for Mercosur's poorer regions but lacks the resources for this, the total funding available is €23 million for 2007–2010. The European Parliament called for the Mercosur IP to be altered as it deemed it (correctly) to be far from the poverty reduction spirit of the regulation (European Parliament, 2007). This was resisted and the proposed agreement remains 'the centrepiece of our policy towards Mercosur' according to the Commission (Strategy Paper 2007f, 21).

7.4 The European Development Fund: Still Unique

Given the failure of the Commission's efforts to incorporate the EDF fully into the EU system, the 10th EDF retains its own particular financing system. At the stormy European Council of December 2005, in which the EU's budgetary framework for the next 7 years was eventually agreed, the member states also agreed the level of €22.682 billion for the 10th EDF(Official Journal 2006c).[3] EU relations with Sub-Saharan Africa have been problematic in recent years, the dominant factor being tough negotiations on the Economic Partnership Agreements (EPAs). December 2007 was the official deadline for the EPAs but this was not fulfilled. Instead the EU had to settle for signing individual interim trade agreements with several countries.[4] Others relied on the general preferences the EU has committed to for developing and least developed countries. The EU is continuing its push for EPAs, seemingly ready to make significant concessions on the staging of liberalizations provisions and on infant industry as long as the basic legal relationship is established. The high-level Lisbon Summit of December 2007 witnessed a renewal of the avowals of a special relationship between the two regions. The EDF operates on similar lines to before with the addition of an explicit incentive tranche to reward countries whose governance conforms to the EU's principles. (It was argued in chapter 5 that the EDF is an indirect instrument of structural power in that it works mostly for development and generic liberalization rather than specific EU interests). If country allocations were made conditional on signing up to EPA agreements then it would be a more direct instrument but the EU vehemently denies that this will happen. ACP states are demanding extra assistance, beyond regular EDF aid to

---

3   21, 966 for the ACP states and the remainder for the Overseas Territories .

4   Botswana, Lesotho, Swaziland, Namibia and Mozambique in the Southern African Development Community. Kenya, Uganda, Tanzania, Rwanda and Burundi in the East African Community. Zimbabwe, Seychelles Mauritious, Comoros and Madagascar in Eastern and Southern Africa and the Ivory Coast and Ghana in ECOWAS. Only in the Carribean was a full regional agreement signed.

enable them to sign EPAs. There have been some declarations from EU member states about extra aid for trade from their own coffers but nothing concrete enough to affect negotiations. The programming of EDF CSPs took place in 2006 and 2007 and proved a more controversial process than before. Development NGOs argued that it was essentially an exclusive process and that 'there are clear indications that certain aid priorities have been imposed to ACP governments in this process' (CONCORD 2007).[5]

Such rancour has not been apparent in the case of Ghana which remains a favoured partner despite the unwillingness of its ECOWAS group to sign an EPA. It signed an interim agreement in December 2008 its trade minister noting that this 'was a necessity in order to avoid serious trade disruption' (Delegation of the European Commission to Ghana 2008). Ghana is allocated €373.6 million for 2008-2013, which is a relatively large amount (Commission 2007e). The CSP is complementary regarding Ghana's government, regarding it as in many ways an example for its region, although failings in governance, budgetary management and economic policy are noted. EU aid is again harmonized with domestic and international policies. The EU aid strategy is based on the government's poverty reduction strategy and the African peer review of governance (Commission 2007e, 16). The three major aid interventions are derived from the former and the landmark Ghana Joint Assistance Strategy which the major donors have agreed (Ibid, 33). 26% of funding goes to governance reform, 48% for continuation of the multi-donor direct budgetary support and 21% for transport and regional interconnectivity. Notions that regional aid would be reduced as a form of punitive conditionality for failure to agree an EPA, appear wrongheaded. The strategy for ECOWAS has not been completed at the time of writing but the funding envisaged is increased from 235 million in the previous period to 478 million (Commission official, 2008). This is further evidence that EDF aid is not used as a blunt instrument to push EPAs, while it is funding activities to support the EPA process.

Conclusions

From a panoramic and historical perspective, the 2006 reforms actually amount to limited change. Above all they do not change the fundamental structure of European aid, in which EU-level aid policy is combined with autonomous member state aid policies. While there have been further landmarks towards coordination at the global level, and coordination and complementarity of aid policies (Orbie 2003; Carbone 2007), the full Europeanization of aid policy is not on the agenda. As to EU-level aid policy, the balance of power between the member states and the Commission remains unchanged. Carbone argues convincingly that the

---

5   This is not to suggest that the EDF programming process has become more exclusive than it already was, the greater opposition is a result of greater awareness of such issues due to NGO activity.

Commission has exercised leadership in EU and European policy-making, but only in certain specific areas and under certain propitious circumstances (Carbone 2007, 124–126).

The fact that the Commission's designs were knocked back by the member states (most obviously in keeping the EDF unique) and even by the Parliament (in decoupling commercial cooperation from development cooperation for the DCI) illustrates that its power to shape policy is sharply limited. But it is still indisputably the central actor in operating this policy. As to the changes in policy, it can be concluded that these reforms were not primarily about further facilitating the direct use of aid for structural power. There were strong countervailing forces to re-orientate aid towards normative developmental objectives. As before, aid is a compromise between these different considerations and motivations. In fact even if the EU has reworked its aid policy to directly promote development, the linkage of aid with other EU trade and cooperation policies would justify a description of aid as an indirect instrument of structural power. What has actually happened is a rebalancing, where apart from the ENPI, aid instruments are more explicitly focused on development but they still retain the flexibility to be used for EU structural objectives. This is to be expected in an era of heightened geoeconomic competition. In this context the EU has revamped its aid framework and increased its coherence and efficiency, though not by as much as the Commission's original plan would have involved. In regard to the new instruments the DCI and the EDF offer little new in terms of forms of aid or strategic methodology. The role of conditionality has not been increased; this implies recognition that this particular mechanism has its limits. Only the ENPI offers a potentially qualitative change in terms of depth of engagement and precise linkage with other EU policies.

Conclusion

Over this period of global geopolitical turmoil, the European Union has continued and refined its efforts at inducing structural changes in the developing world. Although its aid policy is not monolithic, empirical research bears out the assumption that it is used to gain structural power. Even most internal evaluations (which, needless to add, are hardly from a radical perspective) note how this strong tendency to support EU interests hampers dialogue and detracts from the focus on poverty, gender equality and environmental objectives. The power projection element of EU aid involves efforts to reform the state, laws and institutions, change the socio-economic power structure more generally and develop regional integration. This reforming of states and regions along lines favourable to the EU's power may or may not involve democratization, although it certainly involves political liberalization. Aid policy is playing a large role in the EU's gradualist 'foreign policy' and is relatively insulated from the political problems of European integration and the vicissitudes of the EU treaties and reforms.

Conditionality is one of the means by which aid works. Yet this study further confirms that crude conditionality (either as punishment or incentive) is a relatively unimportant tool. The complex institutional set-up of the EU makes it difficult for it to use this kind of mechanism. It lacks the capability of a state donor such as the US to quickly redirect aid resources. This is probably for the best, as EU funding is not large enough to act as a punishment or incentive for most of the countries important to it, and the resultant realistic gradualist approach has more chance of success. More important are the series of 'micro-conditionalities' involved in specific projects and programmes. The aid itself is a direct intervention to inject finance and expertise (and prestige) to local institutions which it favours and ensures contact between European and local elites. Regardless of the specific effects of aid, EU aid is an important process in itself; it forms relationships between EU institutions/personnel and their counterparts and inserts the EU into the national/regional context.

Geography matters greatly in EU aid policy. Its most elaborate and purposeful external relations policies have been for those regions closest to it and this has resulted in the most strategically refined aid instruments that are most precisely attuned to EU interests. TACIS and MEDA, and now the ENPI are explicitly political instruments in terms of conception, legal basis and operation. EDF aid is less intimately linked with the EU's structural diplomacy although it still pursues economic and political changes commensurate with this policy. Public opinion and civil society pressure for a more purely developmental focus to aid have had little effect on EDF policy. In Latin America and Asia, the ALA and now the DCI, have been relatively distant from EU diplomacy and relatively underfunded both in per capita terms and in relation to the size of the economies and polities it seeks to influence.

How Effectively is the EU using Aid for Reform and Expansion?

Accordingly although EU aid is mostly ineffective regarding development and democracy support, it is having a substantial impact on legal structures and economic policies. While the resources devoted to aid are often relatively slight, it operates in tandem with broader efforts at legalized and institutionalized economic and political cooperation. This is the real added-value of EU aid and is the main reason why EU-level aid continued to increase in the 1990s, despite the widespread low opinion of the Commission's aid management. The latter has improved substantially as an aid organization in the past decade in nearly all respects. Accordingly the EU can be considered as an 'actor', and not just a source of funds or a large market. EU efforts are also facilitated by its not inconsiderable prestige worldwide and the Commission's own experience in intervening in European states and supporting integration within Europe. It still lacks the research capacity of an institution like the World Bank or the expertise of a dedicated aid agency such as DFID or USAID, but it can use the IFIs and other donors for the intellectual work for many of its activities. It is not the most rigorous in its approach to programming methodology but this is not always a serious drawback as it allows for a degree of policy and intellectual flexibility (aid conditionalities invariably come down to bargaining at any rate).[1]

Other constraints relate to the limits of European integration more generally. The EU's aid and trade efforts are still not backed up by a coherent foreign and security policy. Internal efforts to consolidate EU policy-making and foreign policy in particular, have run aground as voters have rejected the European Constitution and the Lisbon Reform Treaty. A unified foreign policy is not necessarily vital for the success of its structural policies (and in fact overweening power and identity could restrict its ability to push for reform as it would detract from its 'non-threatening' status). Yet its lack of 'hard power' does mean, as discussed further on, that EU policy becomes hostage to other actors and factors. More seriously, even regarding 'low politics' the EU is not always as cohesive as one might presume. The member states have delegated sufficient power to the EU institutions to pursue credible external policies, but they do not always support this wholeheartedly and thus the EU may amount to less than the sum of its parts. Specifically, in regard to aid policy, the member states retain their autonomous aid policies which pursue their own national inclinations and interests and have been thus far imperfectly aligned with the collective EU programme. Also member states will often rely on the EU to put the pressure on governments to reform when it comes to sensitive political

---

1   It does hamper the use of conditionality to support human rights as there should be very clear conditions and benchmarks linked to international law here.

and economic areas. For example, in the Mediterranean, Commission officials felt that after 9.11, member state ministers eased up on the reform agenda, and sent implicit signals that security cooperation was the most important issue (Interviews, European Commission, 2003/2004).

Beyond the idiosyncrasies of the EU, there are generic constraints on the capability of international/exogenous actors to shape the political and economic development of even the weaker states. In theory the major powers' external promotion of neo-liberal policies is an effective means of increasing their influence as successful neo-liberal reforms denude the power blocks within the partner country (be they centred on the state or other sectors of society) while their own political control over markets and their politico-economic power networks (within the EU or US) are untouched. In practice this is difficult to achieve. First of all 'reform' is a perilous project in major powers such as China and Russia, due to the sheer scale of the economy and public administration and the politicized nature of economic power. Also such states and other energy rich states have gained from massive revenue increases in the 21st century which reduces the leverage of international donors (Aslund 2008, 169–172). The bulk of developing and transitional states remain needful of EU aid, and lack the leverage energy resources supply. However, even these regimes still have substantial autonomy, and many cards to play as they must implement the reforms. This poses enormous challenges to would-be outside reformers – as articulated by Hellman and Dillman (Hellman 1998; Dillman 2001). As recounted here, this can lead to the refraction of aid resources in such a manner that reconfigures existing power blocks rather than diffuses them, leading to relatively superficial change overall. A particular feature of this, which is strikingly apparent in EU efforts, is its relative success in gaining the formal changes to legislation and administration but failure to affect more informal institutions. Indeed this situation is not unfamiliar to other parts of the European Commission as despite the reality of European integration, actual compliance with EU law is often problematic and it faces ongoing battles to realise the single market that member states agreed to in 1986. In any case, with regard to external partners this means that the aid and reform drive, combined with endogenous forces, tends to develop the partner institutions in a form that is suboptimal in terms of liberal values and EU power.

Forming an intellectual response to this challenge is difficult as, (given the underlying liberal ideology), planners tend not to focus systematically on the power dimension. In any case it is not clear that there is a viable solution to this within the neo-liberal paradigm, which does not allow for the proactive use of public power to directly promote development. Greater financial resources, with a large part devoted to economic development, would not only make positive conditionality more potent but also offer the realistic prospect of economic transformation needed to overcome vested interests and popular fear of reform. Within Europe, EU aid has played a major role in supporting reform and integration but the financial investment is incomparably greater. The small, relatively prosperous, country of Portugal was allocated over 19 billion in structural and cohesion funds to enable it to compete within the European market from 2000–2006 (Official Journal 1999; DG Regio 2008). The EU wants countries such as Ukraine, Egypt and Morocco to develop along similar lines but offers less than a twentieth of this funding to these countries that have infinitely greater challenges (urban poverty, rural underdevelopment, political instability…). Budgetary limitations are also salient with regard to supporting regional integration where the role of EU aid is relatively technical and cannot impact on the fundamental economic structures. Innovative programmes, such as the European Payments Union set up by the US that provided hard currency to encourage trade within Europe after World War II (Milward 1992, 348–349), are not possible with the limited resources available.

EU Structural Power?

In theory, the objective of EU aid policy is that traditional political-economic power blocks in states such as Morocco, and Ukraine are diffused, internationalized while the EU retains its own (albeit much more subtle) configuration of economic and political power. While this has occurred to an extent, the reality is more complex. In evaluating the use of aid policy to develop power, it is worthwhile referring back to the Marshall plan, the original and most successful use of aid for this purpose. Although even its effectiveness has been debated (Hogan 1987, 433–455), most accept that this conditional injection of US finance and expertise into post-war Europe had a massive effect on Western Europe's political and economic development. Aid effects included the bolstering of capitalist economies and liberal political systems and the setting in train of European Integration. Such a framework, although in some ways competitive with America, essentially worked for its long-term cold war interests and the US retained structural power in the economic, financial and military spheres (Lundestad 2001). After the cold war the EU has begun to compete for structural power but not in a manner that threatens the essential welfare of America, whose leadership in security issues it still accepts. As the EU is not a superpower on the scale of the US after World War II and is operating long-term aid policies rather than a massive one-off programme, we could not expect its aid policies to achieve anything like what the Marshall Plan did, but the latter remains a benchmark for success.

As outlined in chapter 2 structural power can be delineated in terms of the EU's power in the partner country/region and on the global level. The neighbouring regions are the most important, they offer the most opportunity, but also present major challenges due to the power resources and complexity of the regimes in question. The countries of the Mediterranean have been in the EU's economic orbit for a long period. The EU's aid and trade policies have further institutionalized and legalized this situation. Any future intra-Mediterranean integration is inextricably linked with the Euro-Mediterranean framework due to the legal free trade agreements established. Aid and reform projects of the US and the IFIs also serve to reinforce the EU's position as it is by far the dominant economic pole and will remain so for the foreseeable future. However, as these regimes are not wholly liberalizing or integrating with the EU, it will remain a source of economic power but is not shaping the deeper socio-economic and political trajectory of the region. To Europe's East the re-emergence of Putin's Russia and its fusion of political and economic power (especially over energy) is a text book example of the kind of eventuality that the EU is trying to prevent. It is obviously too late for Russia, although the extensiveness of economic interaction gives the EU potential leverage. Russia was 'lost' in the 1990s but in this century the EU has worked hard with its aid and cooperation instruments in the rest of the near abroad, to develop the socio-economic and political structures amenable to European power. It has achieved this to an extent; Ukraine, Moldova, Georgia and the Caspian region are developing along lines amenable to the EU and are implementing Action Plans for further integration. As with the Mediterranean there are still complications and power blocks and the case of Ukraine shows that reform is clearly not a uni-linear trajectory. The EU would have to consider offering membership for a deeper transformative effect.

In Latin America and Asia, the EU's role is better described as 'presence' or 'influence' than structural power. Aid has played a role from an early stage in developing a relationship with ASEAN. Aid is probably the only means by which the EU can directly influence the internal evolution of China. This influence is limited but combined with its economic diplomacy and the weight of the rest of the international community it is not negligible. In Latin America the EU has acted as a more effective agent of globalization than George Bush's America and continued to increase its economic weight in the Southern Cone. The fact that most commentators tend not to notice the EU presence (as opposed to the US, Chinese and even Iranian presence) is by no means a problem for the EU. In the case of Mercosur, the EU has subtly but comprehensively inserted itself into the process through its aid policy, despite the political shift to the left in Mercosur countries.

In Africa the EU is not always able to exert relational power, for example the EU had to cave in and allow Zimbabwe to attend the EU-Africa summit in Lisbon 2007, against its wishes. Yet assertions that 'Europe needs Africa more than Africa needs Europe' (Versi 2008, 13) are wide of the mark. EU aid has further entrenched liberal economic institutions and helped maintain partners on a cooperative track with Europe. Although the full economic integration agreements have not been signed up to, the EU has signed interim EPAs with most of the more developed countries (including Ghana) and has inserted itself in the regional integration process (through its aid relationship and trade deals) to the extent that it is hard to visualise regional integration developing in a manner exclusive of EU interests. It is not surprising that China, which offers much more in many respects, is growing in influence but this growth would be much greater were it not for the structural power of Europe. China is not offering a specific, coherent development model for development and in time will come across the same resentment as other great powers in Africa (Taylor 2005, 125–126).

On the global level, these instruments have helped the EU further increase its trading weight in the global economy. Also the euro has become a reserve country of choice for many countries, particularly those with strong trade and aid relationships (Atkins 2007). A strong currency is in itself is a form of structural power (as is widely recognised it is the dollar's special position that has enable the US to defy 'economic rules' for so long). It is likely that the euro would be already challenging the dollar's special position were it not for the fact that a collapse of the dollar would lead to a global crash (Taggart-Murphy 2006). The EU is also spreading its own regulatory models worldwide and continuing to shape global economic governance. The situation is complex here as emerging nations are increasingly robust in WTO negotiating rounds. Yet it must be remembered that the WTO is more than a series of, inevitably 'crisis-ridden', negotiations (Wilkinson 2006), and is an accumulated body of law, which the EU has had a major role in shaping. Thus the situation is a kind of stalemate in which EU efforts to further shape the world trade regime and other aspects of global governance are resisted but the pre-existing regimes are still extant. Generally, disappointing gains from neo-liberal policies, and the success of authoritarian states such as China have stemmed the tide of neoliberal globalization. The latter's trajectory has been diverted as this century has witnessed a reinvigoration of territorial power, with sovereignty-jealous strategic states such as Russia and China engaging with the global economy on a selective basis. The most striking example of this is the emergence of 'sovereign wealth funds', the public investment funds of these and other energy rich developing states, that have taken controlling stakes in many major businesses of the capitalist core. Yet globalization's demise has been greatly exaggerated, and these phenomena only debunk the 'straw man' hyper-globalist thesis. As discussed in chapter 2, the more subtle understanding was always that globalization involved a reconfiguration rather than a uni-linear track of transnationalization and deterritorialization (Held et al. 1999). The EU remains one of the more durable nodes of globalization and its numerous trade and economic partnerships offer a kind of insurance (or insulation) from the vagaries of multilateral economic governance.

All of this means that, despite its own economic weaknesses, events and decisions within the EU will continue to shape the economic choices of hundreds of millions outside of Europe. Meanwhile the EU's web of relationships also increases its own structural power within Europe as it further ensures that a large proportion of member state foreign relations is under an EU framework. Thus for example the foreign policy posturing of the new French President and his plan for a 'Mediterranean Union' (involving European Mediterranean states and partners) in 2007 was quickly watered down as core economic and other issues are already handled at the EU level. On the ideational plane, while to say that the EU has 'ideological power' would be an overstatement, it is increasingly accepted internationally, as a source of authority on numerous public policy issues. Significant here is that many do not perceive it as an actor in the sense that major states are viewed, thus its own webs of control have tended to elicit less paranoia and resistance than these other actors.

Of course the EU still lacks power in the security sphere, and remains subservient to the US within an Atlanticist framework. This constrains the EU from achieving anything like superpower status and US foreign policy in the NIS and the Mediterranean sometimes hampers the EU's structural diplomacy. At least as important to the development of the EU's power, is that the EU lacks a feasible model for promoting development in its partners (Gowan 2005, 139). For example, the rapid food prices since January 2008 have the potential to undercut all of the gradual economic and governance reforms the EU has nurtured, but there is little it, as currently configured, can do to relieve this. A recurring theme of the regional studies here, has been that the EU's failure to engender sustainable development (in both senses of the term) detracts from its broader objectives. In a sense the EU, which was established to promote the European interest above all, is an intrinsically ingenerous partner. It must aggregate the interests of its own core stakeholders before reaching outside. Thus the institutions and forces which drive the EU's search for structural power also constrain it from achieving this.

Ontological and Ethical Conundrums

This study has sought to help answer a basic but essential question about the EU's capability as an external actor. Of course it makes no claim to be the final word on the issue, and indeed the assumptions implicit can be critiqued from numerous perspectives. Most obviously, treating of the EU as an actor and a locus of power may seem to involve over-confident neo-positivist assumptions about the possibility and form of knowledge. A more constructivist approach would address the complex overlapping identities and the reflexivity of relationships. Even within the structural power framework, the cognitive dimension has been admittedly under-researched. This would require a discourse analysis and comprehensive interviewing and surveying of elite strata in the various regions (regarding perceptions of the EU's authority and their own countries relationship to it), and would have been beyond the means available to a single author. The conclusions of this book regarding EU capability and power can be complimented by deeper constructivist accounts of the EU's relationships. From another perspective, it may be argued that the concept of 'structural power' is in itself meaningless without a deeper theory of politics and international relations. Neo-Marxist approaches would single out class as the dominant factor, and there are powerful arguments here (Robinson 1996; Pijl 1998). Yet this would prejudge the outcome to a degree and detract from the openness of the research agenda. Relatedly, many may feel that the focus on the EU as the locus of power obscures the deeper processes of globalization and transnationalism (Ibid, Hardt and Negri, 2001). This book has sought to give these phenomena their due weight but does not presume that globalization has denuded territorial configurations of power, and as discussed in the previous section, the tide of opinion has swung dramatically against the hyper-globalist view.

Lastly, there are profound ethical dilemmas regarding the EU's instrumental use of aid, which this book has not hitherto addressed. While EU policy-makers see themselves as promoting (long-term) democratization and development in step with EU interests, there is no question that the use of aid for said interests distorts the altruistic element of aid policy. In reality, the poverty and insecurity of hundreds of millions of human beings is seen as a blank canvass by the EU, upon which it can impose its models of society and governance. To put it mildly, this falls short of the ethical standards claimed to be at the heart of 'European values'. Yet, the EU is not alone in its proclivities, and its efforts to shape the international context could be viewed as an entirely legitimate, 'natural' mode of behaviour. Also, while there is a great deal of cant written by pro-Europeans, the EU does offer a model of cooperation between entities and a new form of 'public power'. For these reasons alone it could be considered an essentially progressive force. Its efforts in developing global environmental governance illustrate the more positive international role it could play.

The EU's search for power has been moderately successful in limited spheres but is increasingly unachievable in a world of emerging developing countries, and, at the risk of sounding teleological, appears to be counter to the currents of history. As it stands, the forms of power it has achieved are quite constrained, and the security benefits of its activities are even more debatable. It is often intensifying the pressure on societies and governance and thus potentially exacerbating the various security threats that stem from this. What are its options? It could seek to further refine its use of aid and trade policies for its own interests. However, as discussed above, there are fundamental limitations to the use of these instruments to shape other societies. As outlined in the previous chapter there are forces, centred on NGOs, the European Parliament and some member states, which work towards a more ethical and purely developmental aid policy. Although there is no quick fix for development the EU would do well to focus on this. It may of necessity need to sacrifice some power for a more sustainable form of influence and a more genuinely cooperative world. Realistically, this is unlikely to occur: the EU will continue attempting to balance its use of aid for ethical and self-interest objectives, and the former are unlikely to prevail.

Bibliography

AECI/Agencia Española de Cooperación Internacionale (2006), 'Cooperación Española en Marruecos', <http://www.aecimarruecos.org/>, accessed 12 September 2006.

Africa Trade Network (2006), 'Declaration of the 9th Annual Meeting of the Africa Trade Network', <www.epa2007.org/upload/documents/atn-declarationenglish.doc>, accessed 15 August 2007.

Aggarwal, V. (2004), *EU trade strategies; between regionalism and globalism*, (Palgrave: Macmillan).

Amnesty International (2000), 'Country Report: Morocco', <http://web.amnesty.org/report2000/ar2000>, accessed 4 April 2002.

Anderson, P. (2007), 'Jotting on the Conjuncture' *New Left Review,* 48, November-December 2007, 5–37.

APRODEV (2002), 'Rapid survey of 40 ACP Country Support Strategies: What about civil society participation?' <www.aprodev.net/devpol/cotonou.htm >, accessed 3 August 2007.

Archer, M. Bhaskar, R. Collier, A. Lawson, T. (eds.), (1998), *Critical Realism: Essential Readings* (London: Routledge).

Aslund, A. (2008), *Russia's capitalist revolution: why market reform succeeded and democracy failed* (Washington: Peterson institute).

Atkins, R. (2007), 'Euro's global importance grows as it gains ground on the dollar', *Financial Times*, 31 December 2007, Page 1.

Attina, F. and Stavridis, S. (2001), *The Barcelona Process and Euro-Mediterranean Issues from Stuttgart to Marseilles,* (Milan: Giuffre).

Ayubi, N. (1995), *Over-Stating the Arab State: Politics and Society in the Middle East* (London: IBN Taurus).

Babarinde, O. and Faber, G. (2004), 'From Lomé to Cotonou: Business as Usual?' *European Foreign Affairs Review* 9:1, 27– 47.

Bach, D. (1999), 'The revival of regional integration in Africa', Documentos de Trabalho no 56, CESA, Lisboa, <http://pascal.iseg.utl.pt/~cesa/files/DocTrab_56.PDF>, accessed 12 October 2006.

Bache, I. (1998), *The politics of European Union regional policy: multilevel governance or flexible gatekeeping* (Sheffield: Sheffield academic press).

Baker, G. (1999), *The taming of the idea of civil society, Democratization* 6: 3, 1–30.

Balcerowitz, L. (1995), *Socialism capitalism transformation* (London: CEU).

Baranovsky (1994), 'The EC as seen from Moscow: Rival, Partner, Model' in Malcolm (ed.), 59–78.

Barnett, M. and Duvall, R. (2005), 'Power in International Politics' *International Organization,* 59: 1, 39–75.

Bayart, J. (1993), *The state in Africa: the politics of the belly* (Longman).

Bayart, J. Ellis, S and Hibou, B. (1999), *The Criminalisation of the State in Africa* (Oxford: James Currey).

Ben Osmane, K. (2004), 'Priority Areas in Reforming Governance and Public Administration in Morocco', UNPAN (United Nations Public Administration Network) Working Paper. <www.unpan.org/innovmed/documents/priorities/Morocco.doc>, accessed 10 February 2005.

Bhaskar. R. (1998), 'General Introduction' in Archer et al. (eds.).

Bicchi, F. (2006), 'Our Size Fits All: Normative power Europe and the Mediterranean.' *Journal of European Public Policy,* 13: 2, 169–181.

Bojcun, A. (2001), Ukraine and Europe: a difficult reunion (London: Kogan Page).

Bojcun, A. (2004), 'Trade Investment and Debt: Ukraine's Integration into World Markets' in Robinson (ed.).

Brabant, J. (1998), *The political economy of transition,* (London: Routledge).

Braguinsk, S. and Yavlinksy, G. (2000), *Incentives and Institutions,* (Princeton: Princeton University Press).

Bretherton, C. and Vogler, J. (1999), *The European Union as a Global Actor,* (London: Routledge).

Browne, A. et al. (2001), 'The Status of Sector Wide Aproaches', Overseas Development Institute Working Paper 142. <www.odi.org.uk/publications/working_papers/wp142.pdf>, accessed 07 May 2003.

Browne, S. (2006), *Aid and Influence: Do Donors Help or Hinder?* (London: Earthscan).

Brynen, Rex B. Korany, and Noble, P. (1998), *Political Liberalisation and Democratization in the Arab World:Volume 1 Theoretical Perspectives* (London: Lynne Rienner).

Brzezinski, Z. and Sullivan, P. (1997), *Russia and the CIS: Documents, data and analysis* (London: M.E. Sharp).

Bukkvoll, T. (1997), *Ukraine and European security* (London: Pinter).

Burgat, F. (2002), *Face to face with political Islam* (London: I.B. Tauris).

Burgat, F. and Dowell, W. (1995), *The Islamic Movement in North Africa* (Austin: Center for Middle East Studies – University of Texas).

Burnell, P. (2004), 'The Domestic Political Impact of Foreign Aid: Recalibrating the Research Agenda', *European Journal of Development Research,* 16: 2, 396–416.

Burnell, P. (2000), *Democracy Assistance: International Cooperation for Democratization* (London: Frank Cass).

Burnell, P. (2000), 'Democracy Assistance: The State of the Art' in Burnell, (ed.).

Burnham, P., Karin G., Grant, W., Layton-Henry, Z. (2004), *Research Methods in Politics* (Basingstoke: Macmillan).

Burnside, C. and Dollar, D. (2004), 'Aid, policies, and growth: revisiting the evidence', Policy Research working paper no. 3251 <http://www.worldbank. org/html/dec/Publications/Workpapers/WPS1700series/wps1777/wps1777. pdf>.

Busse, M. Borrmann, A. and Großmann, H. (2004), *The Impact of ACP/EU Economic Partnership Agreements on ECOWAS Countries: An Empirical Analysis of the Trade and Budget Effects,* Final Report for the Friedrich-Ebert-Stiftung Hamburg, July 2004.

Buzan, B. Waever, O. and De Wilde, J. (eds.) (1998), *Security: A New Framework for Analysis* (London : Lynne Rienner).

Callaghy, T. Kassimir, R. Latham, R. (2001), *Intervention and transnationalism in Africa: global-local networks of power* (Cambridge, Cambridge University Press).

Callinicos, A. (2002), 'Marxism and Global Governance' in Held and McGrew (eds.).

Cameron, F. and Rhein, E. (2005), 'Promoting Political and Economic Reform in the Mediterranean and Middle East', European Policy Centre Issue Paper 33. <http://www.epc.eu/en/pub.asp?TYP=TEWN&LV=187&see=y&t=13&PG= TEWN/EN/detailpub&l=12&AI=490>, accessed 9 January 2006.

Cammack, P. (2005), 'The Governance of Global Capitalism: a New Materialist Perspective', in Wilkinson (ed.).

Caporaso, J. and Haggard, S. (1989), 'Power in the international economy', in: Stoll and & Ward (eds.).

Carbone, M. (2007), *The European Union and international development: the politics of foreign aid* (London: Routledge).

Carranza, M. (2006), 'Clinging together: Mercosur's ambitious external agenda, its internal crisis, and the future of regional economic integration in South America' *Review of International Political Economy* 13:5, 802–829.

Carothers, T. (2000), 'Struggling with semi-authoritarians', in Burnell (ed.).

Carothers, T. (1999), *Aiding Democracy Abroad - the learning curve* (Washington: Carnegie Endowment for International Peace).

Chafer, T. (2002), 'Franco-African Relations: No Longer So Exceptional?' *African Affairs* 101, 343–363.

Chen, S. And Ravallion, M. (2004), 'How Have the World's Poorest Fared since the Early 1980s?', *The World Bank Research Observer* 19: 2, 141–170.

Chow, G. (2007), *China's economic transformation* (Oxford: Blackwell).

Christiansen, T., K.E., Jorgensen, and A. Wiener (1999), 'The Social Construction of Europe', *Journal of European Public Policy*, 6: 4, 528–544.

Cini, M. (ed.), *European Union Politics* (Oxford: OUP).

Cline-Cole (2005), 'Paths through socio-economic change, livelihoods and development in West African worlds' in Cline-Cole and Robson (eds.).

Cline-Cole, R. and Robson, E. (2005), *West African Worlds* (Harlow: Pearson).

Collingwood, S. (2006), Contribution of the Head of Trade Negotiations and Development Unit, Department of Trade & Industry, United Kingdom, to the High-level Conference on EU-ACP Trade Relations: The Development Challenge of Economic Partnership Agreements Brussels 12 October 2006, 78. <http://www.acp-eu-trade.org/library/files/South-Centre_EN_121006_South-Centre_Development-Challenge-of-EPAs.pdf>, accessed 9 August 2007.

CONCORD (2006), Recommendations on the Development Cooperation (& Economic. Cooperation) Instrument January 2006 <http://www.concordeurope.org>, accessed 15 June 2007.

CONCORD (2007), 10th EUROPEAN DEVELOPMENT FUND: the Partnership under Threat Briefing paper, 17 November 2007 <http://www.concordeurope.org>,, accessed 12 August 2007.

Coombes, D. (1970), *Politics and Bureaucracy in the European Community: a portrait of the Commission of the E.E.C.* (London: Allen and Unwin).

Council of the European Union (2005), 'The European Consensus on Development: joint statement with the European Parliament and the Commission' <http://ec.europa.eu/development/icenter/repository/eu_consensus_en.pdf>, accessed 24 March 2006.

Cox, R. and Sinclair, T. (eds) (1983), *Approaches to World Order* (Cambridge: Cambridge University Press).

Cox, R. (1983), 'Gramsci, hegemony and international relations: an essay in method', in Cox and Sinclair (eds).

Cox, R. (ed.) (1997), *The New Realism: Perspectives on Multilateralism and World Order* (Basingstoke: Macmillan Press).

Cox, A. et al. (1997), *How European Aid Works A Comparison of Management Systems and overall effectiveness* (London: Overseas Development Institute).

Cram, L. (2001), 'Whither the Commission? Reform, Renewal and the Issue-attention Cycle', *Journal of European Public Policy*, 8: 5, 770–786.

Crawford, G. (1996), 'Whether Lome? The Mid-Term Review and the Decline of Partnership' *The Journal of Modern African Studies*, 34: 3, 503–518.

DAC/Development Assistance Committee of the OECD (1998), Peer Review of the European Union 1998. <http//www.oecd.org/dac/peerreviews>, accessed 16 November 2001.

DAC/Development Assistance Committee of the OECD (2002), Peer Review of the European Union 2002, <http//www.oecd.org/dac/peerreviews>, accessed 19 May 2003.

DAC/Development Assistance Committee of the OECD (2005), Peer Review of the European Union 2005, <http//www.oecd.org/dac/peerreviews>, accessed 17 February 2007.

DAC/Development Assistance Committee of the OECD (2008), Aid at a glance charts: Ukraine, Morocco, Ghana. <http://www.oecd.org/countrylist/0,3349,en_2825_495602_25602317_1_1_1_1,00.html>, accessed 14 January 2008.

Damina, A and Boltvinik, J. (2006), 'A table to Eat on: the meaning and measurement of poverty in Latin America' in Hershberg, E. and Rosen, F. (eds.).

Dannreuther, R. (2006), 'Developing the Alternative to Enlargement: The European Neighbourhood Policy', *European Foreign Affairs Review*, 11: 2, 183–201.

D'Averso, F. and Palazion, M. (2003), 'Making Transport More Competitive and Efficient: EU Support to Transport Sector Reform in Morocco', Private Participation in Mediterranean Infrastructure. Newsletter Issue no. 21.

Dearden, S. (2002), 'Does the EU's Development Policy Have Any Future?', European Development Policy Study Group: Working paper 24, <www.edpsg.org>, accessed 23 March 2003.

Delegation of the European Commission to Ghana (2008), Press Release; Ghana and EU initial Interim Economic Partnership Agreement. <http://delgha.ec.europa.eu/en/news/PR_item080101.pdf>, accessed 11 March 2008.

Delegation de la Commission Europeene au Maroc (2002b), Bulletin D'Information No. 170, <http://www.delmar.cec.eu.int/fr/presse/bulletins.htm>, accessed 8 August 2007.

Delegation de la Commission Européenne au Maroc (2004a), Bulletin D'Information No. 176. <http://www.delmar.cec.eu.int/fr/presse/bulletins.htm>, accessed 11 May 2005.

Delegation de la Commission Europeene au Maroc (2002b), Conclusions de la reunion de la Comite D'Association. <http://www.delmar.cec.eu.int/fr/bi170/bi170_p05.htm - 20k>, accessed 7 June 2005.

Denoux, G. (2000), 'The Politics of Morocco's Fight Against Corruption' in *Middle East Policy* 7: 2, 165–189.

Desrues, T. (2005), 'Governability and Agricultural Policy in Morocco' *Mediterranean Politics* 10:1, 39–65.

Derrer, M. (2005), 'Growth potential of the Ukranian economy' in Hayoz (ed.).

Development Initiatives (2002), *The Reality of Aid 2002: Conditionality and Ownership*, <www.devinit.org/realityofaid/kpolchap.htm>, accessed 15 March 2003.

Devarajan, S. Dollar, D. Holmgren (eds.) (2001), Aid and Reform in Africa: Lessons from Ten Case Studies (Washington: World Bank).

DFID/UK Department for International Development (2007), *Ghana Joint Assistance Strategy (G-JAS)* February 27, 2007, <http://www.dfid.gov.uk/countries/africa/ghana/ghana-gjas.pdf>, accessed 22 August 2007.

DG Regio (2008) Breakdown of financial policy <http://ec.europa.eu/regional_policy/funds/procf/cf_en.htm>, accessed 24 May 2008.

Dillman, B. (2001), 'International markets and partial economic reforms in North Africa: What impact on democratization?' in Gillespie and Youngs (eds.).

Dillman, B. (2000), *State and Private Sector in Algeria: The Politics of Rent-Seeking and Failed Development* (Boulder: Westview Press).

Dinar, A. Balakrishnan, T. and Wambia, J. (1998), 'Political Economy and Political Risks of institutional reform in the water sector', World Bank Policy Research Working Paper. < http://econ.worldbank.org/resource.php?type=5>, accessed 24 March 2002.

Docksey, C. and Williams, K. (1997), 'The European Commission and the execution of Community policy', in Edwards and Spence (eds.).

Doctor, M. (2007), 'Why Bother With Inter-Regionalism? Negotiations for a European Union-Mercosur Agreement' *Journal of Common Market Studies* 45: 2, 281–314.

Duchêne, F. (1994), *Jean Monnet: the first statesman of interdependence* (London: Norton).

Duchêne, F. (1972), 'Europe's role in World Peace', in Mayne (ed.).

Duffield, R (2005), 'Governing the borderlands: decoding the power of aid' in Wilkinson (ed).

Dyker, D. (1994), 'Economic relations with the rest of Europe' in Malcolm (ed.).

ECA/European Court of Auditors (2002), 'Special Report No 1/2002 concerning macro financial assistance (MFA) to third countries and structural adjustment facilities (SAF) in the Mediterranean countries', OJEU C121/1. <http://eca. europa.eu/portal/page/portal/publications/auditreportsandopinions>

ECA/European Court of Auditors (2004), 'Special Report No 10/2004 concerning the devolution of EC external aid management to the Commission Delegations', OJEU C 72/01 <http://eca.europa.eu/portal/page/portal/ publications/auditreportsandopinions>

ECA/European Court of Auditors (2005), 'Special Report No 2/2005 concerning EDF budget aid to ACP countries: the Commission's management of the public finance reform aspect', OJ C 249 <http://eca.europa.eu/portal/page/portal/ publications/auditreportsandopinions>

ECOFIN/ Economic and Financial Affairs DG of the European Commission, (2008), 'Financial operations and instruments in support of EU policies', <http://ec.europa.eu/economy_finance/financial_operation_instruments/ market_operations398_en.htm>, accessed 18 March 2008.

Edwards, G. and Regelsberger, E. (1990), *Europe's Global Links: the European Community and Inter-Regional Cooperation* (London: Pinter).

Edwards, G. and Spence, D. (eds.) (1997), *The European Commission* (London: Catermill Publishers).

El Badaoui, A, (2004), *Les Rentiers du Maroc Utile* (Casablanca: Publisher unknown).

Emerson, M. et al. (2006), *The Prospect of Deep Free Trade between the European Union and Ukraine*, Centre for European Policy Studies (CEPS), Brussels Institut für Weltwirtschaft (IFW), Kiel International Centre for Policy Studies (ICPS), <http://www.ceps.be/Article.php?article_id=20>, accessed 9 June 2008.

Emerson, M. (2006), *A New Agreement between the EU and Russia: Why, what and when*, CEPS Policy Brief No. 103 <http://www.ceps.be/Article.php?article_ id=18>, accessed 19 September 2007.

Emerson, M. (ed) (2006), *The Elephant and the Bear Try Again Options for a New Agreement between the EU and Russia*, CEPS publication. <http://www.ceps. be/Article.php?article_id=18>, accessed 13 February 2007.

Emerson, M. (2005), *EU-Russia: Four Common Spaces and the Proliferation of the Fuzzy*, CEPS Policy Brief No. 71 < http://www.ceps.be/Article.php?article_id=18>, 18 March 2006.

Emerson, M. and Noutcheva, G. (2004), 'Europeanisation as a Gravity Model of Democratisation', CEPS Working Document No. 214/November 2004. < http://www.ceps.be/Article.php?article_id=18>, accessed 16 April 2005.

Emerson, M. (2004), 'European Neighbourhood Policy: Strategy or Placebo?' CEPS Working Document No 215. < http://www.ceps.be/Article.php?article_id=18>, accessed 21 January 2005.

Erdmann, G. (2002), 'Neo-Patrimonial Rule – Transition to Democracy had not succeeded', *InWent Magazine of Development and Cooperation*, No.1, January/February 2002, 8–11. < http://www.inwent.org/E+Z/index-eng.html>, accessed 8 June 2003.

Erdmann G. and Engel, U. (2006), 'Neopatrimonlialism revisited: beyond a catch all concept', *German Institute of Global and Area Studies Working Paper No. 16* <papers.ssrn.com/sol3/papers.cfm?abstract_id=909183> accessed 12 July 2007.

EuroMed Special Feature no 12, (2000), 'The Association Agreement with Morocco'.<http://europa.eu.int/comm/external_relations/euromed/publication.htm>, accessed 19 March 2002.

EuroMed Special Feature no 34 (2002), 'European Commission support to the implementation of Association Agreements'. <http://europa.eu.int/comm/external_relations/euromed/publication.htm>, accessed 28 May 2003.

EuroMed Special Feature no 41 (2004), 'MEDA II: Reinforced effectiveness'.<http://europa.eu.int/comm/external_relations/euromed/publication.htm>, accessed 19 January 2005.

Europeaid (2002), Ukraine Action Programme 2002,<http://ec.europa.eu/europeaid/where/neighbourhood/regional-cooperation/enpi-east/annual-programmes_en.htm#ukraine>, accessed 14 June 2007.

Europeaid (2003), Ukraine Action Programme 2003,<http://ec.europa.eu/europeaid/where/neighbourhood/regional-cooperation/enpi-east/annual-programmes_en.htm#ukraine>, accessed 14 June 2007.

Europeaid (2004a), Russia Action Programme 2004,<http://www.delrus.ec.europa.eu/en/p_309.htm>, accessed 14 June 2007.

Europeaid (2004b), Ukraine Action Programme 2004,<http://ec.europa.eu/europeaid/where/neighbourhood/regional-cooperation/enpi-east/annual-programmes_en.htm#ukraine>, accessed 14 June 2007.

Europeaid (2004c), External Assistance Reform: Four Years On. (Brussels: Europeaid publication) , April 2004.

Europeaid (2005a), Russia Action Programme 2005,<http://www.delrus.ec.europa.eu/en/p_309.htm>, accessed 14 June 2007.

Europeaid (2005b), Action Programme for Ukraine 2005,<http://ec.europa.eu/europeaid/where/neighbourhood/regional-cooperation/enpi-east/annual-programmes_en.htm#ukraine>, accessed 14 June 2007.

Europeaid (2006a), Georgia Action Programme 2006,http://ec.europa.eu/europeaid/where/neighbourhood/regional-cooperation/enpi-east/annual-programmes_en.htm#belarus.

Europeaid (2006b), *Annual Report 2006 on the European Community's Development Policy and the Implementation of External Assistance in 2005,* <http://ec.europa.eu/europeaid/multimedia/publications/publications/annual-reports/2006_en.htm - 21k>, accessed 18 May 2007.

Europeaid (2007), *Annual Report 2007 on the European Community's Development Policy and the Implementation of External Assistance in 2006,* <http://ec.europa.eu/europeaid/multimedia/publications/publications/annual-reports/2007_en.htm>, accessed 5 October 2007.

Europeaid evaluation unit (1997), *TACIS Interim evaluation: synthesis report,* <http://ec.europa.eu/europeaid/how/evaluation/evaluation_reports/tacis_reports_en.htm>, accessed 11 June 2007.

Europeaid evaluation unit (1998a), *Ukraine - Evaluation of EC Country Programme Final Report Volume I: Main Report,*<http://ec.europa.eu/europeaid/how/evaluation/evaluation_reports/tacis_reports_en.htm>, accessed 21 June 2007.

Europeaid evaluation unit (1998b), *An evaluation of EU Aid to ACP countries,* <http://europa.eu.int/comm/europeaid/evaluation/reports/acp/951338.pdf>, 12 August 2007.

Europeaid evaluation unit (1999a), *Evaluation of the MEDA regulation Final Report,* <http://ec.europa.eu/europeaid/how/evaluation/evaluation_reports/index_en.htm>, accessed 16 May 2002.

Europeaid evaluation unit (1999b), *Evaluation of EC development aid to ALA states,*<http://ec.europa.eu/europeaid/how/evaluation/evaluation_reports/index_en.htm>, accessed 12 December 2007.

Europeaid evaluation unit (2000), *Evaluation of Tacis Inter-State Energy and INOGATE Programmes and Related Actions implemented in the Framework of National Programmes, Final report: volume 1,* <http://ec.europa.eu/europeaid/how/evaluation/evaluation_reports/index_en.htm>, 14 June 2007.

Europeaid evaluation unit (2002), *Evaluation of ALA Regulation 443/92.* <http://ec.europa.eu/europeaid/how/evaluation/evaluation_reports/index_en.htm>, accessed 2 December 2007.

Europeaid evaluation unit (2003a), *Evaluation de la Strategie Pays de la Commission Europeene pour le Maroc* <http://ec.europa.eu/europeaid/how/evaluation/evaluation_reports/index_en.htm>, accessed 7 February 2004.

Europeaid evaluation unit (2003b), *Evaluation of the European Commission's Country Strategy for Ukraine.*<http://ec.europa.eu/europeaid/how/evaluation/evaluation_reports/index_en.htm>, accessed 20 June 2006.

Europeaid evaluation unit (2004), *Evaluation of the EC support to the Mercosur,* <http://ec.europa.eu/europeaid/how/evaluation/evaluation_reports/index_en.htm>, accessed 22 August 2007.

Europeaid evaluation unit (2005a), *Mid-term evaluation of the MEDA II programme: Final report* (Brussels: European Commission).

Europeaid evaluation unit (2005b), *Ghana: Country Strategy Evaluation/ Volume I*, <http://ec.europa.eu/europeaid/how/evaluation/evaluation_reports/index_ en.htm>, accessed 12 May 2006.

Europeaid Evaluation Unit (2005c), *Evaluation de la Strategie Regionale de la CE en Amerique Latine*, <http://ec.europa.eu/europeaid/how/evaluation/ evaluation_reports/index_en.htm>, accessed 21 August 2007.

Europeaid Evaluation Unit (2006), *Evaluation of Council Regulation 99/2000 (TACIS) and its implementation, Synthesis report Volume 1*, <http://ec.europa. eu/europeaid/how/evaluation/evaluation_reports/reports_by_country_region_ en.htm#regions>, accessed 12 March 2007.

Europeaid Evaluation Unit (2007a), *Evaluation of the EC Co-operation and Partnership with the People's Republic of China*, <http://ec.europa.eu/ europeaid/how/evaluation/evaluation_reports/index_en.htm>, accessed 10 October 2007.

Europeaid Evaluation Unit (2007b), *Evaluation of the European Commission's Country Level Cooperation with the Republic of India*, <http://ec.europa. eu/europeaid/how/evaluation/evaluation_reports/index_en.htm>, accessed 7 January 2008.

European Commission (1994), *Strengthening the Mediterranean Policy of the European Union: Establishing a Euro-Mediterranean Partnership*, Com 1994/ 427.

European Commission (1996), *Maroc Programme Indicatif 1996-1998*, Internal Document, Brussels 28.10.1996.

European Commission (1997), *Guidelines for the negotiation of new cooperation agreements with the African, Caribbean and Pacific countries*, COM(97)537.

European Commission (1998), *Commission staff working paper concerning the establishment of an inter-regional association between the European Union and Mercosur* <http://www.ec.europa.eu/external_relations/mercosur/ bacground_doc/work_paper0.htm>, accessed 12 September 2006.

European Commission (2000a), *Community Cooperation: Framework for Country Strategy Papers*, SEC 2000/1049.

European Commission (2000b), *The European Community's Development Policy*, COM 2000/212 final.

European Commission (2000c), *Document de strategie par pays 2000–2006 - Maroc* (Internal Document).

European Commission (2001a), *Regional Strategy Paper 2002–2006 and Regional Indicative Programme 2002-2004 for the Mediterranean*, <europa.eu.int/comm/external_relations/sp/index.htm>, accessed 3 March 2003.

European Commission (2001b), *Maroc Document de Strategie 2002–2006 et Programme Indicatif National 2002-2000* < europa.eu.int/comm/external_ relations/sp/index.htm>, accessed 3 March 2003.

European Commission (2001c), *Union Européenne – Maghreb 25 ans de cooperation 1976– 001* (Brussels: European Community).

European Commission (2001d), *The European Initiative for Democracy and Human Rights Programming Document 2002-2004*, <http://ec.europa.eu/europeaid/where/worldwide/eidhr/working-documents_en.htm>, accessed 4 May 2003.

European Commission (2001e), *Ukraine Country Strategy Paper 2002 –2006 and National Indicative Programme 2002-2003* <http://ec.europa.eu/external_relations/ukraine/docs/index_en.htm>, accessed 5 June 2006.

European Commission (2001f), Guidelines for the implementation of Country Strategy Papers,<http://ec.europa.eu/external_relations/reform/document/iqsg_04_01.pdf>, accessed 14 July 2002.

European Commission (2001g), *Russia Country Strategy Paper 2002–2006 and National Indicative Programme 2002-2003*, <http://ec.europa.eu/external_relations/russia/csp/csp2002.htm> , accessed 9 June 2006.

European Commission (2001h), *Ghana: Country Strategy Paper and Indicative Programme for the Period 2001-2007*, <http://ec.europa.eu/development/how/iqsg/documents_library_en.cfm>, 15 August 2007.

European Commission (2001i), *DG Development, DG Relex and Europeaid Cooperation Office*, Interservice Agreement (Internal Document).

European Commission (2002a), *Progress Report on the Implementation of the Common Framework for Country Strategy Papers* SEC 2002 1279. (ANNEX 4 – Results of the IQSG survey on co-ordination in the field in the context of the CSP process 2001/2002).

European Commission (2002b), *The Interservice Quality Support Group Report on the CSP process in 2001* (Internal Document) 18.03.2002.

European Commission (2002c), *Project Cycle Management Handbook*, March 2002 Version 2.0. <http://www.ueonline.it/Finanziamenti/PCM_Train_Handbook_EN-March2002.pdf>, accessed 14 February 2004.

European Commission (2002d), *The European Initiative for Democracy and Human Rights Programming Update 2003*, Commission Staff Working Document, Brussels 17.01.2002. <http://ec.europa.eu/europeaid/where/worldwide/eidhr/working-documents_en.htm>, accessed 13 September 2003.

European Commission (2002e), *Afrique de l'Ouest - Communauté européenne Document de stratégie de coopération régionale et Programme indicatif régional pour la période 2002 – 2007* <http://ec.europa.eu/development/how/iqsg/documents_library_en.cfm>, accessed 12 August 2007.

European Commission (2002f), *Indonesia Country Strategy Paper 2002– 2006,*<http://ec.europa.eu/external_relations/indonesia/csp/02_06_en.pdf>, accessed 12 August 2007.

European Commission (2002g), China Country Strategy Paper 2002–2006 and National Indicative Programme 2002–2004. <http://ec.europa.eu/external_relations/china/csp/index_2002.htm>, accessed 18 October 2007.

European Commission (2002h), *India Country Strategy Paper and National Indicative Programme 2002 – 2006*. <http://ec.europa.eu/external_relations/ india/csp/index_2002.htm>, accessed 12 December 2007.

European Commission (2002i), *European Community-Mercosur Regional Strategy Paper and National Indicative Programme 2002–2006*. <http://ec.europa.eu/ external_relations/mercosur/rsp/02_06_en.pdf>, accessed 12 February 2007.

European Commission (2003a), *Communication from the Commission to the Council and the European Parliament on Wider Europe – Neighbourhood: A New Framework for Relations with our Eastern and Southern Neighbours*, COM 2003/104 final, Brussels 11.03.2003.

European Commission (2003b), *TACIS Regional Cooperation: Strategy Paper and Indicative Programme 2004-2006,* <http://ec.europa.eu/external_relations/ ceeca/rsp/progs_2002.htm>, accessed 13 June 2007.

European Commission (2003c), *National Indicative Programme for the Russian Federation 2004–2006,* <http://ec.europa.eu/external_relations/russia/csp/ csp2002.htm> , accessed 12 June 2007.

European Commission (2003d), *National Indicative Programme for Ukraine 2004– 2006,* <http://ec.europa.eu/external_relations/ukraine/docs/index_en.htm>, accessed 20 June 2007.

European Commission (2003e), *A maturing partnership - shared interests and challenges in EU-China relations*, COM/2003/0533.

European Commission (2003f), *A New Partnership with South East Asia* Com 399/4. <ec.europa.eu/external_relations/library/publications/09_sea_en.pdf>, accessed 4 June 2006.

European Commission (2004a), *Maroc Programme Indicative National 2005– 2006*, < europa.eu.int/comm/external_relations/sp/index.htm>, accessed 04 January 2005.

European Commission (2004b), *European Initiative for Democracy and Human Rights – Programming for 2005 and 2006,* <ec.europa.eu/external_relations/ human_rights/doc/2006com_23_en.pdf>, accessed 18 January 2005.

European Commission, (2004c), *Regional Strategy Paper and Regional Indicative Programme for the Mediterranean,* <europa.eu.int/comm/external_relations/ sp/index.htm>, accessed 18 January 2005.

European Commission (2004d), *Plan Propose D'Action UE Maroc*, <http://europa. eu.int/comm/world/enp/index_en.htm>, accessed 9 March 2005.

European Commission (2004e), *European Neighbourhood Policy Country Report Ukraine Brussels*, 12.5.2004 COM (2004)373.

European Commission (2004f), *Argentina Country Strategy Paper 2000–2006: mid-term review 2004* <http://ec.europa.eu/external_relations/argentina/ csp/00_06_en.pdf>, accessed 17 October 2007.

European Commission (2004g), *Indonesia National Indicative Programme 2005– 2006* <http://ec.europa.eu/external_relations/indonesia/csp/nip_05-06.pdf>, accessed 24 August 2007.

European Commission (2004h), *China National Indicative Programme 2005–2006*, <http://ec.europa.eu/external_relations/china/csp/nip05_06.pdf>, accessed 12 October 2005.

European Commission (2004i), *Strategy Paper and Indicative Programme for multi-country programmes in Asia in 2005–2006,* <http://ec.europa.eu/external_relations/asia/rsp/rsp_asia.pdf>, accessed 24 August 2007.

European Commission (2004j), *Commission Communication on the Instruments for External Assistance under the Future Financial Perspective 2007-2013,* Brussels: European Commission, COM(2004)626 final, 29 September 2004.

European Commission (2004k), *Taking Europe to the world 50 years of the European Commission's External Service,* <http://ec.europa.eu/external_relations/library/publications/07_50_years_broch_en.pdf>, accessed 18 January 2005.

European Commission (2005a), *Progress Report on the Mid-Term Review of the First Generation of Country Strategy Papers,* Brussesl SEC (2005) 1002.

European Commission (2005b), *Tenth Anniversary of the EMP: A Work Programme to Meet the Challenges of the next Five Years.* Published as Euromed Report No. 89, 14/04/2005.

European Commission (2005c), *Ukraine-EU Action Plan,* <http://ec.europa.eu/world/enp/pdf/action_plans/ukraine_enp_ap_final_en.pdf>, accessed 14 June 2006.

European Commission (2006a), *ENP Progress Report: Morocco,* SEC(2006) Brussels, 4.12.2006.

European Commission (2006b), *ENP Progress Report Ukraine* SEC (2006) 1505/2.

European Commission (2006c), *Communication from the Commission to the Council and the European Parliament on strengthening the European Neighbourhood Policy Overall Assessment,* COM (2006) 726 final} Brussels, 4 December 2006.

European Commission (2007a), Table summarising the allocation of TACIS resources 91-99.<http://ec.europa.eu/external_relations/ceeca/tacis/index.htm>, accessed 8 June 2007.

European Commission (2007b), European Neighbourhood and Partnership Instrument (ENPI): Funding 2007-2013, <http://ec.europa.eu/world/enp/pdf/country/0703_enpi_figures_en.pdf>, accessed 20 May 2007.

European Commission (2007c), *Morocco Country Strategy Paper 2007-2013 and National Indicative Programme 2007-2010,* <http://ec.europa.eu/world/enp/documents_en.htm#1>, accessed 6 December 2007.

European Commission (2007d), *Ukraine Country Strategy Paper 2007 –13 and National Indicative Programme 2007–2010,* <http://ec.europa.eu/world/enp/documents_en.htm#1>, accessed 6 December 2007.

European Commission (2007e), *Ghana Country Strategy Paper and National Indicative Programme for the period 2008-2013,* <http://ec.europa.eu/

development/how/methodologies/strategypapers10_en.cfm> accessed 6 December 2007.

European Commission (2007f), *Mercosur Regional Strategy Paper and Regional Indicative Programme for the period 2007-2013,* <http://ec.europa.eu/external_relations/mercosur/rsp/07_13_en.pdf> accessed 6 December 2007.

European Commission (2007g), Tables summarising the allocation of Tacis resources, 1991–2005, <http://ec.europa.eu/europeaid/projects/tacis/financial_en.htm>, accessed 30 June 2007.

European Parliament (2007), Resolution of 7 June 2007 on the draft Commission decision establishing Regional Strategy Papers and Regional Indicative Programmes for Mercosur and Latin America, <http://www.europarl.europa.eu/sides/getDoc.do?type=TA&reference=P6-TA-2007-0236&language=EN>, accessed 6 June 2008.

Eurostat (2006), *External and intra-European Union trade - Statistical yearbook - Data 1958-2005* (Brussels: Eurostat).

Eurostat (2008), Economy and finance: balance of payments database,<http://epp.eurostat.ec.europa.eu/portal/page?_pageid=0,1136173,0_45570701&_dad=portal&_schema=PORTAL>

European Council (2003), *A secure Europe in a better world: European Security Strategy*, Brussels, 12.12.2003.<register.consilium.europa.eu/pdf/en/03/st15/st15895.en03.pdf>, accessed 6 December 2004.

European Council (2005), *The EU and Africa: Towards a Strategic Partnership,*<register.consilium.europa.eu/pdf/en/06/st16/st16630.en06.pdf> accessed 6 August 2007.

European Council on Foreign Relations (2007),*A Power Audit of EU-Russia relations* <http://www.ecfr.eu/content/entry/eu_russia_relations/>,.accessed 3 December 2007.

Evaluation Partnership (1998), The ACP-EU Trade Development Project (mid-term evaluation), <http://ec.europa.eu/europeaid/how/evaluation/evaluation_reports/index_en.htm> accessed 6 August 2007.

Featherstone, K. (1994), 'Jean Monnet and the Democratic deficit in the EU', *Journal of Common Market Studies*, 32: 20, 149-170.

FEMISE Network (2005), *The Euro-Mediterranean Partnership 10 years after Barcelona: achievements and perspectives*, February 2005. <www.femise.org> , accessed 15 March 2005.

Ferrero-Waldner, B. (2006), Opening address to the conference 'Towards an EU external energy policy to assure a high level of supply security' Brussels 20 November 2006 < http://ec.europa.eu/commission_barroso/ferrero-waldner/speeches/index_en.htm>, Accessed 14 June 2007.

Fioramonti, L. (2007), 'Different Facets of a Strategic Partnership: How the EU is Viewed by Political and Business Elites, Civil Society and the Press in *India*' *European Foreign Affairs Review* 12: 3, 349–362.

Flikke, G. (2008), 'Pacts, Parties and Elite Struggle: Ukraine's Troubled Post-Orange Transition' Europe-Asia Studies, 60: 3, 375–396.

Fontagné, L. and Péridy N. (1997), *The EU and the Maghreb* (Paris: OECD).

Forss, K. (1999), 'Building Aid Organisations with a Capacity to Learn', in: O. Stokke (ed.).

Foster, S. (2001), 'While American Slept: The Harmonization of Competition Laws Based Upon the European Union Mode', *Emory International Law Review* 15: 2, 467–519.

Francis, D. (2005), 'Expanding the frontiers of integration: regional economic and security dynamics'in Cline-Cole and Robson (eds.), 129–150.

Fraser, P. (1994), 'Russia, the CIS and the European Community: building a relationship', in Malcolm (ed.).

Friedman, M. (2002), *Capitalism and freedom* (Chicago: University of Chicago Press).

Frimpong-Ansah, J. (1991), *The vampire state in Africa: the political economy of decline in Ghana* (London: James Currey).

Gallina, N. (2005), 'Beyond the Eastern Enlargement of the EU: The case of Ukraine' in Hayoz (ed.).

Galtung, J. (1973), *The European Community – A Superpower in the Making* (London: George Allen & Unwin).

Garnett, S. (1999), 'Like oil and water' in Kuzio et al. (eds.).

Gibb, R. (2000), 'Post- Lomé the European Union and the South', *Third World Quarterly* 21:3, 457–481.

Gibbon, P. (1993), 'The World Bank and the new politics of aid', in Sorenson (ed.).

Gilpin, R. (2001), *Global Political Economy*, (Princeton: Princeton University Press).

Gillespie, R. (1997), 'Spanish Protagonismo and the Euro-Med Partnership Initiative,' *Mediterranean Politics*, 2: 1, 34–35.

Gillespie, R. (2000), *Spain and the Mediterranean*, Basingstoke: Macmillan.

Gillespie, R. and Youngs, R. (eds.) (2001), *The European Union and Democracy Promotion*, (London: Frank Cass).

Ginsberg, R. (1989), *Foreign Policy actions of the European Community - the politics of scale* (London, Admantine press).

Goldstein, A. (2003), The Political Economy of Regulatory Reform: Telecoms in the Southern Mediterranean OECD Development Centre, Working Paper No. 216 <www.oecd.org/dataoecd/23/43/31652310.pdf>, accessed 6 December 2004.

Government of Morocco (2006), *50 Years of Human Development, Summary of the General Report* <http://www.rdh50.ma/eng/Note_synthese_anglais.pdf>, accessed 9 January 2007.

Gowan, P. (2005), 'Pax Europaea' *New Left Review* 34 May-June 2005: 134–142.

Gowan, P. (1995), 'Neoliberal theory and practice for Eastern Europe', *New Left Review* I/213, September-October 1995, 3–60.

Gower, J. (2000), 'Russian and the European Union' in Webber (ed.). Government of China, (2003), China's EU Policy Paper (translation) <http://ec.europa.eu/external_relations/china/intro/index.htm>

Grilli, E. (1993), *The European Community and Developing Countries* (Cambridge: Cambridge University Press).

Guizzini, S. (1993), 'Structural Power: the limits of neorealist power analysis' *International Organization* 47: 3, 443–478.

Haas, E.B. (1958), *The Uniting of Europe: Political, Social and Economic Forces 1950-57* (Stanford: Stanford University Press).

Hager, W. (1973), 'Europe and the Mediterranean', in Kohnstamm, and Hager, (eds.).

Hammoudi, A. (1997), *Master and Disciple: The Cultural Foundations of Moroccan Authoritarianism* (Chicago: University of Chicago Press).

Haran, O. and Pavlenko, R. (2005), 'Ukraine's foreign policy under Kuchma' in Hayoz (ed.).

Harasymiw, B. (2002), Post-Communist Ukraine (Toronto: Canadian Institute of Ukrainian Studies Press).

Harbeson, J. and Rothschild, R. (ed.) (1995), *Africa in world politics: post-cold war challenges* (Boulder: Westview Press).

Hard, J. and Rodkey, G. (1996), 'Global integration and the convergence of interests among key actors in the West, Russia, Ukraine and the CIS' in Kaminski (ed.).

Hardt, M. and Negri, A. (2001), *Empire,* (Cambridge (Mass): Harvard University Press.).

Harrison, G. (2001), 'Post conditionality Politics and administrative reform: reflections on the cases of Uganda and Tanzania' *Development and Change* 32: 4, 657–679.

Hayek, F. (1962), The road to serfdom (London: Routledge).

Hayoz, N. and Lushnycky, A. (eds.) (2005), *Ukraine at a Crossroads* (Pieterlen: Peter Lang Publications Inc).

Held, D. and McGrew, A. (eds.) (2002), *Governing Globalisation* (Cambridge: Polity Press).

Held, A McGrew, D Goldblatt, D. and Perraton, J. (1999), *Global Transformations: Politics, Economics and Culture* (Cambridge: Polity Press).

Hellman, J. (1998), 'Winners Take All: The Politics of Partial Reforms in Post-. communist Transitions,' *World Politics* 50: 2, 203–234.

Herbst, J. (1993), *The Politics of Reform in Ghana, 1982–1991* (Berkeley: University of California Press) <http://ark.cdlib.org/ark:/13030/ft2199n7n7/>, accessed 4 August 2007.

Herrberg, A. (1998), 'The European Union and Russia: Towards a new Ostpolitk' in Rhodes (ed.).

Hershberg, E. and Rosen, F. (eds.) (2006), *Latin America after neoliberalism : turning the tide in the 21st century?* (London : New Press).

Hershberg, E. and Rosen,F. (2006), 'Turning the Tide?' in Hershberg, E. and Rosen, F. (eds.).

Hibou, B. (2002), 'The World Bank: Missionary deeds and misdeeds', in Schraeder (ed.).

Higgott, R. (2000), 'Studying Regions: Learning from the Old, Constructing the New.' in *New Political Economy,* 5: 3, 333–52.

Hill, C. (1998), 'Closing the capability expectations gap', in Peterson and Sjursen, (eds).

Hill, C. (1993), 'The capability-expectations gap, or conceptualizing Europe's international Role', *Journal of Common Market Studies*, 31: 3, 305-328.

Hirst, P. and Thompson, G. (1999), *Globalisation in Question* (Polity Press).

Hogan, M. (1987), *The Marshall Plan: America, Britain, and the reconstruction of Western Europe,* 1947–1952 (Cambridge: Cambridge University Press).

Holden, P. (2003), 'The European Community's MEDA Aid Programme: A Strategic Instrument of Civilian Power?', *The European Foreign Affairs Review*, 8: 3, 347–363.

Holden, P. (2005a), 'Hybrids on the Rim? The EU's Mediterranean Aid Policy' In *Democratization,* 12: 5, 461–480.

Holden, P. (2005b), 'Partnership Lost? The European Union's Mediterranean Aid Programmes' in *Mediterranean Politics,* 10: 1, 19 –37.

Holden, P. (2006), 'Tensions in the organisation of aid policy for foreign policy purposes: a case study of the European Union's Mediterranean Aid Programmes', in *European Journal of Development Research* 18: 3, 387–412.

Holden, P. (2008), Development through Integration? EU aid reform and the evolution of Mediterranean aid policy' *The Journal of International Development* 20, 230–244.

Hoogvelt, A. (2001), *Globalization and the Post-Colonial World* (Basingstoke: Macmillan).

Houdaigui, R. (2003), *La Politique Etrangere sous la regne de Hassan II* (Paris: L'Harmattan).

Hutchful, E. (2002), *Ghana's adjustment experience: the paradox of reform* (Geneva: United Nations Research Institute for Social Development).

ICEGEC (International Centre for Economic Growth) (2006), News of the Month March 2006 <http://icegec.hu/eng/publications/_docs/news/news_2006_ march.pdf>, 15 June 2007.

IMF (2007b), *Ghana: 2007 Article IV Consultation—Staff Report*, IMF Country Report No. 07/210.

IMF, (2007a), *Ukraine: Staff Report for the Article IV consultation*, Country Report No. 07/50.

Inter-American Development Bank (2004), Mercosur Report no 9 <http://idbdocs. iadb.org/wsdocs/getdocument.aspx?docnum=480172>, accessed 17 November 2007.

Jawad, H. (1992), *Euro-Arab Relations: A study in collective diplomacy* (Reading: Ithaca).

Jenkins, R. (1999), *Democratic politics and economic reform in India* (New York: Cambridge University Press.

Joffé, G. (2000), 'Foreign Investment and the Rule of Law', in Joffé and Vasconcelos (ed.).

Joffé, G. and Vasconcelos, A. (eds) (2000), *The Barcelona Process: Building a Euro-Mediterranean Regional Community* (London: Frank Cass).

Kagarlitsky, B. (2002), Russian under Yeltsin and Putin, (London: Pluto).

Kahler, M. (2000), 'Legalization as Strategy: The Asia-Pacific Case' *International Organization* 54: 3, 549–571.

Kahler, M. (1992), 'Europe and its privileged partners in Africa and the Middle East' *Journal of Common Market Studies,* 21, 199–218.

Kaminski, B. (ed.) (1996), *Economic transition in Russia and the new states of Eurasia* (London: M.E. Sharpe).

Karaganov, S. (1994), 'Russia and Europe: possibilities for the future', in Malcolm (ed.) 224–234.

Karaganov, S. (2005), *Russia-EU Relations: The Present Situation and Prospects* CEPS Working Document No. 225, <http://www.ceps.be/Article.php?article_ id=18>, accessed 17 Janury 2006.

Karber Stiftung (2005), Proceedings from the Bergedorf Round Table Lviv (Karber Stiftung: Hamburg).

Katzenstein, P. (2005), *World of Regions: Asia and Europe in the American Imperium* (New York: Cornell University Press).

Kelly, D. (2002), Japan and World Order, *New Political Economy* 7:3, 397-414.

Keohane, R. and Nye, J. (1989), *Power and Interdependence* (Second Edition), (NewYork: Harper Collins).

Keukeleire, S. (2000), *The European Union as a diplomatic actor*Leicester University Discussion Paper 71.

Killick, T. (1998), *Aid and the Political Economy of Policy Change,* (London: Routledge).

Klom, A. (2003), 'Mercosur and Brazil , A European Perspective', *International Affairs* 70: 2, 351–368.

Kohnstamm, M. and Hager, W. (eds.) (1973), *Nation Writ Large: Foreign Policy Problems Before the European Communities* (London: Macmillan).

Krasner, S. (1983), *International Regimes,* (Ithaca, NY: Cornell University Press).

Krawchenko, B (1999), 'The law on the civil service: a case study of administrative reform in Ukraine' in Kuzio, T. Kravchuk, R. and Anieri R. (eds.).

Kubicek, P. (1999), 'Ukranian interest groups, corporatism and economic reform'. in Kuzio, T. Kravchuk, R. and Anieri R. (eds.) Kuzio, T. (1998), *Ukraine: state and nation building* (London: Routledge).

Kuzio, T. (1997), *Ukraine under Kuchma* (Basingstoke: Macmillan).

Kuzio, T. Kravchuk, R. and Anieri R. (eds.) (1999), *State and institution building in Ukraine* (Basingstoke: Macmillan).

Lamy, P. (2002), 'Mexico and the EU: Married Partners, Lovers, or Just Good Friends?' Institute of European Integration Studies, Instituto Technologico Autonomo de Mexico (ITAM), Mexico City, 29 April 2002. <www.delmex. ec.europa.eu/en/speeches_and_articles/speeches.htm>   accessed 05 April 2005.

Lancaster, C. (1995), 'The Lagos three: economic regionalism in Sub-Saharan Africa' in Harbeson and Rothchild (eds.), 163–188.

Laurent, P. (2001), Interview, Euromed Special Feature Number 21, 3 May 2001. <http://europa.eu.int/comm/external_relations/euromed/publication.htm>

Lavelle, K. (2005), 'Moving in from the Periphery: Africa and the Study of International Political Economy' *Review of International Political Economy* 12:2, 364–369.

Lawton, T., Rosenau, J. and Verdun. A. (2001), *Strange Power, Shaping the parameters of international relations and international political economy* (Aldershot: Ashgate).

Legislative observatory (2006), Procedure file on the financing instrument for development cooperation and economic cooperation. COD/2004/0220 www. europarl.europa.eu/oeil/

Legislative observatory (1998), Report on the TACIS regulation, CNS/1998/0368 www.europarl.europa.eu/oeil/

Legislative observatory (1999), Report on the MEDA regulation, CNS/1999/0214 www.europarl.europa.eu/oeil/

Leonard, M. (2005), *Why Europe will run the 21st century*, (London, Fourth Estate).

Lister, M. (1988), *The European Community and the developing world.* (Aldershot: Gower publishing company).

Lister, M. (1997), *The European Union and the South* (London: Routledge).

Lukes, S. (1999), *Power – A Radical View* (London: Routledge).

Lundestad, G. (1998) *"Empire" by integration : the United States and European integration* 1945-1997 (Oxford: Oxford University Press).

Maes, M. (2006), Contribution to the High-level Conference on EU-ACP Trade Relations: The Development Challenge of Economic Partnership Agreements Brussels 12 October 2006, 70. <http://www.acp-eu-trade.org/library/files/ South-Centre_EN_121006_South-Centre_Development-Challenge-of-EPAs. pdf>, accessed 15 August 2007.

Maghraoui, A. (2002), 'Depoliticization in Morocco' Journal of Democracy 13: 4, 24–32.

Maghraoui, A. (2001), "Political Authority in Crisis. Mohammed VI's Morocco", in: Middle East Report No 218.< http://www.merip.org/mer/mer218/218_ maghraoui.html>, accessed 4 May 2004.

Mahrukh, D. (2007), 'Why Bother With Inter-Regionalism? Negotiations for a European Union-Mercosur Agreement' *Journal of Common Market Studies* 45: 2, 281–314.

Malcolm, N. (ed.) (1994), *Russia and Europe: an end to confrontation?* (London: Pinter Publishers for the Royal Institute of International Affairs).

Mandelson, P. (2004), The ACP-EU relationship in the global economy, speech of the EU Trade Commissioner at the ACP-EU Ministerial (Brussels) <http://ec.europa.eu/commission_barroso/mandelson/speeches_articles/sppm006_en.htm>, accessed 14 April 2005.

Mandelson, Peter (2007a), 'The EU and Russia: Our joint political challenge', Speech at Bologna 20 April 2007. <http://ec.europa.eu/commission_barroso/mandelson/speeches_articles/sppm147_en.htm>, accessed 6 June 2007.

Mandelson, P. (2007b), 'Europe and indispensable India' Speech to the EU-India Business Summit New Delhi, 29 November 2007 <http://trade.ec.europa.eu/doclib/docs/2007/november/tradoc_136934.pdf>, accessed 17 January 2008.

Manners, I. (2006), 'Normative Power Europe Reconsidered: Beyond the Crossroads' *Journal of European Public Policy* 13: 2, 182–199.

Manners, I. (2002), 'Normative Power Europe: A contradiction in Terms?', *Journal of Common Market Studies* 40: 2, 235–259.

Martin, G. (1995), 'Francophone Africa in the context of Franco-African Relations' in Harbeson and Rothchild (eds.), 189–208.

Martin, I. (2006), *Morocco: The Bases for a new Development Model?: The National Initiative for Human Development (INDH)* Real Instituto Elcano. <http://www.realinstitutoelcano.org/analisis/947.asp> , accessed 04 October 2006.

Martin-Munoz, G. (2000), 'Political Reform and Social Change in the Maghreb', in G. Joffe and A. Vasconcelos (eds).

Maull, H. W. (2005), 'Europe and the new balance of global order' *International Affairs* 81: 4, 775–799.

Mayne, R. (ed.), *Europe Tomorrow – 16 Europeans Looking Ahead* (London: Fontana).

Mazower, M. (1998), *Dark Continent: Europe's Twentieth Century* (Harmondsworth: Penguin).

McCormick, J. (2006), *The European Superpower*, (Basingstoke: Palgrave).

Middlemas, K. (1995), *Orchestrating Europe*, (London: Hammersmith).

Milward, A. (1992), *The European Rescue of the Nation State* (London: Routledge).

Mintzberg, Q. and Ghoshal, S. (1998), *The Strategy Process* (Hempstead: Prentice Hall Europe).

Moha, F. (2004), 'Quelle nouvelle politique de voisinage? -Entretien avec Sean Doyle', *Liberation* 13 February. <http//www.liberation.press.ma> , accessed 18 March 2004.

Molloy, S. (2007), *The hidden history of realism* (Basingstoke: Palgrave).

Moore Henry, C. (1996), *The Mediterranean Debt Crescent! Money and Power in Algeria, Egypt, Morocco, Tunisia, and Turkey* (Florida: University Press of Florida).

Moore Henry, C. and Springborg, R. (2001), *Globalization and the politics of development in the Middle East* (Cambridge: Cambridge University Press).

Moravcsik A. (2003), 'Preferences and Power in the European Community: A Liberal Intergovernmentalist Approach', *Journal of Common Market Studies*, 31: 4, 473– 524.

Morgan, O. (2007), 'Putin's tough talk over gas may yet flare up in his face' The Observer, Sunday June 10 2007. <http://www.guardian.co.uk/business/2007/jun/10/russia.oilandpetrol>

Mosley, P. et al. (1991), *Aid and Power - the World Bank and Policy-based Lending*, Vol 1 and 2 (London: Routledge).

Moss, T. (2006), 'Briefing: The G8's Multilateral Debt Relief Initiative and Poverty Reduction in Sub-Saharan Africa' *African Affairs* 105, 285–293.

Motyl, A. (1993), *Dilemmas of Independence: Ukraine after Totalitarianism* (New York: Council on Foreign Relations Press).

Mouqit, M. and Sian A. (2004), *Justice in the Southern and Eastern Mediterranean Region*, Draft Report for the Euro-Mediterranean Rights Network. June 2004.

Murphy, C and Nelson, R (2001), 'International Political Economy: a tale of two heterodoxies', *British Journal of Politics and International Relations*, 3:3, 193–412.

Mwenda, A. and Tangri, R. (2005), 'Patronage Politics, Donor Reforms, and Regime Consolidation in Uganda' *African Affairs* 104: 449–467.

Najem, T. (2001), 'Privatisation and the State in Morocco: Nominal Objectives and Problematic Realities' in *Mediterranean Politics* 6: 2, 51–67.

National Coordinating Unit of the Ukrainian Government (2007), Project Database http://www.ncu.kiev.ua/index/a6/b/len/Project-database

Nugent, N. (2001), *The European Commission*, (Basingstoke: Palgrave).

Nugent, P. (2001), 'Winners, losers and also rans: money, moral authority and voting patterns in the Ghana 2000 election', *African Affairs* 100, 405–428.

Nye, J. (1990), 'Soft Power', *Foreign Policy,* 80:1, 153–171.

Nye, J. (2004), *Soft Power: The Key To Success in World Politics* (Washington: Public Affairs).

Nye, J. (2005), 'Soft Power as Strategy: Problems of Implementation' Staff Seminar at the Centre for International Studies Cambridge, 12 May.

ODI/Overseas Development Institute (2007), *Joint Evaluation of Multi-Donor Budget Support to Ghana Based on OECD-DAC methodology, Volume I*, <www.odi.org.uk/pppg/CAPE/publications.html>, accessed 9 August 2007.

ODI/Overseas Development Institute (1999), *The European Community External Cooperation Programmes: Policies, Management and Distribution* (Brussels: European Commission).

Official Journal of the European Communities (1989), Fourth ACP-EEC Convention signed at Lomé on 15 December 1989, OJ L 229/3

Official Journal of the European Communities (1991), Council Regulation no 2157/91 concerning the provision of technical assistance to economic reform and recovery in the Union of Soviet Socialist Republics, L201/2.

Official Journal of the European Communities (1992), Regulation No 443/92 of 25 February 1992 on financial assistance to and economic cooperation with, the developing countries in Asia and Latin America, OJ L 052/1.

Official Journal of the European Communities (1996a), Regulation (EC) No 1488/96 on financial and technical measures to accompany (MEDA) the reform of economic and social structures in the framework of the Euro-Mediterranean partnership, OJ L 189/1.

Official Journal of the European Communities (1996b), EU-Mercosur interregional framework cooperation agreement, OJ L 069/4.

Official Journal of the European Communities (1997), Agreement on Partnership and Cooperation establishing a partnership between the European Communities and their Member States, of the one part, and the Russian Federation, of the other part, OJ L 327 / 3.

Official Journal of the European Communities (1998a), Partnership and Cooperation Agreement between the European Communities and their Member States, and Ukraine, OJ L 049/ 3.

Official Journal of the European Communities (1998b), Agreement amending the fourth ACP-EC Convention of Lomé signed in Mauritius on 4 November 1995 – Second Financial Protocol – Final Act – Joint Declaration on trade development OJ L 156/ 3.

Official Journal of the European Communities (1999), Commission decision fixing an indicative allocation by member states of the commitment appropriations for Objective 1 of the Structural Funds for the period 2000-2006, 1999/501/EC L 194/49

Official Journal of the European Communities (2000a), Regulation (EC) no 2698/2000 Amending Regulation EC no 1488/96, OJ L 311/1.

Official Journal of the European Communities (2000b), Council Regulation No 99/2000 concerning the provision of assistance to the partner States in Eastern Europe and Central Asia, L 12/1.

Official Journal of the European Communities (2000c), Euro-Mediterranean Agreement establishing an association between the European Communities and their Member States, of the one part, and the Kingdom of Morocco, of the other part, OJ L 070/2.

Official Journal of the European Communities (2000d), Internal Agreement between Representatives of the Governments of the Member States, meeting within the Council, on the financing and administration of Community Aid under the Financial Protocol to the Partnership Agreement between the African, Caribbean and Pacific States and the European Community and its Member States signed in Cotonou (Benin) on 23 June 2000, OJ L 317.

Official Journal of the European Communities (2002), Regulation (EC) No 1726/2000 of the European Parliament and of the Council of 29 June 2000 on development cooperation with South Africa, OJ l 198/1.

Official Journal of the European Union (2006a), Regulation (EC) No 1638/2006 of 24 October 2006 laying down general provisions establishing a European Neighbourhood and Partnership Instrument, OJ L 310/1.

Official Journal of the European Union (2006b), Regulation (EC) No 1905/2006 of 18 December 2006 establishing a financing instrument for development cooperation, OJ L 378/41.

Official Journal of the European Union (2006c), Internal agreement between the Representatives of the Governments of the Member States, meeting within the Council, on the financing of Community aid under the multiannual financial framework for the period 2008 to 2013 in accordance with the ACP-EC Partnership Agreement, OJ L 247/32.

Ohmae, K. (1995), *The End of the Nation-State: The Rise of Regional Economies* (New York: The Free Press).

Olsen, J. (2003), 'Europeanization' in Cini (ed.).

Open Europe (2007), EU aid: is it effective? <http://www.openeurope.org.uk/research/#tandd>, Accessed 15 January 2008.

Orbie J. (2006), 'Review Essay. Civilian Power Europe: Review of the Original and Current Debates'. *Cooperation and Conflict* 41:1, 123–128.

Orbie, J. (2003), 'EU Development Policy Integration and the Monterrey Process: A Leading and Benevolent Identity' *European Foreign Affairs Review* 8:4, 395–416.

Panitch, L. and Gindind, S. (2005), 'Superintending Global Capital', *New Left Review* 35 Sep-Oct 2005.

Patten, C. (2002), Speech to the Central Party School, Beijing, 4 April 2002. <www.chrispatten.org.uk/speeches.htm>, accessed 14 October 2003.

Payne, A. (2006), 'Blair, Brown and the Gleneagles agenda: making poverty history, or confronting the global politics of unequal development?' *International Affairs* 82: 5, 917–935.

Phillipart, E. (2001), 'The Management and Design of the MEDA Programme' in Attina, F. and Stavridis, S. (eds.).

Peterson, J. and Sjursen, H. (eds) (1998), *A Common Foreign Policy for Europe? Competing visions of the CFSP* (London: Routledge).

Petras, J. and Veltmeyer, H. (2005), *Social movements and state power: Argentina, Brazil, Bolivia, Ecuador* (London: Pluto Press).

Phillips, N. (2001), 'Regionalist governance in the New Political Economy of development: relaunching the Mercosur', *Third World Quarterly, 22:* 4,565–583.

Piebalgs, A. (2006), Interview to the Euobserver 28 March 2006<http://euobserver.com/863/21252> , accessed 18 March 2006.

Pijl, K. (1998), *Transnational classes and international relations* (London: Routledge).

Popov, Vladimir (2007), 'Russia Redux?' *New Left Review* 44, March-April 2007, 37–52.

Pronk, J. (2001), 'Aid as Catalyst' *Development and Change* 32: 4, 611–631.

Puglisi, R. (2003), 'Clashing Agendas? Economic Interests, Elite Coalitions and Prospects for Co-operation between Russia and Ukraine' *Europe- Asia Studies,* 55: 6, 827–845.

Raffer, K. (2001), 'Cotonou -slowly Undoing Lome's Concept of Partnership', European Development Policy Study Group: Working paper 21. <www.edpsg.org/>, accessed 18 September 2002.

Ray, D. (1986), *Ghana: politics, economics and society* (London: Pinter).

Regalado, R. (2007), *Latin America at the Crossroads* (New York: Ocean).

Reiterer, M. (2006), 'Interregionalism as a New Diplomatic Tool: The EU and East Asia' *European Foreign Affairs Review*, 11: 2, 223–243.

Rhodes, C. (1998), *European Union in the world community* (Boulder: Lynne Rienner Publishers).

Richards, A. and R. Waterbury (1998), *Political Economy of the Middle East* (Oxford, Westview).

Riddell, R. (2007), *Does foreign aid really work?* (Oxford: Oxford University Press).

Robinson, W. (1996), *Promoting Polyarchy : Globalization, US Intervention, and Hegemony* (Cambridge: Cambridge University Press).

Robinson, N. (1999), 'The global economy, reform and crisis in Russia' Review *of International Political Economy* 6:4, 531–564.

Robinson, N. (ed.) (2004), *Reforging the weakest link : global political economy and post-Soviet change in Russia, Ukraine, and Belarus (*Aldershot: Ashgate).

Robles, A. (2004), *The political economy of interregional relations: ASEAN and the EU* (Aldershot : Ashgate).

Rosamond, B. (2000), *Theories of European Integration* (London: Macmillan).

Sachs, J. (1995), 'Consolidating Capitalism', *Foreign Policy*, no. 98, spring 1995.

Sakwa, R. (2008), *Putin: Russia's choice* (London: Routledge).

Santiso, C. (2002), "Promoting Democracy by Conditioning Aid?"International Politics and Society No.3 2002, 07 –133. < http://www.fes.de/ipg/sets_e/arc_ e.htm>

Santiso, C. (2003), Responding to Democratic Decay and Crises of Governance: The European Union and the Convention of Cotonou, *Democratization* 10: 3, 148–172.

Sargent, J. (1963), 'Aid, Growth and Trade', *New Left Review* 1:22 December 1963.

Sater, J. (2002), 'Civil Society, Political Change and the Private Sector inMorocco: The Case of the Employers' Federation Confédération Générale des Entreprises du Maroc (CGEM)' *Mediterranean Politics*, 7: 2, 13–29.

SCAC/Service de Coopération et Action Culturel (2005). Les grands orientations du service scientifique et technique. <http://www.ambafrance-ma.org/cooperation/ds_presentation.cfm> , accessed 4 March 2006.

Schlumberger, O. (2000), 'Arab political economy and the European Union's Mediterranean policy: what prospects for development?' *New Political Economy* 5: 2, 247–268.

Schraeder, P. (ed.) (2002), *Exporting Democracy*. (Boulder: Lynne Rienner Publishers).

Schroeder, G. (1996), 'Economic transformation in the Post-Soviet Republics' in Kaminski (ed.) Secretariat General, (2008), European Commission Comitology Register, http://ec.europa.eu/transparency/regcomitology/registre.cfm?CL=en

Selafi, M. (1989), Speech at the signing ceremony of the fourth Lomé convention, as reported in the ACP-EEC Courier no. 120 March-April 1990.

Shlapentokh, V. (1996), 'Early feudalism--the best parallel for contemporary Russia.', *Europe-Asia Studies*, 48: 3, 392–411.

Shotton, R. (1999), 'Policy and Institutional Analysis and Programming Strategies for Local Development Funds.' *Regional Development Dialogue* 20: 2, 160–172.

Sjursen, H. (2006), 'What Kind of Power' *Journal of European Public Policy* 13: 2, 169–181.

Smith, D. (2007), *The Dragon and the Elephant: China India and the New World Order* (London: Profile).

Smith, K. (2003), *European Union foreign policy in a changing world* (London: Polity).

Smith, H. (2002), *European Union Foreign Policy: What it is and what it does* (London: Pluto Press).

Smith, Michael (1998), 'Does the Flag follow trade?', in Peterson and Sjursen, (eds).

Smith, Michael E. (2003), *European Foreign and Security policy – the Institutionalization of Cooperation* (Cambridge: Cambridge University Press).

Sorenson, G (ed.) (1993), *Political Conditionality* (London: Frank Cass).

Stiglitz, J. (2002), *Globalization and Its Discontents*. (New York: W.W. Norton):

Stokke, O. (ed.). (1999), *Foreign Aid towards the year 2000 – experiences and challenges* (London: Frank Cass). Stoll R. and Ward M. (eds.) *Power in World Politics* (London: Lynne Reiner Publishers).

Strange, S. (1994), *States and Markets* (London: Pinter).

Strange, S. (1995), 'European Business in Japan: A Policy Crossroads?' *Journal of Common Market Studies,* 33: 1, 1–25.

Strange, S. (1997), 'Territory, state, authority and economy. A new realist ontology of global political economy' in: Cox (ed.).

Taggart-Murphy, R. (2006), 'East Asia's Dollars' in *New Left Review* 40, July August 2006.

Takam, M. (2002), Participation of civil society in the preparation of the cooperation strategy of the EU-ACP agreement in Cameroon: a civil society perspective. (Brussels: ADEID/Eurostep).

Tangri, R. (1991), 'The Politics of State Divestiture in Ghana', *African Affairs* 90, 523–526.

Taylor, I. and Nel, P. (2002), 'New Africa, globalisation and the confines of elite reformism: "Getting the rhetoric right", getting the strategy wrong' *Third World Quarterly*, 23:1, 163–180.

Taylor, I. (2005), *China and Africa: engagement and compromise* (London: Routledge).

Tetreault, M. (1980), 'Measuring Interdependence' *International Organization* 34:3, 429–443.

Therien, JP. (1999), 'Beyond the North South Divide, the two tales of World Povery' Third World Quarterly 20:4, 723–742.

Third World Network-Africa (2006), 'No EPA without investment rules and full reciprocity, Falkenberg insists '29 June 2006 <http://www.twnafrica.org/news_detail.asp?twnID=915>, 12 August 2007.

Third World Network-Africa (2003), 'ECOWAS ruptures unity of ACP countries' <http://www.twnafrica.org/news_detail.asp?twnID=311> , 12 August 2007.

Tietje, C. (1997), 'The Concept of Coherence in the Treaty on European Union and the Common Foreign and Security Policy' *European Foreign Affairs Review* 2: 2, 211–214.

Tonra, B. (2003), 'Constructing the CFSP: The Utility of a Cognitive Approach ' *Journal of Common Market Studies*, 41: 4, 731–756.

Tooze, R. (2001), 'Ideology Knowledge and Power' in Lawton, T., Rosenau, J. and Verdun,A. (ed.).

Tovias, A. and Ugur, M. (2004), 'Can the EU Anchor Policy Reform in Third Countries? An Analysis of the Euro-Med Partnership' *European Union Politics* 5: 4, 395–418.

Tovias, A. (1997), 'The Euro-Mediterranean Partnership: A View from the South', *EU/LDC News*, 4 (1), April 1997.

Toye, J. (1991), 'Ghana' in Mosley et al. (ed.).

Tozy, M. and Hibou, B. (2002), 'De la friture sur la ligne des reformes. La liberalisation des telecommunications au Maroc', *Critique internationale*, 14.

Trade DG of the European Commission (2007a), Bilateral Trade Statistics File: Morocco, <http://europa.eu.int/comm/trade/issues/bilateral/data.htm>, accessed 28 November 2007.

Trade DG of the European Commission (2007b), Bilateral Trade Statistics File: Ukraine, <http://europa.eu.int/comm/trade/issues/bilateral/data.htm>, accessed 28 November 2007.

Trade DG of the European Commission (2007c), Bilateral Statistics File: Ghana, <http://europa.eu.int/comm/trade/issues/bilateral/data.htm>,accessed 28 November 2007.

Trade Ministers of the African Union (2007), Statement on the EPA negotiations Addis Ababa, Ethiopia 16 January 2007 <http://server2.matematici.com/epawatch/index.jsp?id=305&language=1>, accessed 20 August 2007.

UEPLAC (2008), Quarterly Newsletter № 6 Spring 2008, <http://ueplac.kiev.ua/en/publications>, accessed 6 June 2007.

UEPLAC (2007), Quarterly Newsletter No 4 Autumn 2007, <http://ueplac.kiev.ua/en/publications>, accessed 3 December 2007.

UEPLAC (2006), Quarterly Newsletter №1 Winter 2006 /2007, <http://ueplac.kiev.ua/en/publications>, accessed 22 July 2007.

UNCTAD (2007), Foreign Direct Investment Database: Country Fact Sheets and Country Profiles for Morocco, Ukraine, Ghana. <http://www.unctad.org/Templates/Page.asp?intItemID=1923&lang=1>, accessed 26 November 2007.

UNDP/United Nations Development Programme (2002), Arab Human Development Report (Washington: UNDP).

USAID (2002), Ukraine: Country Strategic Plan for 2003-2007 <http://ukraine.usaid.gov/arc.shtml#sub5>, accessed 23 June 2007.

USAID (2004), US Foreign Aid: Meeting the Challenges of the 21st Century, White Paper. <http://www.usaid.gov/policy/pdabz3221.pdf>, accessed 8 July 2007.

USAID (2005), Morocco Annual Report 2004. <http://www.dec.org/pdf_docs/PDACA063.pdf>, accessed 15 February 2006.

USAID (2007), Country Profile Tables Morocco <http://www.usaid.gov/policy/budget/cbj2007/ane/ma.html>, accessed 8 July 2007.

Vahl, M. (2001), Just Good Friends? The EU-Russian "Strategic Partnership" and the Northern Dimension, CEPS Working Document No. 166 < http://www.ceps.be/Article.php?article_id=18>, accessed 6 April 2005.

Versi, A. (2008), 'Africa stands firm' *African Business*, Jan 2008 Issue 338, 12–18.

Wade, R. (2001), 'Showdown at the World Bank'. *New Left Review*.7 January-February 2001, 124–137.

Wade, R. (2003), 'What strategies are available for developing countries today, the World Trade Organization and the Shrinking of Development Space', *Review of International Political Economy* 10:4 621-44.

Walker, R. and D. Buck, R. (2007), 'The Chinese Road' *New left review* 46 July August 2007, 39–66.

Waterbury. J. (1973), 'Endemic Corruption in a Monarchical Regime' *World Politics* 15: 4, 533–555.

Waterbury, J. (1970), *The Commander of the Faithful: The Moroccan Political Elite - A Study in Segmented Politics* (New York: Columbia University Press).

Webber, M. (ed.) (2000), *Russia and Europe: conflict or cooperation?* (London: Macmillan Press).

Wedel, J. (1998), *Collision and Collusion- The strange case of Western Aid to Eastern Europe* (New York: St Martins Press).

Wendt, A. and Friedheim, D. (1995), 'Hierarchy under anarchy: informal empire and the East German state', *International Organization* 49: 4, 689–721.

Wendt, A. (1999), *A Social Theory of International Politics* (Cambridge: Cambridge University Press).

White, G. (2001), *A Comparative Political Economy of Tunisia and Morocco: On the Outside of Europe Looking In* (New York: State University of New York Press).

Whitman, R. (1998), *From Civilian Power to Superpower the International Identity of the European Union* (Basingstoke: Macmillan).

Wilkinson, R. (ed.) (2005), *The Global Governance Reader* (London: Routledge).

Wilkinson, R. (2006), *The WTO crisis and the governance of international trade* (London: Routledge).

Wolfers, A. (1962), *Discord and Collaboration: Essays on International Politics*, (Baltimore: John Hopkins University Press).

World Bank (1981), *Accelerated development in sub-Saharan Africa: an agenda for action* (Washington: World Bank).

World Bank (1989), *Sub-Saharan Africa: from crisis to sustainable growth; a long-term perspective study* (Washington: World Bank).

World Bank (1992), Governance *and Development* (Washington DC: World Bank).

World Bank (1999), *Assessing aid: What works what doesn't and why?* (Washington: World Bank).

World Bank (2000), Morocco 'Legal and Judicial Development Project' Project Appraisal Document, <http://wwwwds.worldbank.org/WBSITE/EXTERNAL/EXTWDS/>.

World Bank (2004), 'The Knowledge Bank in Action.' <http://www.worldbank.org/ks/km_overview.html>, accessed November 2004.

World Bank (2005), *Ukraine – Country assistance strategy progress report* Document no. 32250, (Washington: World Bank).

World Bank, (2004a), 'The Knowledge Bank in Action'. < http://www.worldbank.org/ks/km_overview.html>, accessed 15 November 2004.

World Bank, (2004b), 'Morocco Public Administration Reform Loan Project'.

Project Information Document. <http://www-wds.worldbank.org/navigation.jsp?pcont=browcon>, accessed 15 November 2004.

World Bank (2005), *World Bank's Country Assistance Strategy Progress Report: Ukraine 2005* <http://go.worldbank.org/F9XY5DB2I0>, accessed 22 June 2007.

World Bank Institute (2008), World Governance Indicators 1996–2007 (database). <http://info.worldbank.org/governance/wgi/index.asp>, accessed 22 November 2007.

WTO, (2007), *International Trade Statistics 2006* <http://www.wto.org/english/res_e/statis_e/statis_e.htm>, accessed 15 June 2008.

Yekelchyk, S. (2007), *Ukraine: Birth of a Modern Nation*, Oxford: Oxford University Press.

Yongnian, Z. (2004), *Globalization and State Transformation in China,* (Cambridge: Cambridge University Press).

Youngs, R. (2004), 'Normative Dynamics and Strategic Interests in the EU's external identity', *Journal of Common Market Studies*, 42: 2, 415–436.

Youngs, R. (2002), *The European Union as a Promoter of Democracy: Europe's Mediterranean and East Asian Policies*, (Oxford: Oxford University Press).

Young, H. (1999), *This blessed plot: Britain and Europe from Churchill to Blair,* (Basingstoke: Macmillan).

Zaafrane and Mahjoub (2000), 'The Euro-Mediterranean Free Trade Zone' in Joffe and Vasconcelos (eds.), 9–33.

Zemni, S. and Bogaert, K. (2009), 'Trade, security, and Neo-liberal politics: Whither Arab reform? Evidence from the Moroccan case', forthcoming in the *Journal of North African Studies*.

Index